Engagement and Disengagement

Part dialogue, part debate between Howard Schneiderman and a small number of social theorists, *Engagement and Disengagement* represents the culmination of a life's work in social theory. On the one hand, it is about cohesive social, cultural, and intellectual forces, such as authority, community, status, and the sacred, that tie us together, and on the other hand, about forces such as alienation, politics, and economic warfare that pull us apart. With a blend of humanism and social science, *Engagement and Disengagement* highlights this two-culture solution to understanding social and cultural history.

Howard G. Schneiderman is professor of sociology at Lafayette College, in Easton Pennsylvania. He has a longstanding interest in intellectual history, and has written extensively on some of sociology's leading scholars. He has served in a variety of editorial capacities, including Executive Editor of Society, and editorial consultant to Transaction Publishers. His research interests include charisma, authority, and the intersection of both of these with religion, and he has authored many articles, introductions to classic works, and essays in social theory. This full-length volume, more fully develops many of the ideas initially presented in these smaller works.

Engagement and Disengagement

Class, Authority, Politics, and Intellectuals

Howard G. Schneiderman

Routledge
Taylor & Francis Group
NEW YORK AND LONDON

First published 2018
by Routledge
711 Third Avenue, New York, NY 10017

and by Routledge
2 Park Square, Milton Park, Abingdon, Oxon, OX14 4RN

Routledge is an imprint of the Taylor & Francis Group, an informa business

© 2018 Taylor & Francis

The right of Howard G. Schneiderman to be identified as author of this work has been asserted by him in accordance with sections 77 and 78 of the Copyright, Designs and Patents Act 1988.

All rights reserved. No part of this book may be reprinted or reproduced or utilized in any form or by any electronic, mechanical, or other means, now known or hereafter invented, including photocopying and recording, or in any information storage or retrieval system, without permission in writing from the publishers.

Trademark notice: Product or corporate names may be trademarks or registered trademarks, and are used only for identification and explanation without intent to infringe.

Library of Congress Cataloging-in-Publication Data
A catalog record for this book has been requested

ISBN: 978-1-138-29634-3 (hbk)
ISBN: 978-1-138-29635-0 (pbk)
ISBN: 978-1-315-10007-4 (ebk)

Typeset in Adobe Caslon
by codeMantra

To Mary, my dearest friend and companion, and to my son, Ben, and to my daughter, Maggie.

Contents

Author's Preface	IX
Introduction: Authority, Leadership, and Egalitarianism	1
1 Authority and Legitimacy	17
2 Charisma and Authority	31
3 Authority Patterns in Colonial New England	45
4 The American Dream	60
5 Political Clubs, Parties, and Radicalism	69
6 The Strange Career of Political Sociology in America	84

7 Liberalism and the Democratic Spirit — 107

8 Talent, Wealth, and Power — 126

9 Success and Leadership — 140

10 Class and Authority in the Oval Office — 155

11 The Horatio Alger Myth and the Supreme Court — 173

12 Life and Death of the Protestant Establishment — 193

13 Stress, Crisis, and Psychohistory — 213

14 Hindrances to Good Citizenship — 220

15 Legislating Social and Political Mores — 246

16 Pacifism and Utopian Thought — 266

17 Authority versus Conviction — 281

References — 291
Index — 303

Author's Preface

This book is part dialogue, and part debate between myself and a small number of social theorists who have influenced my way of thinking about culture, class, and authority over the long haul of a richly rewarding career. Among these theorists who have made a deep and lasting impression on me are a handful whom I have known personally as friends and colleagues: E. Digby Baltzell, Philip Rieff, Irving Louis Horowitz, and Donald N. Levine. Their influence is manifest throughout this book. Others who have helped to shape my thoughts in one way or another are Robert K. Merton, Erving Goffman, Bernard Rosenberg, Robert Nisbet, Bruce Mazlish, and Harold Bershady. Then there are those whose influence comes strictly through their writing. Readers of this book will see just how much I lean upon European sociologists, such as Max Weber, Georg Simmel, Ernst Troeltsch, Karl Mannheim, and Emile Durkheim, and American sociologists from William Graham Sumner, Charles Horton Cooley, and Robert Park to Edward Shils, Daniel Bell, and Seymour Martin Lipset. Beyond sociologists, some of the most influential writers whose thinking has become an essential part of my own are Alexis de Tocqueville, James Bryce, James Truslow Adams, George Orwell, William James, Walter Lippmann, Kenneth Burke, and Richard McKeon. While I am not sure that I've ever had a really original thought, the composite influence of these thinkers upon me gives me the sense that together they have given me a unique perspective about the nature of society and social relations.

Engagement and Disengagement is on the one hand about cohesive social, cultural, and intellectual forces, such as authority, community, status, and the sacred, that tie us together, and on the other hand, about forces such as alienation, politics, and economic warfare that pull us apart. Many of the chapters in *Engagement and Disengagement* have appeared before in either slightly or wholly different form. Others appear in print here for the first time. Among all the chapters in this book, two deserve a special comment because they were originally coauthored with my friend and colleague, the late E. Digby Baltzell. These are Chapter 10, "Class and Authority in the Oval Office," and Chapter 11, "The Horatio Alger Myth and the Supreme Court." The first of these was in *The Protestant Establishment Revisited* and the second in *Judgment and Sensibility: Religion and Stratification*. Our collaboration on these two chapters was initiated in each case by me writing the first drafts, then an ongoing discussion between us about those drafts, leading to Digby editing and adding to them, followed by further dialogue and a rewriting line by line until we were both satisfied with the results. Thus, credit for authorship of these two chapters is deservedly shared by us both.

Other chapters in this book have either been written especially for the volume, or they have been rewritten from earlier drafts and iterations that have appeared elsewhere. Among the newly written essays are the Introduction, "Authority, Leadership, and Egalitarianism;" Chapter 1, "Authority and Legitimacy;" and Chapter 2, "Charisma and Authority." Among the previously drafted essays are Chapter 3, "Authority Patterns in Colonial New England," which was originally presented at a conference on "Religious Regimes and State Formation" honoring the 90th birthday of Norbert Elias, held in Amsterdam. Chapter 4, "The American Dream," was published in a different form as "James Truslow Adams and the American Dream," a new introduction to *The Epic of America*. Chapter 5, "Political Clubs, Parties, and Radicalism," was also published in a different form, as "Crane Brinton, The New History and Retrospective Sociology," a new introduction to *The Jacobins*. Chapter 6, "The Strange Career of Political Sociology in America," first appeared in *Culture and Civilization*.

Chapter 7, "Liberalism and the Democratic Spirit," was published in a different form, as "The Moral Career of a Political Sociologist," part of a *festschrift* honoring Irving Louis Horowitz, *The Democratic Imagination*. Parts of Chapter 8, "Talent, Wealth, and Power," were previously published in "Thoughts Out of Season: E. Digby Baltzell and the Protestant Establishment," my editor's introduction to *Judgment and Sensibility*. Chapter 9, "Success and Leadership," was first presented as a paper at the Annual Meeting of the Philanthropy Roundtable. Parts of Chapter 12, "Life and Death of the Protestant Establishment," were published in my editor's introduction to *The Protestant Establishment Revisited*. Chapter 13, "Stress, Crisis, and Psychohistory," was published in a different form as the foreword to Bruce Mazlish's *In Search of Nixon*, reissued by Transaction in 2016. Chapter 14, "Hindrances to Good Citizenship," was first published in a different form as a new introduction to James Bryce's book by the same name. "Legislating Social and Political Mores" was first published in a different form as "*Folkways* and the Rise of Modern Sociology," in William Graham Sumner's *On Folkways and Mores*. Chapter 16, "Pacifism and Utopian Thought," appeared as a new introduction to *Ends and Means*, by Aldous Huxley. Finally, Chapter 17, "Authority versus Conviction," was published as a new introduction to *Protestantism and Progress*, by Ernst Troeltsch. All of these chapters have been revised and rethought for this volume.

What pleases me more than anything else about this book is that it reflects an interweaving of intellectual themes and personal values with which I have struggled over the years. Everyone I have mentioned above combines deep democratic values with hard-nosed social theorizing. Their blend of humanism and social science, and I hope mine, is what brings out the best of both these realms of thought. I hope that the essays in *Engagement and Disengagement* highlight this two-culture solution to understanding social and cultural history.

I owe a special thank you to Margaret "Molly" Martindale, one of my best students at Lafayette College, who helped me to go through this manuscript, word for word, and page by page. With Molly's help for almost four grueling months, I hope that I was able to bring some measure of thematic continuity to what began as disparate chapters. A note of thanks is also due to Julia Dinella, another student assistant, who worked with me on this book for a short time before she left for a semester abroad. Finally, words cannot exactly express my gratitude to Mary Curtis Horowitz, my best friend, confidant, and editorial advisor. I dare say that without Mary's encouragement and advice, this book might not have made it into print.

INTRODUCTION
AUTHORITY, LEADERSHIP, AND EGALITARIANISM

Authority has always been one of modern sociology's pivotal concepts. Without the existence of theories of authority, it is almost unimaginable that we could understand politics, religion, or even culture. Try to name a social institution that does not engage with authority, either directly or indirectly. Authority is not only vital to social systems as a construct itself, but also because opposition to authority is an engine of change without which cultures and societies would stagnate. I begin *Engagement and Disengagement* with a discussion of concepts of authority that have been developed by modern social scientists.

Beyond the opening chapter, I discuss authority as one of the main social mechanisms by which individuals and institutions engage with dominant values and institutions. I explore how this interplay between authority and the social stability it supports is balanced by forces of disengagement, or release from obligations demanded by authority. Social changes, especially revolutionary ones, are, by and large, about engagement and disengagement, by which I mean involving people and institutions both interactively and symbolically with controlling their emotions, desires, and actions, in ways that most individuals would see as legitimate.

To imagine a society without authority and hierarchy would be utopian and revolutionary, if not chimerical. Such radical thinking ignores the fact that authority and social stratification are indispensable to social organization. After all, a society without leaders and the ideals they stand for would be short-lived, directionless, and without structure. Leadership is inextricably linked with authority, and underlying the world's problems today is a crisis of authority, and hence, of leadership. The problem has been less one of convincing the many that they should be led, than one of convincing the few to take the lead. "Ambitious men in democracies," wrote Alexis de Tocqueville in the 1830s, "are less engrossed than any other with the interests and judgments of posterity; the present moment alone engages and absorbs them…and they care much more for success than for fame" (Tocqueville, 1945, p. 247). Tocqueville feared that the inwardness of egalitarian individualism would drive democratic men away from public life where ambition might have vigor and greatness, and into "the midst of the small incessant occupations of private life" (Tocqueville, 1945, p. 248). Not too much earlier than Tocqueville's visit to America in 1830, the close of the colonial era was presided over by an incomparable group of leaders, chief among whom were Washington, Jefferson, Hamilton, Franklin, Madison, Monroe, Jay, Marshall, John Adams, and Samuel Adams, all of whom found greatness and vigor in their public ambitions.

Tocqueville's America was more egalitarian and open to talent than was America during the late colonial era; contemporary America is even more open and egalitarian today than in Tocqueville's day. Yet the quality of leadership has declined as egalitarianism has increased. Why, it has been asked, is it so difficult to produce leaders as characteristically brilliant as those of the revolutionary epoch? One answer might be found in the cultural values and social structures of the revolutionary generation, which were far more authoritarian, hierarchical, and class-bound than our own. The leaders of Washington's America, indeed the colonies themselves, were steeped in values of hierarchy and inherited authority. For example, Virginia's vaunted leadership in establishing the United States was associated with a semi-aristocratic class system that selected men such as Washington, Jefferson, Madison, Monroe, Marshall, and George Mason to office based on their high family social status, superior education, and extensive experience as leaders (Sydnor, 1952, p. 112).

Superior family and social status are, if not resented today, at least looked upon with suspicion, as are authority and leadership in all their forms. The Revolutionary generation of leaders feared what we now prize and are moving steadily towards in our high-tech computerized world, namely, direct plebiscitary democracy. The Revolutionary generation believed in the need for republicanism and class authority, and felt duty bound to take the lead in translating their values into the particular constitutional forms we have come to know as American.

The contemporary crisis of leadership is a crisis of refusal. Men of ability, of good education, worthy of public trust, now refuse to run for public office or to serve in positions of authority and leadership. The refusal to lead is predicated upon an ethos of egalitarian mistrust of authority coupled with an ethos of radical individualism. These two attitudes were evidently on the rise throughout the nineteenth century, and into the twentieth, when early sociologists such as Charles Horton Cooley saw that many Americans regarded government as a minor part of life, if not a necessary evil, practiced by second-rate men (Cooley, 1918, p. 147).

Anti-authoritarian and ultra-individualist attitudes have made it difficult to convince the talented, the best and the brightest, to take the lead in public affairs, leaving them to prefer individual success in the private sector, often in business pursuits, over public achievement and recognition. Tocqueville noted an ethos destructive of public authority and leadership in America, which he called "individualism," as opposed to "egotism," which he described as

> … a passionate and exaggerated love of self, which leads a man to connect everything with his own person and to prefer himself to everything in the world. Individualism… disposes each member of the community to sever himself from the mass of his fellows, and to draw apart with his family and friends, so that he willingly leaves society at large to itself…[I]ndividualism is of democratic origin, and it threatens to spread in the same ratio as the equality of condition.
>
> (Tocqueville, 1945, p. 98)

Tocqueville is credited with the first use of "individualism" in the English language. Individualism is a keystone of Tocqueville's new science of politics, describing as he does an ethos specifically found in democratic or egalitarian societies that have relatively little respect for tradition and authority. This is not to say that societies, groups, and individuals can live in an unbalanced world where authority goes unopposed, since history shows us that unremitting authority grinds down individuality by becoming repressive and relentlessly demanding. In reality, authoritative ideas and ideals always create the conditions for opposition, as well as obedience. The so-called "American Dream" made popular by James Truslow Adams, and discussed later in this volume, illustrates the tension between authority and revolution. While the dream of hard work and perseverance leading to success may come to fruition for some, perhaps many Americans, enough success is just never enough. The dream is not for success itself, but for a progressive "more success." This, of course, is one of the consequences of Durkheim's concept of *anomie*, which is really about never being able to reach goals that are in constant flux.

Egalitarianism, defying authority and tradition, tends to disconcert the political world by causing indifference to the public interest, sociologically defining the essence of radical individualism. In contrast, Tocqueville understood that more-or-less aristocratic societies, which respect tradition and authority, "made a chain of all members of a community." Although such societies have their egotists under the sway of an individual psychological condition, they are relatively immune to the mass-communal, sociological condition of indifferent individualism. No society has ever been purely aristocratic and hierarchical, nor purely democratic and egalitarian, but all societies have countervailing values of both hierarchy and equality. The chief psychological question is one of emphasis and degree. In all societies, however, egalitarian or hierarchical authority is indispensable.

Ironically, Friedrich Engels, Karl Marx's closest associate, provided an elegant analysis of the functional indispensability of authority for social organization. In the 1870s, when Marx's strictly disciplined and personally centralized authority in the International Working Men's Association was threatened by Mikhail Bakunin's anarcho-communist followers who threatened to break with the International, Engels wrote "On Authority" to defend the organizational and authoritative position. Against Bakunin's followers who opposed all political authority, including the centralized authority of the International and even the authority of the workers themselves after the revolution, Engels argued for the functional necessity of leadership and for the principle of authority.

In principle, authority, in Engels' sense, is a form of domination, an imposition of one's will upon another, leading to his subordination. "Is it possible to have organization without authority?" Engels asked rhetorically. He had but one answer: No. Whether it be work in the modern factory—capitalist or socialist—or work in modern agriculture, or the safe running of railways, or of ships at sea, cooperation and coordination depend on a hierarchy of command, of those who give orders and of those who obey them. Engels saw the relationship of authority and leadership as inevitable and indispensable to organized social life. He did not address the ancillary and equally interesting questions of who should lead and who should follow. Questions about who has authority and who obeys authority, and why, are central to the study of social stratification and have been answered in different ways, some of which we examine in this book.

Equality of conditions is possible, but inequality is inevitable, because to fill their most important positions with the most capable individuals, all societies have to reward leaders differentially, with high wealth and prestige. That is the central thesis of Kingsley Davis and Wilbert Moore's seminal 1945 essay, "Some Principles of Stratification," which set off a heated debate among sociologists, and became a key text in the field of social stratification.

> Among the many responses to Davis and Moore, one article in particular, "Some Notes on the Functional Theory of Stratification," by the Polish sociologist, Wlodzimierz Wesolowski, stands out as germane to my purposes here. Wesolowski took issue with Davis' and Moore's assertion that great differentials in material rewards and prestige were functionally indispensable and constituted the principal motives of those striving after important positions in a society.

Writing in a more economically egalitarian, less affluent society behind what was then the Iron Curtain, Wesolowski did not object to Davis' and Moore's statements concerning the universality and inevitability of hierarchy and stratification. What he disagreed with was their reasoning about differences in wealth and prestige being necessary to the filling of important hierarchical positions. In place of the primacy accorded to material rewards and prestige by Davis and Moore, Wesolowski preferred the term "authority:"

> Among the functional prerequisites of social life, it would be difficult not to take social organization into account. Social life is group life, and group life involves the inner structuralization of the group. This structuralization consists among other things in the emergence of positions of command and subordination…In such a structure authority is unevenly distributed. For as soon as positions of authority are filled, those who occupy the positions have the right (and duty) to give orders, while the others have the duty to obey them…In consequence it may be said that if there is any functional necessity for stratification, it is the necessity of stratification according to the criterion of authority, and not according to the criterion of material advantage and prestige.
> (Wesolowski, 1967, p. 68)

An underlying organizational principle of this book takes Wesolowski's argument a step farther: In a society where authority is institutionalized, well-defined, and deferred to, there is *less* need for rewarding positions of leadership with great wealth and prestige than in a society where egalitarian values have eroded clearly defined hierarchies of authority. I therefore emphasize society's attitudes towards institutions of authority rather than its attitudes towards wealth and prestige. In egalitarian societies that devalue authority and institutionalized hierarchies of authority, positions of leadership will more than likely be used as a means to obtain material rewards. In such societies money talks, and one would have to agree with Davis and Moore that material rewards and prestige are, more or less, the primary motives of those striving after positions of leadership. On the other hand, as Wesolowski claims, in societies with well-established hierarchies of authority and authoritarian values, authority is itself an end towards which people strive.

Ironically, where hierarchies of authority and authoritative values are relatively weak, even high material rewards—as Davis and Moore suggest they should be—are often not enough to induce the ablest and most educated to take on the responsibilities of leadership. When positions of power and leadership are looked down upon with scorn and defiance, and when their authority is devalued, capable individuals will often shy away from such positions, choosing instead to exercise their talents in more private ways that might bring them more respect as well as material rewards.

In late nineteenth-century America, for instance, James Bryce noted that although politics was an avenue to wealth and power, it was scorned and carried little authority. Bryce, whom I shall discuss throughout this book, further noticed that under these conditions the "best men," as he called them, did not go into politics, but rather left the field open to office seekers of a sometimes unscrupulous nature:

> The inducement to undertake political work we have been searching for is at once seen to be adequate, and only too adequate. The men for the work are certain to appear because remuneration is provided. Politics has now become a gainful profession like advocacy, stockbroking, the dry goods trade, or the getting up of companies. People go into it to live by it, primarily for the sake of the salaries attached to the places they count on getting, secondarily in the view of the opportunities it affords of making incidental and sometimes illegitimate gains… [T]he worst succumb to it, and the prospect of these illicit profits render a political career distinctly more attractive to an unscrupulous man.
> (Bryce, 1888, p. 28)

If positions of political power in America are profitable, yet shunned by capable individuals, as Bryce claims, it may be because these positions are wanting in authority, or, better, in a legitimacy that allows mere power to become authoritative. It is notable that Bryce had a profound influence on Max Weber. In *The American Commonwealth*, Bryce coined terms such as "living for politics" and "living off of politics," which Weber adopted as his own. Both understood that "living for politics" is mostly made possible by independent wealth and high status, rather than by character or psychological disposition alone.

As I discuss in the first chapter in this book, legitimacy and authority have been extensively discussed by Max Weber, who described three basic ideal-typical forms that authority has taken historically: traditional, charismatic, and rational-legal. Notably, what Weber calls traditional authority comes closest to class authority, which I discuss throughout this book, but especially in the chapters dealing with the Protestant Establishment. What Weber calls charismatic authority I identify as a form of domination resting upon the belief in the extraordinary quality of a person. Last, the legal form of authority or domination rests on the belief in rationally constructed rules and the functional duties of office, as the reader will discover.

Weber imagined legitimacy as ideal types, and as such we must recognize that all three categories of authority may be combined as part of its justification in a particular time and place, since they are not necessarily exclusive of each other. Of course, the most prevalent forms of authority in the modern democratic nation-state have been and are rational-legal or bureaucratic.

In "The Strange Career of Political Sociology in America" I show how differences in social structure and academic culture experienced by American sociologists, on the one hand, and European sociologists on the other, account for the much greater interest in authority among the latter than the former. This is not to say that American political sociologists have had no interest in authority, as my chapter on the career and reputation of Irving Louis Horowitz shows quite clearly. Early in his career Horowitz had a reputation as a radical sociologist; he found himself labeled, unfairly, as a conservative as time went by. In similar fashion, early in his career E. Digby Baltzell was seen as something of a class traitor, and squarely as a liberal, if only as a sort of nineteenth-century liberal. As the academic sociological culture slid quickly into political correctness and radicalism during the 1960s and 1970s, reputations of liberals such as Horowitz and Baltzell changed radically. This character unmasking was first described by Karl Mannheim in *Ideology and Utopia*. Much like Horowitz and Baltzell, one of sociology's greatest founders, William Graham Sumner, was dismissed as a conservative even though he gave us some of the most important and enduring concepts in the field.

Since the beginning of the twentieth century, democratic societies have become increasingly paradoxical in their views of liberalism, conservatism, and authority. Never before have the many had so much political and economic power, at least in principle. Yet in practice, that power has been largely illusory, since real power is in the hands of an elite few. The twentieth century as well as our own have unmistakably been marked by oligarchic democracy. Although "democracy" in theory is opposed to bureaucratization, or rational-legal authority, in its modern mass forms democracy unintentionally promotes bureaucracy. "The people" in mass democratic associations rarely govern themselves; on the contrary, they are governed by relatively small elite groups. In its modern mass forms democracy cannot do without "organization," which Robert Michels called the rule of bureaucracy.

Following from what he considered an iron law, Michels understood that "organization implies the tendency to oligarchy," the few ruling the many. Hence, the great paradox of our democracies: Democratization has, in general, not led to self-governance by "the people," but to the oligarchic governance *of* "the people" by the few.

Even outside the sphere of politics, oligarchic tendencies have become characteristic of our social institutions, which have become increasingly democratic, that is, egalitarian. As technical and scientific advances have challenged our contemporary values and mores, the world has become relatively incomprehensible to most of us, so it is left to small elite groups of insiders to wield authority by virtue of their knowledge and skills. Beyond the scientific and technical spheres of life, the same can be said about progressive advances and changes in the musical, literary, artistic, and philosophical spheres of life.

In the political realm of public policy and debate, only small groups of specialists can make sense of foreign affairs and policies under the terribly dark shadows cast by worldwide terrorism during the past few decades. In a global economy of multinational corporations, and complex domestic and international financial policies, once again, only the few can even hope to understand the complexities which the many, at least in theory, must sort out and decide upon, democratically.

In such a world, leadership in the state, the economy, and indeed in all spheres of life is not merely inevitably oligarchic, as Michels claims, but it is also necessary. All modern forms of political society are oligarchic, but democratic forms have certain characteristics that set them apart from the others. These characteristics were first discussed by Max Weber, who said,

> ... the political concept of democracy deduced from the 'equal rights' of the governed, includes these postulates: 1. prevention of the development of a closed status group of officials in the interest of a universal accessibility of office, and 2. minimization of the authority of officialdom in the interest of expanding the sphere of influence of 'public opinion' as far as practicable
> (Weber, 1946, p. 226)

Hence, the questions to be asked of democracies are whether the oligarchic elite is drawn from all social classes, and whether that elite is more or less accountable and responsible to the rest of society.

Tradition, rather than bureaucracy or charisma, has tended to support the authority of a ruling social class, and when tradition is relatively strong, class authority tends to become increasingly legitimate. Furthermore, when traditional class authority is strong, rational and legal, hence bureaucratic, forms of authority will be relatively subordinated to it. In chapters dealing with the American presidency and the United States Supreme Court, I explore some of these issues of class authority.

Forms of legitimacy carry within themselves certain checks upon the power of leaders who exercise authority. Charismatic authority is defined by inspirational "callings" that define and set the limits to which the means of power are justified by its ends. Bureaucratic and legal rules set limits upon the use of power by office holders. And tradition is the checking force upon the use of power by those who have class authority. Since the First World War, the problems of responsibility among power-holding authorities in atomized mass societies have been in the spotlight. It may be that in mass societies, upper-class leaders drawn from traditionally privileged families with a commonly held code of conduct, as a group, will develop more responsible attitudes towards positions of leadership. Certainly, the chapters in this volume on good citizenship, authority and legitimacy, and patterns of authority suggest such an outcome.

This possibility was hinted at by the noted anthropologist Ralph Linton as the Second World War approached:

> The lack of a definite aristocratic culture which provides the members of this ruling group with common ideals and standards of behavior and thus integrates them into a conscious society is perhaps the most distinctive aspect of the modern condition. Exploiters and exploited have existed since the dawn of history, but the only parallel to the modern situation is that of Rome in the days of the late Republic. Here also power came to be vested in the hands of a group of self-made men who had no common standards and no feeling of responsibility to each other or to the state.
>
> (Linton, 1936, p. 111)

Responsible leadership has probably been basic to the deference accorded upper classes in societies with strong class authority. Deference to class authority is not limited to politics alone, for an upper class may be hegemonic in other ways as well. Writing about the French nobility before the Revolution, Tocqueville saw that "An aristocracy in the days of its strength does not merely conduct affairs; it still directs opinions, gives tone to the writers and authority to ideas" (Tocqueville, 1856, p. 174). When an aristocracy gives up its societal leadership it becomes, in Tocqueville's words, a privileged but irresponsible caste, more likely to provoke defiance than to earn deference.

Historically, a strong upper-class hegemony, or class authority, has been a force countering the dominant democratic trends towards bureaucratic oligarchy, and office-seeking politics, which George Bernard Shaw described as "bosses who ride roughshod over us" (Shaw, 1965, p. 479). Max Weber was one of the first to discuss what I identify as class authority, calling one special and important form of traditional authority *domination by honoratiores*. Such authority exists "wherever social honor within a group has become the basis of domination…the specific authority of the notable—especially of one distinguished among his neighbors through property, education or style of life—derives from honor." The prime example of rule by *honoratiores,* or class authority, was the English gentry, which, as Weber said, "saved England from the bureaucratization which has been the fate of all continental states" (Weber, 1968, p. 9).

In contrast to British cultural values of hierarchy, deference, and self-containment, which supported the dominion of honoraries, Americans have historically developed what Edward Shils has called "a broad antinomian strand…of an exceptional irreverence and disrespect towards the law" (Shils, 1956, p. 161). In America, distance, deference, and reserve have never been much esteemed.

Democratically governed societies face problems of authority and leadership in two basically different ways. Some democracies, like England and Canada, are deferential towards authority and leadership; others, like America, are relatively defiant. Visitors to America from more deferential European societies have often characterized it to be a defiant democracy.

"Every authority is losing power," wrote Guglielmo Ferrero about America in 1909 in his remarkably instructive, but much-neglected book, *Ancient Rome and Modern America*. Ferrero, a notable historian of the classical world, was invited to visit America by President Theodore Roosevelt. At every turn, he saw a nation which, judged by European standards, defied tradition and authority.

> The people discuss the government and the laws, children take the first opportunity of escaping from the authority of their parents, and the younger generation is convinced that it knows more than the older, and values the latter's experience at zero.
> (Ferrero, 1914, p. 204)

All societies, including those that are more-or-less democratic, are elitist because in all social relations, some lead and others follow. In terms of stratification, societies differ from each other mostly on the basis of attitudes, especially on collective attitudes towards authority and leadership. Where there is defiance in thought, there will be defiance in conduct.

Ferrero's America displayed certain tendencies generally characteristic of defiant democracies:

> Traditions are losing their force and academics their prestige. Everyone holds the opinion he likes in religious, artistic, political and moral questions; just as he is free to regulate his own conduct, at his own risk and peril, as he pleases, with the sole obligation of respecting the limits imposed by the laws, which are for the most part neither numerous nor embarrassing.
> (Ferrero, 1914, p. 204)

America was in its progressive "Age of Reform," when Ferrero visited in 1909. Coincidentally, during this same year the British Ambassador to America, James Bryce, published his Yale Lectures, *The Hindrances to Good Citizenship*, which are discussed later in this book. Like Ferrero, Bryce advanced a theory of defiant democracy in which he saw that things are "claimed by the citizen as due to him, to be held and exercised by him for his benefit and satisfaction." When defiance marked a democracy, the citizen stood "over against the ruling man or ruling class and said defiantly, thus far and no farther! Rights to be won were the cry of battle. Rights to be enjoyed were the crown of victory" (Bryce, 1993, p. 9). It might well be argued, of course, that citizens' rights are called for in all democracies, not merely in defiant ones. To concede this is not to alter the argument, for defiant democracies *emphasize* rights over and above everything else, including the counterweights of responsibilities.

Defiant democracies characteristically set into motion various centrifugal forces which make leadership and authority difficult to establish and harder still to maintain. Egalitarian ideals often put authority under suspicion as evil and cause the citizen to stand against the ruling man or ruling class. Defiance when extended to opinion destroys the hierarchies of truth and tradition, freeing each individual to hold his own, often untutored opinion on everything. Such radical individualism provides a sterile medium for consensus, which is the democratic basis for authority and leadership. As Tocqueville recognized, such individualism leads to an immense appetite for consumption, self-satisfaction, and fulfillment of personal desires among all classes of society. Some might say this describes American cultural values today. Tocqueville, not without a little irony, saw this as "virtuous materialism" which might "enervate the soul, and noiselessly unbend its springs of action" (Tocqueville, 1945, p. 133).

In defiant democracies, plutocracy often replaces aristocracy, and "mob snobbery,"—a term coined by James Truslow Adams, whom I discuss in a chapter on the "American Dream"—replaces deference to upper-class leadership. Placing value on egalitarian, leveling ideals, defiant democracies sanctify "the cult of the second-rate," and consequently get the second-best for public leaders, while the best hide behind their private concerns. Behind the cult of the second-best, wrote Walter Lippmann,

> is a great pride, a great sense of emancipation from ancient error…[T]he doctrine of watchful waiting, of mysterious popular guidance, of purely receptive and purely passive leadership, has an air about it of democratic humility, of unpretentiousness, of nobly serving great things.
> (Lippmann, 1970, p. 214)

Purely receptive, purely passive leadership is an idea that is paradoxical, although in a sense workable. In deference democracies leaders take the lead and educate the citizenry to follow them, while in defiant democracies "leaders" are more or less instruments not of leadership, but of the expression of popular will. Leaders in defiant democracies, according to Lippmann,

> assume that a certain insincerity is necessary to success, that a little less than common sense is appropriate, that the best is the enemy of the better…their own powers of invention and judgment are starved through disuse, while their powers of promotion and salesmanship grow constantly more elaborate.
> (Lippmann, 1970, p. 227)

Natural leaders—Weber called them charismatics—in defiant democracies are afraid to appear as such and "the leaders huddle with the herd." James Truslow Adams says defiant democracies, with their mob snobs, give birth to the "mucker-pose," in which individuals of considerable advantages and abilities imitate the masses rather than leading them. Adams's examples of mucker-poseurs are gentlemen who wish to appear uncultured, and scholars who wish to imitate longshoremen. The bright who purposely appear dull, the rich who try to appear poor, the powerful who want to look weak, and leaders who do not wish to appear as such, all affect the mucker-pose in fear of being different, of standing above the crowd. Jacobin defiance in democracies frightens the most capable into the mucker-pose, making leadership in arts, sciences, morals, politics, indeed in anything, all but invisible.

Writing specifically about the mucker-pose, Adams describes the losses authority suffers in defiant democracy which

> ... has knocked the dignity of its elected officials into a cocked hat...when John Quincy Adams was President, he declined to attend a country fair in Maryland, remarking privately that he did not intend that the President of the United States should be made a side-show at a cattle fair.
>
> (Adams, 1929, p. 206)

As the presidential election of 2016 showed us, today the American people insist that the President be a side show. In defiant democracies such as America today, that popular insistence cuts through social distance and deference as sharply as a cracked whip. Every American President since at least the end of the Second World War has been made to dance under the insistent whiplashes of public opinion, adopting the mucker-pose of the side-show attraction. The chapters about the Presidency and the Supreme Court justices in *Engagement and Disengagement* put much of this in perspective.

Taken as a whole, this book addresses issues concerning authority, many of which are raised in this introductory statement, but the reader will soon realize that the individual chapters have been written over multiple decades. Consequently, they should be seen as snapshots rather than complete analyses of contemporary society today. It is my belief that their theoretical relevancy remains clear. The themes explored in this volume and highlighted in this introduction deepen our understanding of authority, political life, and the intellectuals who have helped shape our understanding of contemporary America.

1
AUTHORITY AND LEGITIMACY

For centuries philosophers have written about authority, but they have been less interested in analyzing authority objectively than in using the term ideologically to further their own intellectual agendas regarding justice, power, domination, and government. After all, as the philosopher Bertrand Russell has said,

> Most philosophy has been a reaction against skepticism; it has arisen in ages when authority no longer sufficed to produce the socially necessary minimum of belief, so that nominally rational arguments had to be invented to secure the same result.
> (Russell, 1950, p. 4)

With Russell's pronouncement in mind, this discussion will concentrate on value-neutral social science theories of authority, rather than surveying the vast philosophical literature on the subject.

German Theorists

Most of our ideas about authority have emanated from the work of Max Weber, who gave us the most basic and up to now most pervasive ideas about how power becomes authority through what he considered its three basic legitimations: traditional authority, rational-legal authority, and charisma. Although Weber is justly famous for his discussions of authority, we should acknowledge that his personal contact with historians, sociologists, and theological thinkers such as Rudolph Sohm, Adolf Harnack, Ernst Troeltsch, and Georg Simmel, all of whom wrote about these three forms of authority before, while, and after he did, played a huge part in Weber's thinking. Indeed, in his well-known work on church history, *Kirchenrecht*, Sohm introduced the term "charismatic organization," which Weber directly adopted for his theory of charismatic authority (Sohm, 1892, p. 26). Adolf Harnack's monumental three-volume *Lehrbuch der Dogmengeschichte*, or *History of Dogma*, was published right after Sohm's book, between 1894 and 1898, and also had a major impact on Weber's thinking about authority in the early Christian church, which he then applied to modern societies. Ernst Troeltsch, a close personal friend, and professional colleague of Weber, wrote extensively about premodern and modern forms of institutional authority. Troeltsch's *Protestantism and Progress* (2012) and his *The Social Teachings of the Christian Churches* (1931) discussed organizational and personal forms of authority in both church and state, and his work influenced the formation of Weber's famous tripartite theory of authority.

Georg Simmel, a German sociologist even more influential than Weber in his day, also wrote about authority, and his excursus on "Superordination and Subordination" remains one of the most inventive ways of thinking about the relationship of authority to power. In this essay, Simmel introduced the concept of the "prestige leader," who seems to wield exactly what Weber would later call "charismatic authority" (Simmel, 1950, p. 185). Robert Michels, Weber's most successful student, published *Political Parties*, which introduced a new term to describe authority, "the iron law of oligarchy," which says that the authority of an oligarchic elite in any democratic institution is inevitable. Michels reminds us of the Weberian-endorsed idea of a value-free sociology regarding the study of authority: "Leadership is a necessary phenomenon in every form of social life. Consequently, it is not the task of science to inquire whether this phenomenon is good or evil, or predominantly one or the other" (Michels, 1915, p. 364). With the unification of Germany into a major modern state in the late nineteenth century, these social science thinkers brought a new analytic interest in power and authority, and this is clearly reflected in their work.

French Theorists

French sociology was also quick to become interested in the nationalistic forces boiling up in Europe, and in the new movements to consolidate power and to create the basis of legitimate authority in France and neighboring states. Gabriel Tarde was the first French sociologist to write extensively about authority and its relationship to power. In his 1899 book, *Les Transformations du Pouvoir*, he defined authority as the *right* to be obeyed. Tarde's well-known three-pronged theory of social order, first introduced in his *Laws of Imitation*, namely repetition, opposition, and adaptation are applied to power and authority in modern societies. Tarde sees the origins of political and social authority of the modern state in the history of the family as a social institution, an idea that was later underscored by the American sociologist Robert Nisbet in "Kinship and Power in First Century Rome" (Nisbet, 1999). Another notable French sociologist, Célestin Bouglé, wrote about authority and social class in his famous treatise, *Essais Sur le Régime des Castes,* reiterating a line of thinking originating with Alexis de Tocqueville's famous analysis of the origins of the French Revolution, *The Ancient Regime and the Revolution*, and leading up to Louis Dumont's work on caste and authority in the 1960s. The most important French sociologist was, of course, Émile Durkheim, who also wrote about authority in his work on law and education. For Durkheim, social authority was not only about roles and statuses in the social order, but also about collective representations and symbols, which exacted obedience to authority through its moral interface with the society. These French sociologists played a part in more contemporary thinking about the cultural and symbolic nature of obedience to authority discussed above.

Italian Theorists

Interest in authority, power, and politics in Italy was set in motion by the three wars of Italian independence fought in 1848, 1859, and 1866 and was further fueled by the unification of the various Italian states as the Kingdom of Italy in 1861. Thus, in Italy as in Germany, the modern bureaucratic state came into existence late in the nineteenth century and created an interest in power and authority among early social scientists. Among the most important Italian social scientists writing about authority were Gaetano Mosca, Vilfredo Pareto, and Guglielmo Ferrero. As Italy underwent its transformation from an array of tiny principalities to a loose confederation of small states, and then to a centralized modern state, social scientists became interested in the process of how centralizing power became centralized authority.

Gaetano Mosca, an Italian political scientist whose *Elementi di scienza politica*, first published in 1895 and later in an English translation as *The Ruling Class*, set forth a theory of elites that added a new dimension to our theories of authority. Mosca's basic assumption is that all societies are composed of small elite ruling classes that demand obedience from large unorganized majority groups. The pivotal question for Mosca is how the leaders who wield authority do so. As he says, in any form of political organization, authority is either transmitted from above downward in the political or social scale (he calls this the autocratic principle), or from below upward (the liberal principle). Mosca also discusses how leaders are chosen to wield authority, or at least from where in the social order they are chosen. The two types of leadership recruitment are aristocratic and democratic. Aristocratic recruitment consolidates power and authority in the hands of a relatively few families over multiple generations, while democratic recruitment emphasizes rejuvenation of elites by bringing up new talented individuals from the lower and middle classes.

Mosca's types of recruitment to authoritative elite positions anticipated Vilfredo Pareto's even more well-known "circulation of the elite." Pareto's best-known work, *Mind and Society (Trattato Di Sociologia Generale)*, published in 1916, analyzed regime change, where authority is transferred from one elite to another because of revolutions from below. Perhaps thinking of the situation in Italy during the second half of the nineteenth century, Pareto was able to generate a theory of how social and political authority changes hands due to a constant pressure to change leaders.

Another Italian social scientist, Guglielmo Ferrero, wrote extensively about power and authority in his historical works about the Roman Republic and the Empire. He also visited America at the invitation of President Theodore Roosevelt, and wrote *Ancient Rome and Modern America* in 1914. In this book, Ferrero said of America that "Every authority is losing power." According to Ferrero, everywhere he turned he saw a nation which, judged by European standards, defied tradition and authority.

> The people discuss the government and the laws, children take the first opportunity of escaping from the authority of their parents, the younger generation is convinced that it knows more than the older, and values the latter's experience at zero.
> (Ferrero, 1914, p. 204)

These observations led Ferrero to distinguish between authority in what he called defiant democracies, and authority in those societies that he called deference democracies. Deference democracies favor legitimate authority, according to Ferrero, while defiant ones bring power to the fore since they question legitimacy incessantly. These theories of how authority circulates throughout the social order later influenced the thinking of American sociologists from Talcott Parsons to E. Digby Baltzell.

British Theorists

Interest in authority among British social scientists is exemplified by James Bryce, but also by Walter Bagehot and Harold Laski. As Perry Anderson astutely observed, there really was no effective effort to build a British sociology until after WWII. Even absent a full-blown sociology, British social scientists showed a lively interest in authority. The English statesman, political scientist, and sociologist James Bryce's study of democracy in the *American Commonwealth* and later in *Modern Democracies* exposed the give-and-take between leaders and citizens in the modern state, and his essay "Obedience" is a remarkable dissection of why and how authority effectively commands obedience on the basis of indolence, deference, sympathy, fear, and reason (Bryce, 1901). Indolence is again emphasized as a reason for obedience in Bryce's 1909 Yale Lectures, *The Hindrances to Good Citizenship*. In his well-known *English Constitution* Bryce's contemporary Walter Bagehot also took up the study of deference and obedience to authority, and comes very close to what Weber later called "traditional authority." In his discussion of tradition and authority, Bagehot says "custom is the first check on tyranny; that fixed routine of social life at which modern innovations chafe, and by which modern improvement is impeded, is the primitive check on base power" (Bagehot, 1867, p. 26). In other words, tradition embedded in custom acts to legitimate power, and it becomes authority. Another English social scientist, Harold Laski, in *Authority in the Modern State*, wrote that the basis for obedience to authority is consent. Laski thus added his voice to many social scientists linking authority to freedom in the contemporary state. If we freely consent to obey authority, its legitimacy becomes more pervasive than if we are forced to obey by dint of raw power.

This brief overview of who among the early European social scientists wrote about authority shows that social science responded to the sociopolitical events dominating the continent. It is interesting that American social science took very little notable interest in authority until the post-WWII period. This American neglect of a major social science concept is neither an accident nor a quirk. It gives us an opportunity to see that social theory is at least in part a mirror for understanding the social and historical conditions of the times and places in which they are produced.

American Theorists

During the second half of the nineteenth century European nations underwent births and rebirths of nationalism, bureaucratization, and centralization, and while these forces were also at work in America, they did not materialize as focal points because politics was subsumed by civil society and treated like any other associational influence. American social scientists generally saw politics as just another part of the associational life. Authority was viewed as just part of the fabric of association in America. Except for E. A. Ross' 1901 book, *Social Control*, hardly any of the great founding generation of American social scientists wrote about authority, and it was not until well after World War I that authority showed up on the American social science horizon. Beginning in the 1930s, Robert MacIver began writing about authority; so did Harold Lasswell, Talcott Parsons, Pitirim Sorokin, and Carl Friedrich, among others who were acquainted with the European literature and began applying it to America. It is notable that these social scientists imported and modified German, French, and Italian theories of authority rather than creating genuinely American theories.

Weberian Concepts

As noted, the most influential discussion of authority is found in the work of Max Weber, one of the founders of modern sociology. It is rare for any social science discussion of authority to omit Weber's analysis of power, authority, and legitimacy. Weber was interested in forms of power, *Herrschaftstypen*, or types of domination. The term *Herrschaft*, which means "rule" or "domination," has come to be popularly translated as "authority," and sometimes as "legitimate power." Indeed, Weber's studies showed that all societies established and maintained authority based on one or another type of legitimacy. Although Weber understood that authority rarely if ever existed in its pure form in any social organization, he categorized these types of authority as traditional, rational-legal, or charismatic.

Traditional Authority

Traditional authority, or what Weber called "*die Autorität des ewig Gestrigen*," "the authority of the eternal yesterday," rests on legitimacy conferred by custom (Weber, 1946, p. 78). He says that traditional legitimacy justifies the use of power by sanctifying the mores by appeals to "ancient recognition" and to accepted practices. Some of the examples Weber uses to illustrate traditional authority are hereditary rulers, religious priesthoods, parents, and elders in extended families. Later American sociologists, such as Edward Shils and Robert Nisbet, further explored the bases for traditional authority, extending the term to explain the overarching authority of the royal family in Great Britain, and the traditional authority of fathers, paterfamilias, regarding citizenship and life-and-death authority over their extended families in ancient Roman society (Shils and Young, 1952; Nisbet, 1999). The sociological theory of traditional authority always takes tradition, custom, hereditary or ascribed status, and social norms burnished over long periods of time into account as essential to this form of legitimacy in relatively small and homogeneous communities with simple divisions of labor.

Rational-Legal Authority

With the transition from medieval to modern societies and states in Europe, there emerged a powerful alternative to traditional authority:

rational-legal authority, or power legitimated by a rational-legal and interdependent division of labor, characterized by economic and occupational specialization, and complex rational-legal systems, where highly specialized and differentiated bureaucracies and associations are commonplace. Weber called this rational justification for obedience to authority, "domination by virtue of legality, by virtue of the belief in the validity of legal statute and functional competence, based on rationally created rules" (Weber, 1946, p. 79). According to Weber, this is the authority "exercised by the modern servant of the state." Aside from bureaucracies, rational-legal authority is situated in constitutions and courts that interest these, as well as achieved offices, such as those held by presidents, governors, and senators, rather than hereditary and ascribed offices held by monarchs and aristocrats. Structural complexity, complex organizations, and constant pressures to change are endemic to the world of rational-legal authority.

Weber's German sociological colleague, Ferdinand Tönnies distinguished between two types of societies: communally and rurally oriented *gemeinschaft-like* rooted in families or neighborhoods and ascribed statuses. In contrast, *gesellschaft-like* are exemplified by associational rather than communal orientations, and achieved statuses. Sociologists have clearly understood that *gemeinschaft* societies are marked by traditional authority structures, and *gesellschaft* societies by rational-legal authority.

A younger colleague of both Weber and Tönnies, Herman Schmalenbach, wrote about a third form of social organization, *des bundes*, communions, that transcended the *gemeinschaft-gesellschaft* continuum and its relationship to traditional and rational-legal legitimations of authority. He showed clearly that these ephemeral forms of association are based on what Weber called "charismatic authority," the third leg of his famous tripartite theory of authority.

Charisma

Charisma, according to Weber, "is the authority of the extraordinary and personal gift of grace." Weber used this ecclesiastical term to denote "the absolutely personal devotion and the personal confidence in revelation, heroism, or other qualities of individual leadership" (Weber, 1946, p. 79). This form of authority is useful for analyzing small, very cohesive inner circles of political, communal, and religious organizations. It is the authority of the revolutionary religious prophet, the political zealot, radically innovative entrepreneurs, and vanguard artists. Unlike traditional or bureaucratic authorities, these are individuals that demand obedience from their followers not on the basis of either ascribed or achieved status, but on their direct and personal connection to mystical powers. Although many social theorists have used the concept of charismatic authority, none have really transcended what Weber said about this form of legitimacy as a certain quality of an individual personality by virtue of which he is set apart from ordinary men and treated as endowed with supernatural, superhuman, or at least specifically exceptional powers or qualities. These are regarded as of divine origin or as exemplary, and based on them the individual concerned is treated as a leader. Religious leaders from Moses, Abraham, Jesus, or the Old Testament prophets are seen as charismatic authorities, but so were more recent leaders on the edge of sanity and the good-and-evil divide, such as John Brown, Jim Jones, or David Koresh. Edward Shils extended the Weberian analysis of charismatic authority to events, places, and things, and Weber's colleague, Joseph Schumpeter, went even farther in applying charismatic authority theories to economic entrepreneurs.

While Herman Schmalenbach, Edward Shils, and Joseph Schumpeter extended Weber's theory of charismatic authority beyond Tönnies' *Gemeinschaft und Gesellschaft* continuum, a later sociologist, Robert Bierstedt, raised the question of whether charisma is a type of authority at all. Arguing that "a leader can only request, and authority can require," Bierstedt made the case that charisma is merely a type of leadership, not a type of authority (Bierstedt, 1974, p. 247). By setting Weber's traditional and rational-legal legitimations of authority along a continuum of organizational status terms, Bierstedt demonstrated that authority exists because statuses that carry authority exist. But because charismatic legitimacy inheres in the person, rather than in roles and statuses, "charismatic authority is not authority at all, but leadership." While this interesting line of reasoning runs counter to Weber's theory of authority and to Edward Shils' extension of that theory beyond leadership to events and things, it also offers a possible obstacle to an ever-expanding list of studies of charisma. In the end, Bierstedt's argument that the entire collective symbolism of the society stands behind the traditional as well as the rational-legal forms of authority, offering no alternatives to obedience, seems in keeping not only with Weber's theory, but also with the French sociologist Émile Durkheim's theory of collective representations. If charismatic leaders cannot bring collective sanctions to bear on disobedience, do they really have authority, as Weber understood that term? This question is still worth pondering.

Obedience and Authority

One important question raised by Bierstedt's discussion of the relationship between authority and leadership is why authority is obeyed. Whether the authority is conferred by status in the society, or by followers in smaller bund-like groups, authority always demands obedience, and its success or failure depends upon followers obeying authoritative demands. So why is authority obeyed?

Legitimacy

Before trying to answer the question of obedience, a baseline assumption is usually made; namely, when authoritative demands are considered legitimate by those who thereby willingly obey them, we have authority. When the demands are obeyed mostly out of fear of force being used, we have raw power. Power is the ability to make people do what they don't want to do, but authority is the ability to make them want to do what they start off not wanting to do. This assumption is problematic because it valorizes one important part of Weber's theory of power at the expense of an equally important but contradictory element of it. The problem is centered on Weber's often ambivalent use of terms, such as *Herrschaft*, or "domination," *Autorität*, or "authority," and *Macht*, or "power." Thus, in Weber's most comprehensive chapter on authority in his magnum opus *Wirtschaft und Gesellschaft*, or *Economy and Society*, Weber says that "Herrschaft ist ein sonderfall von macht" ("Domination is a special case of power"), and a few paragraphs later he discusses "domination by virtue of a constellation of interests," ("die Herrschaft kraft Interessenkonstellation"), as opposed to "domination by virtue of authority," ("die Herrschaft kraft Autorität") (Weber, 1922, 1968).

These ambiguities in Weber's language of domination and authority have been noted and discussed by a number of social theorists including Steven Lukes, Guenther Roth, and Wolfgang Mommsen. This inexactness of terminology is yet to be resolved, and there remains a certain cloudiness that hangs over the social science theories of authority resting on Weberian foundations. Weber himself seems to have understood that legitimate domination, or authority, as we have come to understand the term, is different than power insofar as it is accepted by those over whom obedience is demanded. It is this acceptance to which we must turn to understand obedience to authority.

This Weberian perspective—problematic as it may be—has been emphasized by Hannah Arendt in her article, "What Was Authority?," in which she also demonstrates that there is nothing to be gained by discussing some vague "authority in general" (Arendt, 1968). As she notes, authority is always alloyed to the dialectic of obedience and disobedience in a particular and specific social structure, and it makes no sense to discuss authority in a free-floating and overly general way. For Arendt, as for Weber in his somewhat convoluted but comprehensive treatment of domination, authority must be understood "in contradistinction to both coercion by force and persuasion through arguments" (Arendt, 1968, p. 93). It is in this theoretical context that we must try to understand why we obey authority.

Power

The ability of authority to transform resistance to obedience into acceptance of obedience is usually attributed to what Weber called legitimation or justification of power. This transformation is what I call a social and cultural "transduction." In physics, a transducer is a device that transforms one form of energy into another, as when an electromagnet transforms electrical energy into magnetic energy, or an incandescent bulb transforms electrical energy into light. Weber's forms of legitimacy are socio-cultural devices that transform power into traditional authority, or rational-legal authority, or charismatic authority.

What Weber lacked was an understanding about how these transducing justifications turned power into authority, or, put differently, how a reluctant obedience to power is turned into a willing obedience to authority. Weber was well versed in the work of James Bryce, and was definitely influenced by him. As noted earlier, Bryce's now much-neglected essay "Obedience" had a demonstrable effect on Weber's theory of authority. In "Obedience," Bryce was one of the first social scientists to use the term "legitimate authority" as an analytical tool, and he narrowed down the transformational and transducive qualities that turn power into authority to indolence, deference, sympathy, fear, and reason, all of which would later become important to Weber's understanding of legitimacy.

So why do people obey authority? Traditional values, religious values, rational values, and the like actually become part of who we are, part of our identities, and if they justify obedience to authority, reluctantly obeyed power becomes transformed into happily obeyed authority. To get to deeper and more modern answers to the question about socio-cultural transduction of power into authority, we must turn to later theorists.

Culture

Philip Rieff, a sociologist, understood cultures to be engines of moral demand, or what he called "moral demand systems." Rieff was not the only theorist to see culture as a system of moral demands. In this he was joined by the anthropologist Clifford Geertz, who saw culture as a set of symbolic control mechanisms that govern behavior. Both Rieff's and Geertz's theories of culture benefit from Sigmund Freud's psychoanalytical idea that symbols become introjected into the self, and are made part of an individual's sense of identity.

These cultural theories were anticipated decades ago by social scientists influenced by pragmatist philosophy, such as George Herbert Mead, whose ideas about "significant symbols" lay the groundwork for understanding the transducive quality of cultural values. To this list of theorists, we should add the philosopher Susanne Langer, whose *Philosophy in a New Key* has chapters on "life symbols" as the root of myth and of sacrament that provide key insights into how cultural symbols transform reluctant obedience to power into willing obedience to authority. As she says, "the human brain is constantly carrying on a process of symbolic transformation of the experiential data that comes to it that causes it to become a veritable fountain of spontaneous ideas" (Langer, 1942, p. 34). It is the seeming spontaneity and freedom of our ideas about the need to obey authority that give authority legitimacy.

A very different point of view about the reasons people obey authority was expressed by the social psychologist Stanley Milgram, whose experiments about obedience were both brilliant and controversial. Milgram found that a disturbingly high rate of experimental subjects was willing to obey an authority figure wearing a lab coat and professing to be in charge of a learning experiment. The subjects were instructed to give what they believed were electrical shocks in increasing intensities to a "learner" whenever he got an answer wrong. After finding that a majority of subjects obeyed the authority figure, often in spite of professing to have moral qualms about inflicting pain on the "learner," Milgram tried to explain their obedience, first, in part, by the cultural context of their upbringings, and then by the institutional setting of the experiments. But, what is really interesting about Milgram's explanations, in terms of obedience to authority, is that the subjects responded to the perceived legitimacy of the experimenter. Very much in line with Weber's theory, and that of the culture theorists such as Rieff and Geertz, Milgram says that the first and foremost reason for obedience is "the perception of a legitimate authority" (Milgram, 1974, p. 138). This perception of legitimacy is a direct result of "the internalization of the social order—that is internalizing the set of axioms by which social life is conducted." Thus, from Bryce to Rieff, Geertz and Milgram, we see that we must turn to cultural symbolics of obedience to understand the transducive qualities in the Weberian justifications of authority.

The most basic paradigm for conceptualizing authority was the one set into motion by Max Weber, and he and others addressed how obedience to authority comes to replace obedience to power. The intellectual landscape of authority reveals when, where, and how authority was conceived as a social science concept.

While Western philosophers from Plato and Aristotle through Hobbes, Locke, Rousseau, Machiavelli, Kant, Hegel, Kierkegaard, and Nietzsche, among others, have thought about power and authority, their discussions generally pivot on either justifying or condemning hierarchical civic or political relations. Social science theories of authority, on the other hand, tend to ask and answer the problem-solving questions *What? Why? When? How? Where?* and *Who?* In other words, social science theorists of authority, such as Weber and the other social scientists discussed above, are less interested in justifying or condemning authority, than in understanding it.

2
CHARISMA AND AUTHORITY

Social scientists use the term "charisma" to describe a special form of authority that is based on the belief that a person possesses extraordinary and perhaps divinely ordained powers. The concept is useful for understanding the relatively small, extraordinarily cohesive inner circles of sectarian communities and social movements that develop around revolutionary religious prophets, extremist political zealots, rebellious vanguards and artists, radically creative entrepreneurs, and other nonconformist leaders who attract devoted, sometimes fanatical followers and disciples. In their pure form, charismatic movements are based on intense, shared experiences of rapport and rapture, and are necessarily short-lived. They eventually yield to what the German sociologist Max Weber (1864–1920) called the routinization of charisma and become reintegrated into the social structure, or they disappear with the group's disenchantment with the leader or with the leader's death.

The terms "charisma" (from the Greek *charisma*, favor or gift) was widely used in early Christian thought, and early twentieth-century German theologians used the word when explaining that early Christianity was transformed from an ecstatic prophetic (charismatic) sect into an institutionalized church. The term's meaning in social science was established by Max Weber, who noted that the phenomenon characterized the rise and transformation of various groups that believed that they and their leaders were charismatic and above dealing with matters of everyday life. Remarkably, until about 1950 charisma was a little known and mostly unused concept in English-language publications, while today seemingly countless articles and books in sociology, anthropology, history, political science, psychology, psychoanalysis, and economics consider charisma a powerful force.

Although each of the social sciences has adapted its own interpretation of charisma, Weber's conception is still valid:

> ... a certain quality of an individual personality by virtue of which he is set apart from ordinary men and treated as endowed with supernatural, superhuman, or at least specifically exceptional powers or qualities. These are such as are not accessible to the ordinary person, but are regarded as of divine origin or as exemplary, and on the basis of them the individual concerned is treated as a leader.
>
> (Weber, 1946, p. 329)

The relationship between charismatic leaders and their followers leads to the formation of charismatic communities, which in their pure forms have been called "bunds" (communions) or "fusions." In these groups, charismatics and their followers are bound together by mutually shared inspirational feelings and experiences. Charismatic movements and communities tend to arise during times that call for revolutionary or at least extraordinary behavior. Such movements generally form around "natural leaders in moments of distress—whether psychic, physical, economic, ethical, religious, or political" (Weber, 1968, p. 1112). Charismatic movements such as radical political parties, nonconforming religious sects, avant-garde artistic salons, or utopian communes always stand in opposition to the status quo. This inherently oppositional quality led Weber to see charisma, in its pure forms, as the most primal revolutionary force in social life.

Because of the revolutionary attitude associated with charismatic movements, outsiders often regard them with hostility, especially in the formative stages, when charismatic authority is purest. At these times, charismatic movements are most intense and undiminished by routinization, most threatening to established social values.

The mere fact of recognizing the personal mission of a charismatic master established his power...this recognition derives from the surrender of the faithful to the extraordinary and unheard-of, to what is alien to all regulation and tradition and therefore is viewed as divine—surrender which arises from distress or enthusiasm.

(Weber, 1968, p. 1115)

These concepts are evident in the peculiar case of Jemima Wilkinson and her "miraculous ministry," which I will use as a case study of charismatic authority. During the fall of 1776 word spread from Cumberland, Rhode Island that a young woman, Jemima Wilkinson, had died and had been miraculously resurrected. Furthermore, this young woman had announced that her resurrected body was now possessed by a spirit called the "Publick Universal Friend," and that she was taking up a ministry under that name. Jemima Wilkinson became so successful as an evangelical preacher and founder of a religious cult that in her day she was at least as well known as her more historically famous contemporary, Mother Anne Lee of the Shakers.

By 1785 Jemima Wilkinson had a large following who attended her weekly meetings believing that she had died and been reborn. The size of her following and the fervor of their belief in her is attributable to her charisma. However, the sociologically unusual thing is the fact that she and most of her followers were middle to upper middle class in terms of both their ascribed and achieved statuses. This runs contrary to the more common sociological explanation of charismatic movements as ones fueled by economic and political deprivation. That charismatic religious movements arise in distressing times has been widely noted, but Weber's assertion that such movements are often enthusiastic in origin has largely been ignored. Enthusiasts such as Jemima Wilkinson believe that they are seized and guided in an extraordinary manner by immediate, direct, divine inspiration and revelation. Her case is interesting not just as a study of a charismatic cult movement, but also for the new insights it gives into the relationships of class, culture, and charisma.

The basis for the Weberian conceptualization of charisma is cultural rather than political or psychological (Hennis, 1988). This cultural emphasis helps give charisma a special place in sociological theory. As originally formulated by Weber, charisma is an example of what Robert Merton called a "key concept...bridging the gap between statics and dynamics." This key concept is "that of strain, tension, contradiction, or discrepancy between the component elements of social and cultural structure" (Merton, 1968, p. 122). Both symbolizing and resolving these strains and contradictions, charisma represents a phenomenon to be found at the disjuncture of cultural and social structures. This brings us to the problem of culture.

Following Philip Rieff's lead, I define culture as a "system of moral demands," or better, "a design of motives directing the self outward, toward those communal purposes in which alone the self can be realized and satisfied" (Rieff, 1966, p. 4). To maintain itself, a culture communicates ideals which establish themselves in personality and character as "faith," which Rieff defines as "the compelling dynamic of culture, channeling obedience to, trust in, and dependence upon authority" (Rieff, 1966, p. 12). This definition is supported and augmented by Clifford Geertz, who defines culture as a

> system of symbols which acts to establish powerful, pervasive, and long-lasting moods and motivations in men by formulating conceptions of a general order of existence and clothing these conceptions with such an aura of factuality that the moods and motivations seem uniquely realistic.
> (Geertz, 1973, p. 90)

Charisma founded on faith, and on religious moods and motivations, is a supremely cultural construct.

Both culture and charisma rest firmly on a Kantian foundation. In answering the rhetorical question basic to his philosophy, namely, "How is nature possible?" Kant insinuated a view of reality central to modern sociological thought. In essence, his answer was that nature is possible because human beings can conceive of it as possible. The human mind gives shape and order to the bits and pieces, the things and actions of the world, so as to form a unity which is represented by the term "nature"

(Kant, 1889, p. 77). From this perspective, every cultural symbol is a stylized representation of reality, and what we call "reality" is always merely a stylized representation of reality. We are many things to many people, and, as we shall see, so was Jemima Wilkinson.

Since human perceptions of reality are filtered through the cultural symbols embedded in language, we might well say that it is the function of culture to maintain a symbolic system capable of stylizing the contents of reality in such a way as to give both a sense of meaning and of mastery over social reality. And if we twist Kant's question slightly, and ask "How is a sense of immanence possible?," or "How is a sense of divinity possible?," or "How is the perception of the miraculous possible?," we can derive the general Kantian answer: These are all possible because culture allows them to be conceivable to us. When a society, or some segment of it, bestows the judgment that a person is endowed with exceptional powers of divine origin, it has stylized that person's reality into a symbol as well as an affirmation of the existence of the divine realm itself.

This perspective clearly constitutes the a priori foundation for the concept of charisma. A culture that allows for conceptualization of the divine, of miracles, of immanence, and of prophecy, allows making sense out of the existence of such phenomena. Hence, they can have a place in the social life and experience in a society shaped by the normative order of such a culture. But what use may be made of this cultural perspective of reality by sociologists interested in religion as a social force? More specifically, what use is it to understand a society's reaction to a religious leader like Jemima Wilkinson? In other words, "How was Jemima Wilkinson possible?" In a word, an answer to this general question can be found in the concept of charisma.

Although the term "charisma" itself is well known to sociologists its meaning is not always clear. It is important to the argument advanced here that this concept be understood specifically as Weber used it:

> The term "charisma" will be applied to a certain quality of an individual personality by virtue of which he is set apart from ordinary men and treated as endowed with supernatural, superhuman, or at least specifically exceptional powers or qualities. These are such

as are not accessible to the ordinary person, but are regarded as of divine origin or as exemplary, and on the basis of them the individual concerned is treated as a leader.

(Weber, 1968, p. 329)

Following Weber, we see that "charisma" is a relational term. It represents not merely a "quality of personality," per se, but more importantly, a social relationship in which the person who is perceived to have this extraordinary quality is "set apart" and is treated as a leader by those who believe that these powers are of "divine origin."

As a sociologist, Weber was not interested in judging whether or not the charismatic was actually endowed with supernatural, superhuman powers of divine origin, but only in whether or not such a person was believed to be by followers who subjected themselves to the charismatic's authority on that basis, as did Jemima Wilkinson's. According to Weber, "it is recognition on the part of those subject to authority which is decisive for the validity of charisma" (Weber, 1968, p. 330). Weber, then, understood charismatic authority to extend no further than over those who believe in the divine gift of grace of a particular individual and are willing to subjugate their will to that person.

To this point it is not hard to see that a culture which allows for faith in divinity can support charisma and charismatic movements. But since charismatic claims always challenge the legitimacy of existing social structures they tend to produce strains and tensions by pointing out contradictions and discrepancies between the component elements of social and cultural structures. If this is so, then charisma is disruptive but not deviant because culture, paradoxically, supports and hence warrants the challenge to things as they are, inherent in charismatic claims.

Beyond this we must ask, what specific elements of cultural structure must be present to support charismatic movements? This question leads us to ask, how does a charismatic movement originate, and how does it become legitimized to and by its followers? About the origin of charisma Weber wrote,

> The mere fact of recognizing the personal mission of a charismatic master establishes his power...this recognition derives

from the surrender of the faithful to the extraordinary and unheard-of, to what is alien to all regulation and tradition and therefore is viewed as divine—surrender which arises from distress or enthusiasm.

(Weber, 1968, p. 1115)

If enthusiasm is a primary cause of charisma, we must ask, what is it and how can a culture support it? Simply put, enthusiasm is the belief that one is possessed by an indwelling divine presence. All enthusiasts, Jemima Wilkinson included, are persuaded that they are seized and guided in an extraordinary manner by immediate, and direct, divine inspiration and revelation (Knox, 1950, p. 450). This persuasion of mind leads enthusiasts to claim an unmediated union with the divine. A culture that supports faith in charismatics must allow for belief in direct contact with divinity.

This brings us to the question of how Jemima Wilkinson and her followers came to believe that she had died and been resurrected. Was late eighteenth century American culture able to support such a belief? Of course it was. As a Judeo-Christian culture, it had a theo-lingual heritage of prophets and saviors, mysteries and miracles, God and heaven. Why relatively few people believed Jemima Wilkinson's story is also easily explainable. By the late eighteenth century American culture had tended to emphasize rational forms of worship more likely to be exercised in churches rather than in cults. Besides this, for those more prone to seek out enthusiastic or other nontraditional forms of religion, there were a plethora of competing movements to follow, such as some of those listed by a horrified traditionalist in the *American Mercury* in 1791: "Familists, Libertines, Anti-trinitarians, Anabaptists, Antinomians, Mortalians, Gnostics, Fatalists, Universalists, Seekers, Shakers, &c., &c," (McLoughlin, 1971, p. 918).

Of course, we are still left with the question of why any particular person believed in Jemima Wilkinson. The question is unanswerable. When dealing with charismatic movements such as this, which are long since spent, with no living survivors, we can only speculate about motive. But we can say with certainty that economic and political deprivation are insufficient explanations, at least in this case. Given that few of Jemima Wilkinson's followers were deprived, the cultural conceptualization of charisma better explains this movement.

As background, Jemima Wilkinson was born into a prominent Quaker family in 1752 in Cumberland, Rhode Island. Although not much is known about her childhood, it is clear that she was brought up as a Quaker and that her early religious training influenced her throughout her life. Her youth was later characterized by her detractors as that of a vain child who loved fine clothing and gay company, and who used her great beauty to get her way. She was also characterized as extremely lazy and manipulative to the point of getting her sisters to regularly do her chores for her. This characterization was consistent with the idea held by those who derided her that Wilkinson was a manipulative impostor whose claim about her death and resurrection was a ploy to make herself "the object of their faith" (Wisbey, 1964, p. 31).

When she was about twelve years old Jemima Wilkinson's mother died soon after bearing her twelfth child. There is reason to speculate that her mother's death, apparently related to the strain of child bearing, deeply affected Jemima. This may also help explain why throughout her life, and as the charismatic leader of her own cult, Jemima Wilkinson advocated celibacy. After her mother's death Wilkinson became interested in Quaker history and theology. She read all the standard theological works and knew the Bible so thoroughly that scriptural phrases became a normal part of her everyday speech. This is important, because Wilkinson was never known, even among her followers, as a particularly profound theologian. Most of her sermons were simply rambling compilations of biblical truisms. It was not what she said, but the sincerity of her manner and her self-proclaimed divine calling to say it that constituted her powerful appeal to her followers.

In 1770, at age eighteen or nineteen, Jemima Wilkinson came under the influence of George Whitefield, the most famous revivalist preacher of his day. Although she remained a birthright Quaker, Jemima began to attend meetings of a New Light Baptist group in Cumberland. One of her biographers described the New Light Baptists as

> ... noisy, zealous congregations of persons emphasizing individual inspiration and enlightenment through the Holy Spirit. Hostile to all authority other than the Bible and the Holy Spirit,

they were strict in requiring their members to give clear evidence of a conversion experience.

(Wisbey, 1964, p. 7)

In August 1776, she was expelled from the Society of Friends for attending the New Light Baptist meetings, as well as for not attending the Quaker meetings and for refusing to use plain language, that is, "thee" and "thou," as required of Quakers. Later, during her ministry, Quakers, who turned out to be among her strongest critics, charged her with the heresy of "the exalted character given to her own mission...which savored strongly of pride and ambition to distinguish herself from the rest of Mankind" (Wisbey, 1964, p. 34). They went as far as declaring that it was "a cause for stumbling" to attend one of the Universal Friend's meetings.

During the months following her dismissal from her Quaker meeting, Jemima Wilkinson lost interest in the New Lights as well as in the Quakers. She became withdrawn, and isolated herself from family and friends. She spent much of her time meditating and studying the Scriptures. In October 1776, she became seriously ill with a dangerously high fever and was delirious for a few days. During her illness, which her doctor thought had affected her mind, she claimed to have had a vision in which she saw angels take her soul away, replacing in her body the Spirit of God, which was to be known as "the Publick Universal Friend" (Marlin, 1963, p. 91). Upon recovering, she announced that during the illness Jemima Wilkinson had died and had been resurrected. The body of Jemima Wilkinson contained a new spirit sent directly from God with a mission to preach to a sinful and dying world. She proclaimed that from then on, she was to be called the "Publick Universal Friend" and indeed never again responded to her given name. In Wilkinson's enthusiasm, in which she was persuaded that she was guided in an extraordinary manner by immediate and direct divine inspiration and revelation, we have the origins of her charismatic authority. This self-proclaimed experience was also the symbolic basis for her moral career as a disruptive symbol.

Within days of her enthusiastic experience Jemima Wilkinson began her ministry as the Publick Universal Friend, preaching in the churchyard of the small Baptist meeting house in Cumberland. She told the congregants about the dangers of sin and the need for repentance, and soon she was holding meetings in her home as well as traveling to nearby towns. Among her adherents, who numbered about two hundred and fifty men and women, were quite a few independently rich individuals and families. In fact, a preliminary study of her following shows that most of Wilkinson's adherents were middle or upper middle class in terms of both their ascribed and achieved statuses. Some had sold or left behind thriving and prosperous farms and businesses in New England to follow her into an inhospitable wilderness. Others gave up positions of power and prestige to be with her. For example, Judge William Potter of South Kingston, Rhode Island, freed his slaves and ended his career as Chief Justice of the Court of Common Pleas in Washington County, Rhode Island to follow The Friend.

That neither Jemima Wilkinson, nor most of her followers, were from the lower or more deprived classes, presents a problem for those who consider a chief cause of charismatic cult movements to be economic and political deprivation. This idea, which did not originate with Weber, was probably first made popular in 1929, a decade after his death, both by Karl Mannheim in *Ideology and Utopia* and by H. Richard Niebuhr in *The Social Sources of Denominationalism*. Mannheim's suggestion that charismatic and enthusiastic movements "originated in the oppressed strata of society" (Mannheim, 1936, p. 212) has been echoed many times since, to the point of being taken for granted. Thus, Werner Stark wrote that "all through history, the lowest ranks of society have been the prime recruiting ground of heresies and schisms. Marxists are, by and large, within their rights when they claim that sect movements are phenomena of an ongoing class struggle" (Stark, 1967, p. 5).

Less noticed among sociologists are the arguments of many historians who claim that evidence from the historical record does not support the class struggle thesis. For instance, after sifting through historical accounts of the medieval roots of the German reformation, Guenter Lewy concluded that "the downtrodden and disinherited of medieval Europe… do not in fact form the backbone of religious dissenters" (Lewy, 1974, p. 105). This assertion is backed up by Norman Cohn, who wrote that "it was only very rarely that settled peasants could be induced to embark on the pursuit of the Millennium" (Cohn, 1970, p. 24).

There is obviously no simple resolution to these conflicting points of view. Although it is clear that enthusiastic religious cults often do have a great appeal among the politically and economically distressed classes, this is not exclusively so. Even if political and economic deprivation predisposes the deprived to be susceptible to recruitment by charismatic movements, this does not adequately explain participation in them. If we are to explain participation in such movements by the non-deprived, as in the case of Jemima Wilkinson and her adherents, we must look for other reasons than those the economic determinists offer.

Of greater concern is the tendency of economic determinism to obscure the fact that in most historical cases pre-dating the present era, such as the case at hand, people like Jemima Wilkinson, her followers, and opponents all lived in a world where religion not only counted, but was of overriding importance. To obscure this fact is to lose sight of the single most important element in explaining her compelling attraction. Religion itself may be, in any given society, an irreducible social fact, which like social class or social norms, serves as an explanation for behavior, as opposed to being a phenomenon itself in need of explanation.

If this is the case in late eighteenth and early nineteenth century America, and I posit that it is, charisma is the one concept that can help explain religious movements without obscuring the overarching importance of religion itself. The mere recognition of extraordinary gift and mission was understood by Weber to establish the charismatic's power. There is an unconditional rightness in recognition that causes self-surrender, a "surrender of the faithful to the extraordinary and unheard of, to what is alien to all regulations," (Weber, 1968, p. 1115). This is the revolutionary power of charisma, and the power behind Wilkinson's enthusiastic movement. Evidence suggests that her adherents followed her simply because they believed she was really the mouthpiece of their god. Theirs was a culture, unlike our own, in which at least some could easily believe in revelations and miracles of the sort Jemima Wilkinson claimed to have had.

The two key socioreligious elements which made Jemima Wilkinson the center of a charismatic movement were her claim about having died and then having been resurrected, and her messianism. Clearly, belief in Wilkinson's miraculous resurrection story by her adherents is the basis for her ministry, just as the fact that those who did not believe in her story saw her as either suffering from delusions or as a charlatan. She herself appears to have believed that she did indeed die and become reanimated. She never wavered, as far as we know, in this belief. Moreover, she constantly reminded her followers that Jemima Wilkinson was dead and that the Publick Universal Friend was sent by God to inhabit her body.

Jemima Wilkinson's story of death and resurrection had strong messianic elements, which formed the basis for the declaration on the part of many of her followers that she was the resurrection of Christ himself. These messianic components of her story led to her being branded a blasphemer by some who heard this claim. These messianic pretensions caused her to be brought to trial for blasphemy by one of her former adherents. After a brilliantly sincere performance in court, in which she denied ever having personally made claims to being Jesus Christ or his substitute on earth, she was acquitted. Her followers' adoration was matched by her detractors' derision. The death and resurrection story was disputed by her attending physician as well as by her older brother, Jeremiah, both of whom questioned her sanity.

In Wilkinson's religious movement we have a case history of a charismatic movement fueled by the cultural notions of divinity and faith, which permitted those predisposed to do so to believe in the charismatic's direct link with God. Sociologists do not need to be concerned with the authenticity of her claims, but only with their social consequences. As Weber said, charisma, if it has any specific effects at all, "manifests its revolutionary power from within, from a central metanoia (change) of the followers' attitudes" (Weber, 1968, p. 1117). Enthusiasm, that is belief in direct and immanent revelation and guidance, is largely responsible for such changes. In the case of Jemima Wilkinson, enthusiastic belief in her death and resurrection was a culturally accepted idea, as were the concepts of revelations and miracles. As such, those beliefs transcended social class and economic position to affect a wide range of believers.

In its most extreme manifestations, enthusiasm—the claim to immediate direct revelations such as Wilkinson's—has often led to antinomianism (a disregard for all established social institutions) and to rebellion against both ecclesiastical and civil authorities. It may be that those who claim such an intimate relationship to divinity feel license to break conventional laws and societal morals. From the time of Anne Hutchinson's enthusiastically inspired "antinomian controversy," to the present, this seems to be the case. Following Weber, contemporary sociologists, such as Daniel Bell, Edward Shils, and S. N. Eisenstadt, have noted the connection between charismatic movements and antinomianism.

Underscoring this enthusiastically antinomian component of charisma, Weber said that in its most extreme form, a charismatic movement overturns reason, tradition, and "all notions of sanctity. Instead of reverence for customs that are…sacred, it enforces the inner subjection to the unprecedented and absolutely unique and therefore Divine." In this sense "charisma is indeed the specifically creative revolutionary force of history" (Weber, 1968, p. 1117).

Antinomianism is strongest during the formative phases of charismatic movements. These early phases have been referred to as liminal, representation transitions between old and new identities for both leaders and disciples. Victor Turner, the anthropologist who first introduced the idea of liminality into the language of social theory, recognized that charismatic religious movements often arise outside normal ritual structures, and that "their liminality is not institutionalized." Instead, Turner wrote, this charismatic liminality is "spontaneously generated in a situation of radical structural change…. It is in this limbo of structure that religious movements, led by charismatic prophets, powerfully reassert the values of communities, often in extreme and antinomian forms" (Turner 1974, p. 248). On the other hand, almost from the beginning, the revolutionary tide that accompanies the birth of charismatic movements begins to ebb and is routinized, transformed into an institution such as a church, political party, of profession, with permanent structures and traditions.

Social scientists have not tried to evaluate whether charismatics are actually endowed with supernatural, superhuman powers of divine origin, but only whether the followers subjecting themselves to the charismatic's authority on that basis believe in the leader's powers. The charismatic bond between leaders and followers "finds its limits at the edges of these groups" (Weber, 1968, p. 1113). Many casual observers have attributed charisma to leaders with mass appeal (such as Adolph Hitler). In fact, such leaders often do have charisma, but only in relation to those in their inner circles. When the parties or social movements headed by these leaders are successful, it is because they have been transformed into mainstream rational or traditional institutions. If pure charismatic movements do not yield to routinization, they eventually fail.

Challenges to the established ways of doing things in ongoing communities—from community units as small as families to units as large as nations—are usually first met by resistance. Charismatic movements driven by passion and enthusiasm can be likened to firestorms of change, sweeping across the normative social landscape. Often, they burn out or are put out by the communities that they threaten to change. Sometimes, however, their challenges prevail and the communities change because of them. It is in this sense that Weber saw charisma as the most revolutionary agent in history.

3
AUTHORITY PATTERNS IN COLONIAL NEW ENGLAND

During its entire colonial history, 1636–1790, Rhode Island was dominated by two religious groups, both of which were instrumental in its founding, namely Quakers and Baptists. At their high point the Quakers were clearly the majority religious group in the colony, and their beliefs were translated into secular law and policy for the entire colony. It is estimated that, between 1700 and 1740, Rhode Island's population grew from 5,894 to 25,255 inhabitants. One prominent historian called this period "The Golden Age of Quakerism," estimating that half of the population of Rhode Island was Quaker, and that Quakers held the office of Governor for thirty-six successive terms (Brinton, 1952, p. 183). The majority of the remaining population was Baptist. In 1750, for example, although the Quakers were in the majority, there were at least thirty Baptist churches, twelve Congregational churches, and seven Anglican churches in the colony.

Founded the same year as neighboring Rhode Island, Connecticut was dominated by Puritan Congregationalism, which presided over its secular and political life throughout the colonial period as the established state religion, which it remained until 1818. During the period 1700–1740, Connecticut's population grew from an estimated 25,970 to 89,580 inhabitants. Historians agree that the overwhelming majority of the Connecticut population was Congregational. In 1750, for example, there were one hundred and fifty-five Congregational churches in the colony, but only nineteen Anglican churches, and twelve Baptist churches, most of which were in eastern Connecticut near the Rhode Island border (Gaustad, 1962, p. 167). From the beginning, Connecticut remained largely impervious to Quakerism (Jones, 1966, p. 120).

This chapter explores the influence, often unanticipated and unintended, of religious beliefs upon social action. More specifically, I address the unintended consequences of Puritan beliefs on the pattern of leadership and authority in colonial Connecticut, and of Quaker and Baptist beliefs on the pattern of leadership and authority in colonial Rhode Island.

In *The Protestant Ethic and the Spirit of Capitalism* Max Weber discussed the affinity between those cultures which had been strongly influenced by the rationalist ethos of the ascetic branches of Protestantism and the rise of capitalism. Weber's study of this relationship falls, by and large, into one of the two overarching perspectives about social development, namely the comparative historical approach. Unlike the evolutionary perspective, represented by theorists like Karl Marx and later Talcott Parsons, which assumes a single progressive social development for an abstract "humanity," occurring in stages, higher evolving from lower, the comparative approach of theorists like Weber and Alexis de Tocqueville assumes an abundance of social developments, specific to given times and places (Schneiderman, 1982, p. 95).

Following the comparative historical approach, I assume here, as did Weber and Ernst Troeltsch, that more than one protestant ethic influenced the different social and political developments of Western societies. Furthermore, I am explicitly interested in testing one of the main theses of a much-heralded book which is now part of the Weberian "Protestant Ethic" controversy, E. Digby Baltzell's *Puritan Boston and Quaker Philadelphia*. Baltzell's thesis is that the patterns of elite development in a society are influenced by its attitudes about hierarchy, authority, and leadership. With this in mind he wrote that,

> A normative culture that stresses the desirability of hierarchy, class and authority will instill in its members a stronger desire and capacity to take the lead in both community building and

community reform than a normative culture that emphasizes equality and brotherly love, explicitly *rejecting* the need for hierarchy, class, and authority.

(Baltzell, 1979, p. 6)

Baltzell tested this thesis by examining the very different patterns of leadership that developed among the upper classes in Boston, Massachusetts under the powerful influence of the philo-hierarchical Puritan ethic, as opposed to the upper classes in Philadelphia, Pennsylvania under the equally strong influence of the much more egalitarian ethos of Quakerism. His conclusion was that the Quaker ethic, which emphasized equality, privacy, and private success, caused Philadelphia to suffer a vacuum of authoritative public leadership for almost three centuries, while during that same period Boston's best-qualified citizens, driven by the Puritan obsession with public authority, leadership, and fame, sought out and filled the most important positions of public authority in the city, state, and nation. The differences between the Puritan and Quaker ethic were summarized by Baltzell as follows (Baltzell, 1979, p. 94).

The religious patterns of the Puritans emphasized the Old Testament's Ten Commandments, law, and the authority of the Bible, while the Quakers emphasized the New Testament's Sermon on the Mount, the Gospel, and the Inner Light. For the Puritans, God is transcendent, and emphasis is on the historical Jesus, while for the Quakers, God is immanent, and the eternal Christ is revered. Philosophically, the Puritans considered themselves God's servants who needed to do good works, while the Quakers thought of themselves as friends of God, looking for his grace. Puritans glorified God in the world, and Quakers looked inward to a mystical union with God. Puritans' psychology was filled with anxiety and compulsion due to their notions of honor and duty. The Quaker psychology was about finding peace of mind through honesty. The Puritan mores underscored predestination and election, a highly educated clergy, and value placed on education and learned sermons. Meanwhile, the Quakers placed much stock in charismatic laymen, and on keeping personal journals.

The cultural consequences of the Puritan and Quaker ethics are most interesting for their differing emphases on authority and citizenship. The Puritans practiced hierarchical communalism, and idealized the church dominating the community. The Quakers withdrew from community building to the sectarian ideal of withdrawing to their peers. Puritans were well known for theological intolerance, but also for institution-building, while the Quakers believed in spontaneous perfectionism and tolerance for competing value systems. The ideal social types for Puritans were judges, ministers, and magistrates. The social types most idealized by Quakers were private citizens, personal legal advocates, and martyrs or mystics.

The sociological results of these two religious cultures are as disparate as the theologies themselves. The Puritans valued hierarchy and patrician mores. The Quakers valued equality and plutocratic money-making. In this same vein, the Puritans were opportunists who valued leveling-up patriarchal mores that led to hierarchical social strata, but the Quakers were egalitarians who placed great emphasis on leveling down so that all might be equal.

If Baltzell's thesis is correct, the same dichotomy can be applied to any cohesive social groups which are held together under the sway of religious ethics, like Boston under the Puritan ethos and Philadelphia under the Quaker ethos. In this chapter I will apply it to colonial Rhode Island and Connecticut. It should be emphasized, however, that Rhode Island's early culture, while largely influenced by Quakerism, also included strong Baptist influences.

The colonial American Baptists, like the Quakers, practiced tolerance toward other religions. They were also advocates of a strict separation of church and state. Both of these principles were put into practice in colonial Rhode Island. The Baptists also emphasized individualism. Church membership was dependent upon individual religious experience, and individual conscience was valued above any ministerial authority. Corporately each congregation was considered completely independent of any higher ecclesiastical authority (Harrison, 1959). The cultural results of the Baptist ethos were extreme localism and resistance to all efforts to centralize authority, as well as extreme individualism which enervated the drive to exercise public authority and emphasized private callings.

An examination of the leadership elite in the two colonies reveals that predictions which may have been made from Baltzell's thesis can be borne out. In general, the Puritan society in Connecticut became dominated by public authority figures, while Rhode Island's elite, springing from a

Quaker and Baptist background, consisted in large part of privately successful individuals, such as merchants and manufacturers.

This conclusion is reached from an analysis of a group of individuals born before 1765 included in the *Dictionary of American Biography (DAB)*. The *DAB* is the most authoritative index of America's historical elite. As C. Wright Mills said, "In a certain sense, the persons who appear in the *Dictionary of American Biography* may be considered the historical elite of the United States" (Mills and Horowitz, 1963, p. 110). Baltzell himself used the *DAB* as the basis of his study of Boston and Philadelphia and wrote that "the most useful index of the men and women who have been the foremost contributors to American cultural history is the *Dictionary of American Biography*" (Baltzell, 1979, p. 34).

A total of 13,633 individuals are included in the twenty original volumes of the *DAB*. Of these, 784 (5.8% of the total) were born in Connecticut, and 205 (1.5% of the total) were born in Rhode Island. If we follow Baltzell's methods, however, and correct for population differences to a rate of inclusion in the DAB per 10,000 based on the census of 1830, we get the results for the original thirteen states shown in Table 3.1.

Table 3.1 Number of Individuals in the DAB Born in the Original Thirteen States Per 10,000 Population

State	Number in DAB	Population in 1830	Number in *DAB* per 10,000
Massachusetts	1,868 (13.7)[a]	610,408	31
Connecticut	784 (5.8)	297,675	26
Rhode Island	205 (1.5)	97,199	21
New Hampshire	326 (2.4)	269,328	12
New Jersey	354 (2.6)	320,823	11
New York	1,876 (13.7)	1,918,608	10
Delaware	76 (0.6)	76,748	10
Pennsylvania	1,255 (9.2)	348,233	9
Maryland	340 (2.5)	470,019	7
Virginia	726 (5.3)	1,211,405	6
South Carolina	296 (2.2)	581,185	5
North Carolina	239 (1.8)	737,987	3
Georgia	39 (0.3)	516,823	1
	8,384 (61.5)		

[a] Figures in parentheses are percentages of the total number of individuals in the twenty original volumes of the *DAB* (13,633).

From Table 3.1 we can see that in spite of relatively small absolute numbers, both Connecticut and Rhode Island contributed heavily to the American historical elite in proportion to their population. What we shall be interested in, therefore, is the difference in the types of contributions to the American historical elite made by these two colonies.

In all, 2,586 (18.8%) of the individuals included in the *DAB* were born between 1550 and 1760. The Connecticut sample discussed in this paper is made up of 155 individuals of whom 112 were Connecticut natives, while the other 43 were Auslanders, born outside of the colony. The Rhode Island sample is composed of 78 individuals, 42 of whom were natives, the other 36 being Auslanders. These two samples are composed of almost all the individuals in the *DAB* who became successful in their chosen callings in these two states. Omitted are distinguished individuals born in Connecticut or Rhode Island who made their fame chiefly outside their native colonies. Included are some individuals who while born elsewhere made their careers in either Connecticut or Rhode Island (Table 3.2).

College graduates were rare in colonial society, so much so that only 14.7% (347) of the 2,366 members of the American elite represented in the *DAB* born before 1760 were graduates of American colleges (Pierson, 1969, p. 5). Yet 64.5% (100) of the Connecticut elite had college degrees. In contrast, 16.7% (13) of the Rhode Island elite had college degrees. These differences can be attributed to the different attitudes toward education held by each colony.

Throughout its history, Connecticut reflected the Puritan obsession with education, and in 1701 Yale, the third American college, was founded in New Haven. About 25% of the entire American historical elite represented in the DAB born before 1760 and who were college graduates were educated at Yale. Forty-two percent (65) of the Connecticut elite

Table 3.2 Natives and Auslanders in the Connecticut and Rhode Island Elites

	Connecticut	Rhode Island
Natives	112 (72.3)	42 (53.8)
Auslanders	43 (27.7)	36 (46.2)
Total	155 (100.0)	78 (100.0)

held Yale degrees and 71.4% of all the Connecticut elite who held college degrees were Yale graduates.

Rhode Island, on the other hand, lagged in founding a college of its own. This was largely due to the anti-intellectual influences of the Baptists and Quakers on its colonial culture. Indeed, only one native Rhode Islander graduated from college in the seventeenth century, and Rhode Island College, later to become Brown University, was not founded until 1765, too late to have much influence upon the colonial Rhode Island elite (Table 3.3).

Reflecting what little value Rhode Islanders placed on education, ten of the thirteen members of the Rhode Island elite who were college educated were not natives of Rhode Island. Two were from New Jersey and had graduated from Princeton. Of the five from Massachusetts two had graduated from Harvard, two had graduated from Brown, one of whom had first been expelled from Harvard, while the last held his degree from the University of Pennsylvania. The remaining two were born in England and Ireland and were graduated from Cambridge and Glasgow respectively. Of the three native Rhode Islanders in the elite sample to have graduated from college, two had gone to Harvard, one to Brown.

While only 23% of the Rhode Island elite who held college degrees were natives, 75% of the Connecticut elite who held college degrees were natives of their colony. In fact, as shown in Table 3.2, 72.3% of the Connecticut elite, compared to 53.8% of the Rhode Island elite, were natives of their colony.

Table 3.3 Education of the Connecticut and Rhode Island Elites in the *DAB*

Connecticut		Rhode Island	
Yale	65 (42.0)	Harvard	4 (5.1)
Harvard	20 (12.9)	Brown	3 (3.8)
Princeton	5 (3.2)	Princeton	2 (2.6)
Cambridge	6 (3.9)	Cambridge	2 (2.6)
Oxford	2 (1.3)	Glasgow	1 (1.3)
Trinity	1 (0.6)	Pennsylvania	1 (1.3)
Brown	1 (0.6)	No College	65 (83.3)
No College	55 (35.5)	Total	78 (100.0)
Total	155 (100.0)		

The Connecticut elite were part of a political and cultural community made fast by birth, and given shape by education and religion; they were by and large a group of well-educated natives of their colony, sharing the same religious creed. In comparison, the Rhode Island elite had generally not attended college, held diverse religious beliefs, and were less likely to be natives of their colony.

Just as the Puritan enthusiasm for education led to the founding of Yale, so did the Puritan affinity for law lead to the founding of America's first law school in Litchfield, Connecticut in 1775. During its sixty-year history, it educated over one thousand students representing every state, including two vice presidents of the United States, three U.S. Supreme Court Justices, six cabinet officers, ninety U.S. Congressmen, twenty U.S. Senators, sixteen governors, and at least twenty-seven state Supreme Court justices, including thirteen who were chief justices. While Connecticut from its beginning emphasized law and lawyers ("The Constitution State" is the nickname adopted by Connecticut today, in celebration of the fact that its Fundamental Orders of 1639 was the first written constitution in America), Rhode Island, from its antinomian beginnings, never placed the emphasis on law that its Puritan neighbor did. Indeed, to this day Rhode Island remains the only state in the continental United States with no accredited law school of its own. A comparison of the elite samples from the two states illustrates this difference in attitude toward the legal profession. Notably, 33% of the Connecticut elite had been trained in and practiced law, but only 9% of the Rhode Island elite were lawyers. Furthermore, about 40% of the entire elite sample from Connecticut had either served at the bar or on the bench, while in comparison only 14% of the Rhode Island elite had been lawyers or jurists. Reflecting the indigenous values of their colonies, 87% (53) of the 61 Connecticut elite who were lawyers or jurists, but only 54% (6) of the 11 Rhode Island elite who were lawyers were natives of the state they represented. Keeping with the different educational values of the two colonies, 77% of the Connecticut lawyers and jurists were college graduates, compared to 45% of the Rhode Islanders.

The legal profession has always been partitioned by the line separating the bar from the bench. As Baltzell has pointed out, the bar stands for advocacy and for the defense of private and particular interests, while the bench stands for authority and the defense of the interests of the entire community (Baltzell, 1979, p. 337). Given its Puritan tradition of respect for communal authority and law, Connecticut might well be expected to have had more judges among its elite members than Rhode Island, which had a long history, influenced by its antinomian and sectarian founding, and fostered by its Quaker and Baptist individualism, of respecting the individual conscience over and against communal authority and interest. This expectation is borne out in the careers of the elite members from these two colonies.

Judicial careers in colonial, state, or U.S. Federal courts were followed by 26% (40) of the Connecticut elite, but by only 10% (8) of the Rhode Island elite. Moreover, 14% (22) of the Connecticut elite served as justices of their state's supreme court, with 9% (14) of them serving as chief justice. Six of the Connecticut elite also served in the U.S. Federal judicial system, and one of these elite members, Oliver Ellsworth, served as chief justice of the U.S. Supreme Court. On the other hand, only one member of Rhode Island's elite sample served on the state's Supreme Court.

Considering that Congregational Puritanism was the established religion in Connecticut from its founding in 1636 until 1818, and that the college-educated minister was one of the most respected figures in the colonial society, it is not surprising that there should be so many clergymen in the Connecticut elite. In all, 29% (45) of the elite members were clergymen. Of these, all but one was college educated, and all but seven were Puritan Congregationalists. Of the exceptions, six were Episcopal clergymen, one of whom, Samuel Seabury, was the first Episcopal bishop in America.

Rhode Island, on the other hand, was the most religiously tolerant of all thirteen colonies. Both the Quakers and the Baptists, the two dominant religious sects in the colony, devalued the authority of the ministry while extolling the individual's authority over himself in religious matters. The Rhode Island elite reflects this cultural bias, containing 17% (13) religious leaders, only four of whom were ministers. Among these thirteen religious leaders were four Baptists, two Quakers, and two Episcopal missionaries. The other five were ultra-individualistic sectarians who led small cult-like groups.

Whereas the Connecticut elite was composed largely of individuals who exercised public authority, legal, juridical, or ministerial, Rhode

Island's elite was composed of a greater proportion of private individuals, as evidenced by its proportionately higher number of merchants and manufacturers. Connecticut's elite contained only 16% (25) such persons, while the 35 (45%) merchants and manufacturers were the largest occupational group within the Rhode Island elite.

In terms of intellectuals and artists, we again see the Puritan influence in Connecticut. The authority of the word as exercised by the minister, the college professor, the lawyer, and the judge was also evidenced in Connecticut's elite intellectuals. Over half of the Connecticut elite (81) were authors, among whom were well-known poets, eminent theologians, and historians. One among them, Jonathan Edwards, was recognized as colonial America's greatest philosopher. Most of the Connecticut intellectuals in the *DAB* sample were college educated. Three members of Connecticut's intellectual and artistic elite were artists, among whom was the painter John Trumbull, who made his career and fame a part of Connecticut's cultural history.

Rhode Island's intellectual and artistic representation in the elite reflects its anti-intellectual Quaker and Baptist heritage, which emphasized the sensual world more than did the Puritan ethos. In the entire Rhode Island *DAB* sample, only 15 (19%) were authors. However, among the other elite members were four painters, six silversmiths and craftsmen, and two architects. Among these were but a few native Rhode Islanders, including the famous portrait painter Gilbert Stuart, who eventually left his native colony to become a citizen of the world.

Having seen that Connecticut and Rhode Island's leadership patterns follow Baltzell's predictions, we can ask if the shapes of the two societies fit the pattern as well. Was colonial Connecticut indeed a "community builder" and did Rhode Island explicitly reject the need for hierarchy, class, and authority? Brief highlights of the history of each colony provide an affirmative answer.

One of the most critical and eventful periods in America's history were the years 1774 through 1789, during which the Continental Congress presided over the birth of the nation. In these years, the thirteen colonies declared their independence from England, fought a revolutionary war to secure that independence, and finally united as a republic under the authority of the United States Constitution.

Connecticut and Rhode Island played significant but decidedly different roles in some of the most dramatic episodes of this period. As the nationalist movement grew, Connecticut took a leading part, and eventually played an important role in the Constitutional Convention of 1787. Rhode Island, on the other hand, played its major part early in the period, when independence meant more than nation-building. Rhode Island was the first state to declare independence, but, as the nationalist movement gained momentum, it became the leading anti-nationalist state, thwarted an attempt to give more authority to the national government under the Articles of Confederation, and eventually became the only state to boycott the Constitutional Convention.

Two great events of the critical period, 1774–1789, which produced instant heroes for the American imagination, were the signing of the Declaration of Independence in 1776, and the framing of the Constitution in 1787. The participation of Connecticut and Rhode Island in these events, and in the period between them, was typical of their social and political histories.

From its founding in 1636, Connecticut's settlers had made balance a virtue. The smaller interests of the town were balanced against the larger interests of the colony, both being considered important. In large part, this emphasis on proportion and harmony may be traced to the overwhelming influence of Puritan Congregationalism in the colony. Connecticut congregationalism was institutionally federal, balancing the theological importance of both God and the individual, both the church and the congregant, both the doctrine of works and the doctrine of grace, and both the minister and the congregation. When in the eighteenth century the extension of Parliamentary authority threatened their chartered freedom to govern themselves, Connecticut's citizens, sensing that both their smaller interests as a colony and the larger interests of all thirteen colonies were threatened, directed their congressional representatives to sign both the Declaration of Independence and the Articles of Confederation.

The Articles of Confederation, while creating America's first national government, ensured that it would remain relatively weak by leaving intact the absolute sovereignty of each individual state. When under the exigencies of war, it became apparent that Congress needed more authority at the expense of some of each state's sovereignty, Connecticut, in keeping with its custom of balanced interests, agreed, in 1781, to a proposal to give Congress the power of taxation. Later, in 1787, Connecticut sacrificed some of its smaller interests in favor of larger national ones by proposing a key compromise which was instrumental in the formation of the United States under the Constitution, thus helping to preserve the old relationship of balance between the town and colony in the balance of power between the states and the federal government.

In contrast, Rhode Islanders had from the start made a fetish of smaller interests, and seemed to be hyper-phobic about larger interests. From its founding in 1636 through the colonial period the smaller interests of the town took precedence over the larger interests of the colony. This emphasis on smaller interests may be traced to the sectarian influences of the early Baptists and Quakers in Rhode Island, who placed their confidence in individual conscience over the church, over the congregation, and over ministerial authority. Although Rhode Island was the first colony to declare independence, two months before the fourth of July 1776, Rhode Islanders, sensing that their own self-interests might best be served by uniting with the other colonies, directed their congressional delegates to sign the Declaration of Independence.

Because, and perhaps only because, the Articles of Confederation ensured its continued sovereignty, thus preserving its right to guard its smaller interests, Rhode Island agreed to sign them.

However, while the other colonies were willing to subordinate their smaller local interests to the larger interests of the union of states under the Articles of Confederation, specifically in granting Congress the power of taxation in 1781, Rhode Island vetoed the taxation proposal. Indeed, from the time of that veto upon Congress's power until 1790, when it reluctantly ratified the Constitution by the slimmest possible margin, Rhode Island's slavish devotion to smaller interests made it a constant hindrance to any strengthening of the nationalist movement. Due in large measure to this peculiar obsession, Rhode Island was the only state to send no representatives to the Constitutional Convention in 1787, which balanced small and large interests, a balance which has been the very essence of American government.

The difference between Rhode Island and Connecticut, in attitudes and in contributions to the formation of the new nation, can be explained by the circumstances of their founding, and by the character and philosophy of their earliest leaders. Connecticut was first settled in 1636 by orthodox Puritan Congregationalists who carried the spirit, if not the letter, of the Puritan theocracy of Massachusetts Bay Colony with them into the wilderness along the Connecticut River. The three original Connecticut River towns, Hartford, Windsor, and Wethersfield, were not founded by individual adventurers, but were transplanted communities from Massachusetts. Moreover, in the main, these communities that left Massachusetts had originally been transplanted Puritan congregations from England. They were organized and led by their ministers, and were in large part made up of carefully selected members of the English gentry, military leaders, and spiritually inclined young men and women. Each migration, from England to America, then Massachusetts to Connecticut, pared down these self-chosen, spiritually harmonious groups, into yet more orderly, conforming communities of like-minded believers and neighbors generally in accord with each other.

These Connecticut settlements found it easy to accept authority, in large part due to their common and shared theological beliefs and their consensus about leadership and government in covenanted communities. From the beginning these communities were able to blend local interests with the common interests of all three settlements. In fact, these communities had formed a federation even before they left Massachusetts, and came to the Connecticut River Valley with a government already chosen to look after the common good. Thus, the persistent habit of balancing small, or local, interests with large, or statewide interests, which we saw in Connecticut's participation in the crucial Revolutionary Period, has a long history dating back to its founding era.

Rhode Island's earliest history, on the other hand, was marked by defiance of authority and extreme factionalism in and among the settlements on the Narragansett Bay. Unlike the much-respected Connecticut settlers who had to beg leave of Massachusetts to migrate, and were only granted permission to do so with the greatest reluctance, the founders of Rhode Island were mostly exiles from Massachusetts, banished for their heretical and seditious beliefs. Indeed, the factional strife which differentiates early Rhode Island from politically placid Connecticut can be traced to the antinomian and ultra-individualistic religious convictions of the colony's founders.

First Roger Williams, the only college-educated clergyman in early Rhode Island, was banished from Massachusetts for preaching doctrines considered to be heretical to the Puritan creed and seditious to the Puritan state. Unlike the founders of Connecticut who led entire congregations of the like-minded to well-planned settlements, Williams fled from Massachusetts in the midst of a dreadful snowstorm to avoid deportation to England. With no intention of founding a settlement, let alone a colony, Williams established himself at Providence, at the head of the Narragansett Bay, in what is now Rhode Island, in 1636. Although Williams did not wish to have the company of other settlers, he soon attracted other dissenters from the Congregational way in Massachusetts.

After Williams' banishment, Massachusetts was again in the throes of dissent, in the form of Anne Hutchinson's "antinomian controversy," in which she too preached a heretical and seditious doctrine to which she won many adherents. Among her followers were numbered a good many powerful and wealthy Puritans who were banished along with her in 1638. Looking only for a place to live their private lives as they wished, the Hutchinsonians, led by a wealthy merchant, William Coddington, settled Portsmouth on the northern end of the island of Aquidneck in the Narragansett Bay, just south of Williams' Providence settlement. Unlike the Connecticut settlements, Portsmouth had no church, no congregation, no minister, no authoritative temporal leaders. Shortly after it was settled, Portsmouth was split by dissension over the form of government it would have, and Coddington appropriated the town records and marched to the southern end of Aquidneck Island with a band of followers, where he founded the settlement of Newport. Last among the first founders of Rhode Island was Samuel Gorton, who was unwelcome first in Massachusetts, then in Plymouth, and finally at Providence. Wherever he went, he caused dissension. He preached an extremely antinomian doctrine, which made him dangerous to any Puritan community, and he seemed always to put his own conscience above the law, making him a seditious man in any community. He founded his own community at Warwick, Rhode Island in 1642.

Unlike intolerant Connecticut and Massachusetts, Rhode Island was the first tolerant state. It was settled by a diverse host of sectaries, each at war with authority in all its forms. This tendency toward ultra-individualism carried over into the political arrangements of the settlements in Rhode Island. Originally each town was content, even desirous, to remain isolated from the others. This philo-localism made it difficult to form any colonial federation and government. Only the immediate threat of becoming annexed to Massachusetts led to a reluctant colonial government, which failed over and over again to unite the colony, until 1663, when a royal charter was obtained. Thus, from the beginning Rhode Island had strong local factions jealously protecting smaller, local interests against larger state interests. This combination of extreme localism and extreme factionalism was characteristic of Rhode Island right up to its reluctant ratification of the Constitution in 1790.

Thus, in each colony, the religious ethics had the unintended, although important, impact on the secular sphere which Baltzell had shown them to have in Boston and Philadelphia. Further, both the Connecticut/Rhode Island and the Boston/Philadelphia examples demonstrate the influence of religious ideas on the systems of power. They emphasize the interdependence of the religious systems of each, and the development of the structures of culture, politics, and power.

4
THE AMERICAN DREAM

The "American dream" is a term so widely used as to obscure its intellectual background as the chief metaphor for the virtues of American life today. Coined by a best-selling historian, James Truslow Adams, early into the Great Depression, the "American Dream" emphasizes values such as developing one's capabilities to their fullest, and the enhancement of individuality unhampered by class obstacles characteristic of European civilization from its medieval roots well into the twentieth century.

Adams introduced the term "American Dream" in his widely read 1931 book *The Epic of America*. The American Dream mandates that all the aforementioned values can be accomplished through hard work and individual effort. Indeed, Adams sought to have his publisher call this book *The American Dream*, instead of *The Epic of America*. Despite his failure to name the book as he pleased, the notoriety and far-ranging citations of Adams' *Epic* have been largely due to the American dream metaphor.

Counterintuitively, perhaps, the timing of the publication of Adams' book could not have been better. In 1931 America was still in the early stages of the Great Depression. Wall Street had melted down, personal savings and investments had been vaporized, businesses were going bust, and unemployment was rampant. America was in the midst of its worst economic disaster when *The Epic of America* was published. But the book was more than just a history of America, beginning before Europeans began exploring and colonizing it, and ending in the then-contemporary early 1930s. In its way, it was something of an historical time capsule, filled with hope, national pride, and reminders that what Adams called the American dream was still alive and worth aspiring to, despite the nightmare Americans were living through. The book was an instant success. Notably, in the couple of decades after *The Epic of America* was published, sociological journals carried articles that employed the concept of the American Dream, by Howard Odum, Harry Elmer Barnes, Kimball Young, Read Bain, Horace Kallen, Louis Wirth, John Dollard, Harold Lasswell, Alex Inkeles, and Robert Cooley Angell.

Not only did *The Epic of America* top the bestseller lists, it also was a leading title in the relatively new Book-of-the-Month-Club, assuring it an even more broadly-based readership. Spreading from and beyond the book, Adams' famous metaphorical phrase "the American Dream" took off like a rocket, and it was soon being used in academic articles, as well as in popular magazines such as the *Saturday Review of Literature*. Once Adams used the metaphor, sociologists began using it, and the sociological literature has been rife with the term since the 1930s. Some of this literature was highly focused on the normative aspects of the dream, as in Leo Rosten's 1939 study of Hollywood, published in *Public Opinion Quarterly*, in which he showed how the American dream had formed the backbone of modern American movies. More famously, in a revision of his 1938 sociology of knowledge article, "Social Structure and Anomie," Robert Merton discussed the American dream in terms of Americans' unfulfilled aspirations for success.

Indeed, two of the most important American community studies ever undertaken—Robert and Helen Lynd's *Middletown in Transition*, and W. Lloyd Warner's *Yankee City* series—made extensive use of the American dream as a tool for understanding values held in these communities. While Robert Lynd's solo study of Muncie, Indiana, *Middletown*, was published in 1929, two years earlier, and therefore could not have referenced the American dream metaphor, the second study, *Middletown in Transition*, published in 1937, did. The Lynds not only integrated the "dream" into the analysis from beginning to end, but, also showed through quotations from those interviewed, that the metaphor had speedily become part of their everyday way of thinking (Lynd and Lynd, 1937, p. 476).

Furthermore, the generational differences in the class and status structure of Muncie between the first and second studies highlighted the importance of the American dream to understanding stratification in America. In the first study Middletown was dominated by successful businessmen who formed a functional elite running the economic and political structures of the city. When they returned to Middletown, the Lynds found that some of the families of the successful businessmen had formed an upper class in the city's status hierarchy. In a few generations, these families rose "from comparative poverty to great wealth, [and] they fit perfectly the American success dream" (Lynd and Lynd, 1937, p. 76).

Unlike the Lynds, who were concerned with the objective economic aspects of class in Muncie, W. Lloyd Warner's *Yankee City* studies in Newburyport, Massachusetts, focused more on the subjective status elements of class, and the open opportunities to succeed that are so important to a belief in the American dream. Warner provided us with one of the great analyses of the cultural values supporting the American dream.

> They believe that a man by applying himself, by using the talents he has, by acquiring the necessary skills, can rise from lower to higher status, and that his family can rise with him. The opportunity for social mobility for everyone is the very fabric of the 'American dream.'

Warner went on to say that "the American dream is not a mere fantasy that can be dismissed as unimportant by those who think realistically, for it does provide the motive power for much of what Americans do in their daily lives" (Warner, 1953, p. 106). In describing and analyzing the first factory strike in Newburyport's shoe-manufacturing industry, and the erosion of the status structure that helped bring it about, Warner showed that for most of the workers, "the 'ladder to the stars' was gone and with it much of the fabric of the American dream" (Warner, 1953, p. 136).

While the American dream has been useful in community and social class studies, it frequently emerges in other studies of American values. The range of uses is far and wide. For instance, in *The Nature and Destiny of Man,* the theologian Reinhold Niebuhr suggests that "a very youthful and creative American civilization compounded the Christian vision of the

Kingdom of God with the 'American dream'" (Niebuhr, 1943, p. 346). In a quite different sort of work, *Out of Our Past*, the historian Carl Degler showed how the American dream blunted the cutting edge of socialism in America. Thus, the dream has been a valuable intellectual concept, as well as metaphor, for a plethora of intellectuals, as well as social scientists.

Outside academia the American dream took on a different and far more normative meaning, especially in the area of civil rights. For instance, sharp-edged political uses of the metaphor were put forth by the two most famous, if not most important icons of the civil rights era, Martin Luther King, Jr. and Malcolm X. The American dream metaphor was a central feature in King's "I have a dream" speech, delivered on August 28, 1963 in Washington D.C. at the Lincoln Memorial. "So even though we face the difficulties of today and tomorrow, I still have a dream. It is a dream deeply rooted in the American dream." Months later, on February 3, 1964, King again invoked the dream metaphor, in another speech called "The American Dream," which he delivered at Drew University. On the other side of the civil rights divide, Malcolm X used the dream metaphor in his own famous speech, "The Ballot or the Bullet," delivered at Cory Methodist Church, in Cleveland on April 3, 1964. "I'm speaking as a victim of this American system. And I see America through the eyes of the victim. I don't see any American dream; I see an American nightmare." One of the latest evocations of the dream in the post-Civil Rights era has been Barack Obama's 2006 autobiographical work, *The Audacity of Hope: Reclaiming the American Dream* (Obama, 2006).

Thus, from social scientists to social reformers, Adams' "American Dream" has been a useful, maybe indispensable concept on the one hand, and a tool for mobilization on the other.

As Merton pointed out, the American dream implies as-yet-unfulfilled aspirations, and in the same vein, Barack Obama's use of the dream implies hope for the future. In both cases, there is something quintessentially American about this notion of growth, progress, hope, and aspiration. To dream the American dream implies that the future—both individual and social—can be made better. Even Malcolm X's twisting the dream into a nightmare implies that a future better than the present may yet be achieved. Having had such a major influence on American culture, what was Adams' original use of the American dream all about?

In the preface, Adams laid out his aims in writing *The Epic of America*, among which was to "trace the beginnings... of that American dream of a better, richer, and happier life for all our citizens of every rank which is the greatest contribution we have as yet made to the thought and welfare of the world."

In an early chapter on the earliest European settlers in America, "The Men of Destiny," Adams suggests that by the early seventeenth century,

> the American dream was beginning to take form in the hearts of men. The economic motive was unquestionably powerful, often dominant, in the minds of those who took part in the great migration, but mixed with this was also frequently present the hope of a better and freer life, a life in which a man might think as he would and develop as he willed. ... The dream was as yet largely inchoate and unexpressed, but it was forming.

Adams brilliantly shows that the American class system had its beginning in pragmatic social solutions to the early frontier environment. As Adams put it, the early settlers

> came from prisons, from hovels, from little farm cottages, from town shops, from country manor houses and rectories, but never from palaces. The aristocracy remained in England, and, with scarcely an exception, the thousands who came were from the middle and lower classes, fleeing from persecution or hard social and economic conditions.

When they arrived here, they found only wilderness—endless forests and uncleared land. These conditions had a leveling-down effect, so that "the man with money found himself brought far nearer the level of the laborer than he had ever dreamed of being in England." If there was no Protestant work ethic before, it would have had to be invented here. Adams describes laws in several colonies that reinforced incipient norms against idling and insisted on work. The early colonists, according to Adams, "were not engaged in building a Utopia. Their hope was for a civilization, which should be, as soon as might be, like that they had known, but in which they would each be freer, richer, and more independent." From the start, therefore, the American dream was not about the elimination of social class distinctions, but for mobility through those ranks based on hard work. Indeed, any discussion of the American dream today still must hinge on the high value placed on work and achieving upward mobility through it.

Adams, who had won the 1922 Pulitzer Prize in history for his still useful book, *The Founding of New England*, was a sharp-eyed observer of the Puritan mind. In his analysis of the American dream, Adams reminded his readers that the Puritan leaders "had no intention of allowing democracy in their government or liberty in worship. The American dream owes more to the wilderness than to them." Without minimizing the place of religion, or specifically of Puritanism, Adams underscored this idea—"it was this 'land in the woods' as a possibility for almost every inhabitant of America that was to prove one of the most powerful of the forces which worked toward the shaping of our American dream" (Adams, 1921, p. 119).

Although the English translation of Max Weber's *Protestant Ethic and the Spirit of Capitalism* had been published the year before, in 1930, Adams shows no knowledge of this now-indispensable analysis of the relationship of religion to social structure. Nevertheless, in *The Epic of America*, Adams offers what amounts to an intervening variable in the relationship of the Puritan work ethic to the economy, namely the transmutation of hard work into a moral virtue and leisure into an evil. In what in another context might be an important and testable sociology of knowledge proposition, Adams suggested that man rationalizes and idealizes the sort of life that is imposed upon him. Given the frontier circumstances in early America, wealth as well as the comforts it brings had to be created out of the wilderness by hard work. Therefore, we may surmise that necessity preceded theological ideology, or at least accompanied it. The roots of hard work as a key to success in the American dream metaphor are as deep as the first European settlements here.

The supremely middle-class value placed on hard work was not the only identifiable aspect of the early development of the American dream. In his chapter about the burgeoning institutions of the early American frontiers, "A Civilization Established," Adams describes the place of law and respect for it as essential not merely for the dreams and aspirations for a more successful future, but also for the development of capitalism. The chapter also introduced the place of slavery in the colonial economy. But most importantly, Adams herein began to discuss America as an incipient "business civilization," which has been the bedrock not only of American society and the American economy, but also of the American dream. With no apparent knowledge about Weber's famous thesis, Adams writes a parallel history of the relationship of the work ethic—tethered more to frontier conditions than to Protestantism—and the American dream of success.

As in any one-volume history of America, there is no pretense at being comprehensive. Adams pushes forward and stays on track, through the centuries, as if he himself was a pioneer on some vast historical frontier. What makes this book so readable, and valuable as a sort of historical ready reckoning of centuries of American history from the early seventeenth to the early eighteenth centuries, is Adams' point of view. From Tacitus to modern philosophers of history, such as Wilhelm Windelband, Heinrich Rickert, and Georg Simmel, the idea that history depends upon the vantage point established by the historian is now a given. James Truslow Adams alloyed his point of view to the American dream, and the entire history of America is told with the dream metaphor as the organizing principle. No wonder that the book was so popular during the Great Depression, when dreams of the future were sweeter than the bitter economic dregs of the present.

One might wonder if Adams invented the American dream, or if he discovered it. If he invented it he married the strange with the familiar. If he discovered it he merely gave a new and compelling name to a preexisting social *force majeure*. The evidence indicates that Adams rediscovered a real set of American values, and brought these under the umbrella of the new phrase. Almost a century before, Alexis de Tocqueville saw the same emphasis on success in America, and wrote about it in *Democracy in America*. A half-century before, in *The American Commonwealth,* James Bryce also wrote about the extreme value that Americans placed on monetary success, and even showed how this emphasis kept the most able Americans from entering politics. Thus, it would be difficult to conclude that Adams invented the American dream. Nevertheless, by rediscovering it, and naming it felicitously, as he did, Adams focused our attention on a particularly American set of values that has influenced the course of our history for nearly four centuries.

Adams' family personified the American dream so well that one may suspect that *The Epic of America* was written with them in mind. He was born in Brooklyn, New York, then America's third largest city, on October 18, 1878. Adams represented the eighth American generation of his father's Adams side of the family, and the fourth American generation of his mother's Truslow side. Although he wrote a wildly successful book on the well-known Adams family of New England, he had to constantly remind his readers, and others, that he was unrelated to *that* Adams family (Adams, 1930).

Indeed, James Truslow Adams came from a business and banking family that was well-off, but not wealthy, gentrified and upper-middle class, but not politically minded or powerful. In almost each generation since 1638, when Francis Adams arrived in Maryland from England as an indentured servant, the family fit the mold of the American dream, "of a land in which life should be better and richer and fuller for every man, with opportunity for each according to his ability or achievement."

The first four generations of the family fulfilled the dream by acquiring land, and becoming planters in Maryland and Virginia. Beginning with Adams' great grandfather, Francis Adams, in the fifth generation, the family moved into the shipping trade, and then into banking. After running the family's shipping business in Venezuela, and marrying into a distinguished Spanish family, Adams' grandfather, William Newton Adams, moved his family to New York City, and then across the East River to Brooklyn as he devoted himself to the banking business. James Truslow Adams' grandfather on his mother's side, James Linklater Truslow, was a millionaire businessman, who owned and ran the Armstrong Cork Company, in Brooklyn, in the shadow of the nearly completed Brooklyn Bridge. Thus, Adams had first-hand impressions through his grandfathers, about living the American dream of success.

Adams' father, on the other hand, studied finance in Germany before becoming a Wall Street stockbroker, but seems to have had little talent for reading the stock market; he had a hard-luck career, at best—a sure setback for the Adams family in living the dream. In large part the family's economic circumstances kept Adams from attending an Ivy League college, and instead he lived at home and enrolled in Brooklyn Polytechnic Institute, from which he graduated in 1898. At Brooklyn Poly, where he majored in English, Adams wanted to teach philosophy and enrolled at Yale as a graduate student. He found academic life at Yale to be boring, and he quit his studies after a year, and worked at his father's brokerage firm until he was thirty-five years old.

While working as a stockbroker by day, Adams cultivated his interest as an historian in his spare time, resulting in two books: one on currency, in 1908, the other about the stock exchange, in 1913. In 1913, at the age of thirty-five, he retired from the brokerage firm, and began writing as a vocation. He published two local histories of Long Island communities, which were quite successful in terms of reviews and sales. After a tour of duty in the Army during World War I as a captain in the Military Intelligence Office, Adams returned to civilian life, and began the second phase of his career as an independent scholar.

In quick succession Adams published three books that established him as an important historian: *The Founding of New England* (1921), *Revolutionary New England* (1923), and *New England in the Republic* (1926). *The Founding of New England* won the Pulitzer Prize and rave reviews from prominent academic historians. Adams was now making enough money from his published books to make a living as an independent scholar. He followed the New England trilogy with *Provincial Society* (1927), *The Adams Family* (1930), and *The Epic of America* (1931). But this wasn't all, because Adams was a prolific writer. Adams was now a famous historian, as well as a popular one. He published a two-volume history of America, *The March of Democracy*, in 1933 and 1934, followed immediately by *America's Tragedy*, about the Civil War (1934).

Between 1940 and 1960 Adams edited and contributed to two five-volume reference works that remain valuable today: *Dictionary of American History* and the *Album of American History*. Aside from these and other books, he published a steady stream of over five dozen articles in academic and popular journals and magazines, such as *American Historical Review*, *Atlantic*, *Harper's*, *Yale Review*, *Saturday Review of Literature*, and *The New York Times*. Some of his early articles were collected into two books of his essays, *Our Business Civilization* (1929) and the *Tempo of Modern Life* (1931).

From a privileged, but not overly privileged beginning, James Truslow Adams developed his skills as a writer, and educated himself as an historian. His success in both these related endeavors allowed him to fulfill the American dream, as well as to write about it.

5
POLITICAL CLUBS, PARTIES, AND RADICALISM

Crane Brinton's *The Jacobins* was published in 1930, at the end of the first recognizably modern decade in American history, and at the beginning of the decade known for the worst economic disaster in that history. Both decades were revolutionary, each in its own manner, sparking the interest of then contemporary social scientists. Many of these intellectuals, already preoccupied by the events of the Russian Revolution and by Joseph Stalin's rise to power in the new Soviet state, were very much interested in theories of change in general, and more particularly, in revolution.

Indeed, other than—and accompanying—Brinton's *Jacobins*, there were numerous books published within a few years of each other that looked deeply into violent means of change, and ideological radicalism. In 1925, Brinton's colleague at Harvard, Pitirim Sorokin, published *The Sociology of Revolution*, soon followed by Lyford Edwards' 1927 study *The Natural History of Revolution*. In 1929 and 1930 a host of now-classic works on revolution and ideology were published. Among these were Karl Mannheim's *Ideology and Utopia*, Harold Lasswell's *Psychopathology and Politics*, Ortega y Gasset's *Revolt of the Masses*, and Sigmund Freud's *Civilization and Its Discontents*. Another classic study of social change, albeit of a non-revolutionary sort, was Robert and Helen Lynd's *Middletown*, published in 1929. Besides these indispensable works on ideas and change, another of Brinton's colleagues at Harvard, Talcott Parsons, published his English translation of Max Weber's *The Protestant Ethic and the Spirit of Capitalism*, in 1930. Certainly, Weber's *Protestant Ethic* must be numbered among the greatest and most important studies of how ideas interact with and can change social, political, and economic structures. All told, these were a few very fruitful years in social science history.

Brinton's book on Jacobinism was the first of three volumes on revolution he wrote during the 1930s, which, taken collectively, helped him become the most prominent theorist of revolution for decades to come. The best known of these three books, *The Anatomy of Revolution*, published in 1938, was revised twice and continues in print today as one of the most highly cited works on the subject. The third of Brinton's books on revolution, *A Decade of Revolution*, specifically about the revolutionary events in France beginning in 1789, was published in 1934, and remains a useful volume for those interested in the subject.

Brinton was fascinated by two strains of thought which he weaved together in *The Jacobins*. The first was the subject itself, in its particular focus upon the Jacobins as a revolutionary party, and as a case study in how such parties are organized and how they operate. The second strand of thought was about how one can gather pertinent information to describe and analyze a political party such as the Jacobins.

As he worked his way through the material at hand, Brinton based much of his thinking on a narrow band of the day's available social science theories. He only mentioned three social scientists, Vilfredo Pareto, James Bryce, and Moisey Ostrogorski (these last two were mentioned in passing). These three were emblematic because they crossed disciplinary lines easily and with intellectual alacrity, and because they each wrote definitively about things essential to understanding the Jacobin movement.

Although we might not think of him as such today, Pareto was the most well-known and discussed sociologist of the late 1920s through the 1930s. Today, Pareto is read and cited mostly by economists, among whom his Pareto efficiency, or Pareto optimality theory, is considered indispensable. In Brinton's day, Pareto, who was ubiquitous in the sociological literature as well as in the popular press, was best known for his theories of residues and derivations, which, for lack of a coherent sociology of knowledge approach in American sociology back then, set the stage for understanding the relationship between ideas and behavior. More important to Brinton was Pareto's theory of "the circulation of the elites," which helps us to make sense of much of the data about the revolutionary Jacobin party presented in *The Jacobins*.

Bryce, the author of what may be one of the two best books ever written about American political society, *The American Commonwealth*, was the first president of the British Sociological Society, and the fourth president of the American Political Science Association. His pioneering studies of public opinion and of political parties had an obvious influence on Brinton's thinking about the Jacobins. Ostrogorski was a lawyer, historian, political scientist and sociologist, whose *Democracy and the Organization of Political Parties* was one of the founding works in political sociology, and obviously known to Brinton. Based on his understanding of these theorists, Brinton was able to conceive of *The Jacobins* as a work of "retrospective sociology," and "an essay in the New History."

Among other things, the New History was about the place of "great men" in historical context, an issue still argued about today, but widely so a century ago. In March of 1906, William James famously addressed faculty and students on Founders' Day at Stanford University. "The wealth of a nation," he said, "consists more than anything else in the number of superior men that it harbors" (James, 1911, p. 182). During that same year, one of Columbia University's well-known historians, James Harvey Robinson, was already formulating his thoughts about what would soon become known as the "New History." In an article, "Recent Tendencies in the Study of the French Revolution," published a month after James' speech at Stanford, in the April issue of *The American Historical Review*, Robinson called for a more pragmatic and populist history that leaned on the social sciences, and that hived itself off from the military and political modalities that most often led to mere biographies of superior men. Indeed, Robinson's new history was a leveler: down with the high and mighty, up with the average man. While both James and Robinson were a generation ahead of Brinton, their differing views about elites and elitism would have a notable effect upon him.

While James emphasized the creative and leadership roles of superior individuals, Robinson emphasized the history of common men and women. James died in 1910 after a brilliant career in philosophy and psychology at Harvard University, during which he became one of the founders of Pragmatism, America's only home-grown school of philosophy. James represented the prevailing opinion of social scientists in the late nineteenth and early twentieth centuries, that great men were the engines of social change and progress. Thus, in a famous essay published in 1880, "Great Men, Great Thoughts, and the Environment," James likened genius to Darwin's notion of variation:

> ... the relation of the visible environment to the great man is in the main exactly what it is to the variation in the Darwinian philosophy. It chiefly adopts or rejects, preserves or destroys, in short *selects* him. And whenever it adopts and preserves the great man, it becomes modified by his influence in an entirely original and peculiar way. He acts as a ferment, and changes its constitution, just as the advent of a new zoölogical species changes the faunal and floral equilibrium of the region in which it appears.
>
> (James, 1880)

But this elitist viewpoint was about to come under fire by the New Historians, such as James Harvey Robinson.

Two years after James' death, Robinson published *The New History*, which challenged historians to become more like quantitatively-oriented social scientists, and less like biographers of superior men and notable events. Indeed, Robinson laid out his populist manifesto for history in *The New History*, in which his chapter "History for the Common Man," amounts to a call for a history *of* the common man.

In 1915, three years after Robinson's *The New History* was published, Clarence Crane Brinton entered Harvard University as an undergraduate. Brinton returned to Harvard in 1923 to teach history after having received a PhD from Oxford University that same year. In 1930 Brinton published *The Jacobins: An Essay in the New History*, and thus began a decade-long opening act in a remarkable career that made him one of the leading American public intellectuals from the 1930s until his death in 1968.

An acolyte of Robinson's new history, Brinton began his book on Jacobinism by suggesting that history could no longer make the study of exceptional individuals an end in itself. Furthermore, he wished to relegate "kings and courtiers, statesmen and generals to the more graceful talents of the new biographers" (Brinton, 1930, p. 1). Thus, the home-side of James' pragmatism was echoed in Brinton's idea that the historian must "study the behavior of many men in the past because he ultimately wishes to understand the behavior of many men in the present" (Brinton, 1930, p. 5). But, the far-side of James' philosophy that considered the study of superior men essential to the workings of democracy was a challenge to Brinton's outlook as a new historian. Mere chronology was not enough, according to Brinton. The discovery of laws that predicted the uniformity of human behavior was the stuff of the new history. If all of this sounds a lot like historical and political sociology, that is because it is sociology. Brinton's own evaluation of his book as a study in "Retrospective Sociology," is a key for us to unlock the meaning of *The Jacobins*, and beyond that to think about why sociology drifted away from making better use of its own "great man" theory: Max Weber's theory of charisma.

Who were the Jacobins? Or, perhaps, a better question would be, what were the Jacobin clubs? The original, and eponymous, Jacobin club was named such because the Dominican convent in which it was housed was located on Rue St. Jacques, Paris. The club took its name from the Latinate form of Jacques: *Jacobus*. As Brinton nicely put it for his American readers,

> They were unofficial political groups, similar in many ways to the Anti-Corn Law League, the Anti-Saloon League, or the Ku Klux Klan. They got things done. They were, in short, the sort of agencies of political action made familiar by the studies of Bryce and Ostrogorski.
>
> (Brinton, 1930, p. 4)

With this last reference, of course, Brinton suggests that the Jacobin clubs were first and foremost political parties. This is a key point, because as a party the Jacobins vied for power in the government, but they were not the governing body itself.

Before Brinton's time sociologists as varied as Herbert Spencer, Lester Ward, John Commons, Moise Ostrogorski, James Bryce, Max Weber, and Robert Michels had published analyses of parties that are still relevant today. Brinton, who modeled his work so as to be able to call it retrospective sociology, was aware of at least significant parts of this literature, and he was well aware that parties take many shapes, one of which was represented by the Jacobins. Through political organization, propaganda, and violence, the Jacobins promoted paranoid visions of enemies within France, and were by and large responsible for bringing on the Reign of Terror soon after the Revolution had begun. These extremist visions led to the public executions of King Louis XVI, Queen Marie Antoinette, and many thousands more during the thirteen months of the Terror, which lasted from June 1793 through July 1794. At its end, the Terror turned upon its own leaders, including St. Just and Maximillian de Robespierre, who were themselves executed by their infamous guillotine that had beheaded thousands, perhaps tens of thousands of "enemies of the Revolution."

Robespierre was surely the most famous Jacobin, but he isn't mentioned by Brinton until the middle of the second chapter of *The Jacobins*, and then only in passing. For many old-school historians and biographers, it would have been inconceivable to understand the political force and importance of the Jacobin clubs to the French Revolution without placing Robespierre at the head of the line. Thus, John Morley's *Robespierre*, published in 1886, Jules Michelet's 1899 biography, *Robespierre*, and Hilaire Belloc's *Robespierre: A Study*, published in 1901, are representative pre-New History works concentrating on the Jacobins through their most famous representative. Brinton, who knew that there were hundreds of thousands of Jacobins spread throughout thousands of clubs during the Revolution, relegated Robespierre to a mere signpost pointing to a chronology of events that readers would have to turn to biographers to learn more about. It speaks volumes about the new history that it took Max Weber, a sociologist rather than an historian, to capture the irreplaceable and ironic part played by Robespierre to the Revolution, when he wrote that "the charismatic glorification of 'Reason,' which found a characteristic expression in its apotheosis by Robespierre, is the last form that charisma has adopted in its fateful historical course" (Weber, 1968, p. 1209). Brinton and the New Historians were enamored with quantitative analysis, while charisma, a singular manifestation of the "great man" theory of historical change, which couldn't be easily quantified, was all but ignored.

Other than it being written by one of the foremost historians of the twentieth century, what is the specific value of *The Jacobins*? There are two answers to this question. First, Brinton does a brilliant job uncovering the demographic, ideational, and historical nature of the Jacobins' political movement. He carefully combed through the innumerable primary and secondary sources to firmly supplement the biographical material available about Robespierre and the other Jacobin leaders. Taken together, the older type of political and biographical history and the new, more sociological history gives us a remarkably in-depth view into the nature of the Jacobin movement. Second, by offering such a detailed and useful collective portrait of the Jacobins, Brinton ignites fireworks between the old and new histories. By doing this Brinton sheds light on an essential difference between history and sociology that still needs to be resolved, namely the relationship of theory to explanation, and vice versa.

In the mid-1960s, when discussions in the social sciences were often focused on "the new sociology," and the old clash between qualitative versus quantitative approaches to the work at hand, George Homans, a longtime friend and colleague of Brinton, published a small book called *The Nature of Social Science*. As young scholars at Harvard, both Homans and Brinton had been key figures in the Pareto seminars organized and led by Lawrence Joseph Henderson, a biologist turned sociologist. Homans dedicated *The Nature of Social Science* to Henderson, his mentor, as well as Brinton's at Harvard. How to reconcile the scientific aspects of social science with the humanistic elements was a question dealt with by Homans, and by Brinton in *The Jacobins* and in his other books.

Homans sums up the problem of theory and explanation in history and sociology as follows:

> History... possesses an enormous range of empirical findings, findings, that is, of a rather low order of generality... The historians have looked for general propositions in their subject matter, found none that they recognized as such, and concluded that they had no theories.
>
> (Homans, 1967, p. 29)

Homans wasn't through yet, and he later suggests that "If history has many explanations and no theories, sociology sometimes appears to have many theories and no explanations" (Homans, 1967, p. 30). In many ways Homans' critique of both history and sociology is derived from his early study and embrace of Vilfredo Pareto's theories about the place of reified ideas, or what he called "sentiments," to sociological explanation. Homans learned this, as did Brinton under Henderson's tutelage. Both incorporated these concerns over theory and explanation in their work, and we see this as early as 1930 in *The Jacobins*.

Brinton's description and analysis of the organization of the Jacobin clubs relies in part on his knowledge of the sociology of voluntary associations. It is clear that he was acquainted with the burgeoning literature in this area, including Simmel's *Soziologie*, especially the chapter on "The Secret and the Secret Society," and Charles Horton Cooley's *Social Organization*. Indeed, Brinton's own contribution to this body of theory, his 1930 essay on "clubs," in the *Encyclopedia of the Social Sciences*, demonstrates his expertise in this subject, which is so crucial to his work on the Jacobins.

In his chapter on the organization of the Jacobin clubs, Brinton suggests that our preconceived view was that these revolutionary clubs represented something new because voluntary political associations could not have a place in a state under the kingship of Louis XIV (Brinton, 1930). True, but, as he shows, the real antecedents of the Jacobin clubs were not political bodies, but the well-known literary societies, on the one side, and the mostly Masonic secret societies, on the other.

As Brinton describes them, the literary societies, *chambres littéraires*, started out as clubs for bourgeois scholars in the seventeenth century, but by 1760 they were ubiquitous in both the urban centers and provincial towns. What had begun as associations for intellectuals to spread egalitarian and reformist propaganda, as Brinton called it, had now become social clubs, and among their members were middle-class lawyers, merchants, doctors, and *rentiers*. In the three decades between 1760 and the outbreak of the Revolution "the literary societies closely organized by committees of correspondence, and united by a central committee, did by propaganda, caucuses, electioneering and public manifestations influence political events" (Brinton, 1930).

If the literary societies constituted, in Brinton's words, a "political machine," the secret societies, such as the freemasons, were a cultural one. Warning his readers that reliable information about secret societies is difficult to obtain, Brinton nevertheless ventures forth and shows that "many freemasons were among the founders of the first Jacobin clubs" (Brinton, 1930).

More important than sheer numbers of masons who were Jacobins is the ritual and normative effect that the freemasons had on the clubs. Here Brinton allows the reader to flesh out some of Simmel's brilliant insights into secret societies in general, and freemasonry in particular. Although Simmel is not mentioned by name in *The Jacobins* we know that Brinton was very much acquainted with his work because he cited it prominently in his article on "Clubs" cited above, published in the same year. Simmel says that "there are perhaps no other external traits, which are so typical of the secret society... than the high valuation of usages, formulas, and rites." Simmel uses the freemasons to show that "the vow of secrecy refers exclusively to the form of the Masonic ritual," rather than to its contents (Simmel, 1950, p. 358). Brinton's discussion of the Masonic origins of Jacobin practices underscores Simmel's point. Hence, among other rituals, both the masons and the Jacobins shared the "fraternal embrace" between high officials and guests, the use of "Brother" as a form of address, and the use of "blackballing" as part of the secret voting procedure for admission to the clubs. As with the masons, the Jacobins had elaborate secret codes for recognizing each other, detailed examples of which are given by Brinton.

Having shown that the Jacobin clubs did not arise *de novo*, but out of the wellsprings of long-established middle-class voluntary associations such as the Masonic and literary societies, Brinton turns his attention to the enormous pleasure that the Jacobins took in participating in politics. Brinton shows no acquaintance with Max Weber's essay "Politics as a Vocation," published a decade before in Germany, but his description of the exuberance of the Jacobins for political life with no financial rewards evokes Weber's dichotomy of "living for" as opposed to "living off" of politics, as only an upper-middle-class leadership could do. As Brinton puts it, the Jacobins "had talked about politics, and read about politics for years, but until this blessed Revolution they had never been able to give themselves the illusion that they were in politics" (Brinton, 1930, p. 20).

To round out the organizational aspects of the Jacobin movement, Brinton gives the reader a detailed description of the estimated number of clubs, which he thinks may be near 7,000, and the number of members, which during the Terror may have ranged from 500,000 to a million. More valuable than these estimates are Brinton's honest admissions that although they are based on the best data he could find, the gaps in the historical record prevent a more accurate picture. Perhaps Brinton's most sociologically advanced thinking about the Jacobins concerns the relationship of leaders to the rank and file. He shows that only a very small minority among the Jacobins actually took the lead in one club after another. These elite groups manned the committees and formed what Brinton calls an "undisguised oligarchy." Brinton's discussion of this oligarchy echoes the ideas of Vilfredo Pareto about the "circulation of elites," which is not surprising, since Pareto was the most prominent sociologist during the late 1920s through the 1930s. Besides the general fascination with Pareto among social scientists during this time, Brinton was, as mentioned above, a prominent figure in the famed Pareto Circle at Harvard University. Indeed, *The Jacobins* might be read as a case study in "the circulation of elites," as middle-class Jacobins replaced aristocrats and the monarchy in positions of authority.

According to Pareto, the circulation of the elite could induce social changes in leadership in either a gradual pattern of replacement, or by violent revolution. Brinton takes up this question of how changes in the elite occur in his chapter on membership in the Jacobin clubs. "There is a current theory," he wrote, "that all violent revolutions are the work of men who are disconnected with the society from which they rebel almost wholly because they are failures in that society." One would have thought that Tocqueville's beautifully researched and argued theory that revolutions are more likely to occur in places where the people have rising expectations rather than among the more permanently poor would have forestalled what Brinton called "the maladjustment theory" of revolution (Brinton, 1930, p. 46). The effect of Brinton's analysis of the membership of the Jacobin clubs was to underscore Tocqueville's premise, namely that the most active areas of violence during the French Revolution were those where the middle classes were on the rise. According to Brinton, "the names of Jacobins are almost never found among the poor" (Brinton, 1930, p. 53).

So "the Jacobin was neither noble nor beggar" (Brinton, 1930, p. 70). In fact, as Brinton carefully shows, the Jacobin clubs cut across class lines, sometimes accepting nobles as members, sometimes those who were working class, and mostly those who were middle and upper-middle class. These revolutionaries were by and large successful in their occupations and communities. These observations brought Brinton closer to Tocqueville than to Marx.

The middle-class orientation of the Jacobin clubs was consistent with their tactics. One of the earliest and most enduring elements of political action associated with the clubs was the shaping of public opinion through propaganda. Brinton uses both public opinion and propaganda in a thoroughly modern way because he thought that these methods of mass appeal and manipulation were often believed to be "primitive until quite recent times." This, wrote Brinton, is "quite false, like so many other assumptions based on the dogma that men were never ingenious before the industrial revolution" (Brinton, 1930, p. 76).

Brinton's understanding of contemporary hubris about our supposed superiority leads the reader to rethink commonplace assumptions about progress and modernity. The many thousands of Jacobin clubs became centers of news and views. They had reading rooms filled with newspapers from across France, as well as pamphlets and books. They all had committees of correspondence, and Brinton demonstrates that the clubs spent a small fortune on printing and mailing packets of propaganda circulars and pamphlets. This emphasis on the power of the word harks back to the Jacobin clubs' antecedents in the literary societies, and underscores the middle and upper-middle-class backgrounds of most of their members.

The revolutionary propaganda efforts of the clubs extended to public education of young and old alike about the rights of man, popular sovereignty. They sponsored prizes for reading aloud *Rights of Man*, which Brinton calls the "new gospel." The Jacobins' insight about using propaganda methods for mass persuasion shows them to be many times more modern than we might think at first blush. This observation extends to the political acumen of these societies. Brinton carefully shows that the success of the Jacobins in pushing their agenda in elections and in policy making was "due to the simple fact that they were organized and disciplined, that they voted as a unit" (Brinton, 1930, p. 86). Here we could easily see the relevance of the political sociology of Michels, Ostrogorski, Bryce, and Weber, all of whom saw that politics is driven by these tactics.

Up to 1793 the Jacobin clubs were more or less "at peace with the government," according to Brinton, even though as a collective political party they tried to unseat incumbent officials in elections (Brinton, 1930, p. 89). During the thirteen months of the Reign of Terror stretching from the summer of 1793 through the summer of 1794, the Jacobins had effectively eliminated all opposition, and their members had taken control of the government. In the year-long Terror, according to Brinton, "all government officials, both elective and appointive, were for the moment of the same party; all were Jacobins" (Brinton, 1930, p. 117). During this period, we could easily make use of Pareto's work on the circulation of the elites to understand how the Jacobin clubs "provided a reservoir from which the new officialdom could be drawn," as Brinton put it (Brinton, 1930, p. 120).

Even before the Terror, and certainly during it, the Jacobins' use of violence, both physical and mental, was notable, especially in the form of rioting and hazing against their opponents. The numerous examples Brinton provides allow us to see just how apt is Lord Acton's famous phrase, "Power tends to corrupt, and absolute power corrupts absolutely." Without significant opposition during the period of the Terror, the Jacobins used violent means to get their way in the public life of France, as well as to insinuate their ideas into the private realm, interfering with morality, on the one hand, and exerting pressure on individuals to conform to collectivist economic positions, on the other. A locked-box hold on power always seems to open up real possibilities for totalitarian temptations to come to the fore. The Jacobins were neither the first nor the last movement to monopolize power and use violent means for glorified ends. From the Inquisition centuries before to the Nazi and Communist monopolies of power centuries after, the Jacobin-inspired Terror demonstrates what can happen when viable opposition parties disappear.

While various forms of radicalism have been institutionalized throughout history, the Jacobins mounted one of the most successful campaigns to insinuate their ideas into the institutions of their society. In his attempt to create an "ideal typical" understanding of the Jacobins, Brinton sums up the aims of his average model:

> An independent nation-state, a republican form of government, universal manhood suffrage, separation of church and state; equal civil rights for all, and the abolition of hereditary distinctions and social privileges; a competitive industrial and agricultural society, with private ownership of property, but without great fortunes and without dire poverty; a virtuous, hard-working society, without luxuries and without vices, where the individual freely conforms to standards of middle-class decency.
> (Brinton, 1930, p. 142)

Brinton's description of the average or ideal-type Jacobin' makes him seem to be much like an average contemporary European or American. Herein lies the eternal problem of reconciling ends and means, and the issue is not the aims, but the means by which one pursues those ends. Radicals such as the Jacobins rarely seem to trust people to arrive at the same conclusions, or to share the same goals that they have without forcing them to move in those directions. Contrarily, liberals seem more readily to trust that individuals can and should make up their own minds about value-laden issues, and that they can be persuaded through reason to share the same goals.

In America, from the Revolution on, liberalism has been prevalent, while radicals have been positioned to the left and right of the prevailing liberal center. Not so for the Jacobins. Not only were they cultural Puritans, as Brinton put it, but they were radicals who wanted to force their ideologies upon everyone else. Nothing new here under the sociological sun; think of radicals on the left and right such as Maoists, Soviet and Chinese Communists, Nazis, Khmer Rouge, and McCarthyites. Brinton, an old-school academic liberal, understood that the Jacobins, middle-class and well-intentioned, had become dangerous radicals who fostered terrorism. *The Jacobins*, published almost on the eve of the European democratic meltdown that would lead to the unspeakable horrors perpetrated by Hitler, Stalin, and their like, is a sound guidebook for understanding an earlier, different, but, kindred meltdown of democratic morality and liberalism.

Certainly, one of the most notable parts of *The Jacobins* is Brinton's chapter "Ritual." A commonplace concept today among social scientists, "Ritual" was a relatively new addition to their theoretical toolbox when Brinton published this book. Here again we see his debt to Pareto, who discussed ritual extensively as a social need to express one's sentiments through actions, as part of his third type of "residues." Three of the most prominent participants in Lawrence J. Henderson's Pareto seminars at Harvard all remark about the importance of ritual to Pareto's theory of society: Brinton himself, in his 1954 retrospective article "The Residue of Pareto" in *Foreign Affairs*; Talcott Parsons, in *The Structure of Social Action*, and in reviews of Pareto's *Mind and Society;* and George C. Homans, in his 1941 article on "Anxiety and Ritual" in *American Anthropologist*.

Others at Harvard who were heavily influenced by Pareto, especially his thoughts about ritual, and who were well-connected to Brinton at this time were Elton Mayo, whose office was next to Henderson's in the Business School, and W. Lloyd Warner, an anthropologist whom Mayo brought to Harvard. The fifth and final volume of Warner's still important Yankee City series, *The Living and the Dead*, shows that he found ways to link Pareto's to Durkheim's work on ritual, in one of the great ethnographic accounts of American rites. As a footnote to the rippling and enduring influence of Pareto, consider the now well-known influence of W. Lloyd Warner on Erving Goffman, his student at the University of Chicago, whose work relied on the ritual concept that Warner derived in part from Pareto and Durkheim. Brinton's chapter on ritual among the Jacobins is an earlier, but no less important manifestation of the ritual concept.

As the Revolution progressed toward its most famous phase, the Terror, Jacobin rituals progressed too, from the pedestrian to the almost fanatical. At the beginning these rituals entailed mostly communal meals, festivals, planting liberty trees on town squares, and other cultish imitations of religious rites. As Brinton writes, "There were civic marriages, civic baptisms, civic burials. Revolutionary songs were written, and the songs became hymns. The Declaration of the Rights of Man took on the authority of scripture" (Brinton, 1930, p. 189). In time, these rites of revolution were underscored with statuary—busts of the apostles of the Revolution were placed throughout the Jacobin meeting halls, and Brinton makes the obvious connection for his readers between Jacobinism and forms of fanatical religion, and he shows clearly that the divide between political ritual and religious rites can easily be blurred in what the anthropologist Victor Turner would later call "liminal periods."

This exercise in the New History, or what Brinton eventually called retrospective sociology, offers less of an alternative to the older narrative forms of history than it does an addition to it. Brinton's collective biography of the Jacobins is an early trendsetting example of what Lawrence Stone described and labeled "prosopography," in his well-known eponymous 1971 *Daedalus* article. Thus, Brinton's book is an important contribution to the social sciences as a successful example of a new methodological technique, a correction to previous historical assumptions of the lower-class origin of the Jacobins, as a contribution to help sociologists understand how elites circulate, and as an exploration of the use of ritual in revolutionary movements.

Based on his early work on revolution in the three books on this subject that he published in the 1930s, Brinton became one of the most popular commentators on revolutionary activity during the middle part of the twentieth century. His work extended beyond revolutions to the history of ideas, and among his many other books he is known for publishing *Nietzsche* in 1941, *Ideas and Men: The Story of Western Thought* in 1950, *A History of Western Morals* in 1959, *The Shaping of the Modern Mind* in 1963, and *The Americans and the French* in 1968.

Brinton was also one of the most prolific public intellectuals writing in influential journals and magazines. Thus, he published a staggering number of articles and reviews—over a hundred in all—in *The Saturday Review of Literature* during the 1930s and 1940s. Brinton also published twenty-nine essays and reviews in *The New York Times* between 1946 and 1965. He also published articles in such diverse but important venues as *Daedalus*, *Journal of the History of Ideas*, *The Sewanee Review*, *The Journal of Modern History*, *The American Historical Review*, *The Journal of Economic History*, *The Harvard Theological Review*, *Foreign Affairs*, *Political Science Quarterly*, and *The Journal of Higher Education*, among others. He served as President of the American Historical Association in 1963. In February 1968, Brinton testified at the Fulbright Senate hearings during the Vietnam War about the nature of the Viet Cong. He died in September 1968 at the age of 70, having just retired from Harvard University.

6

THE STRANGE CAREER OF POLITICAL SOCIOLOGY IN AMERICA

Political sociology is both a key part of the American sociological tradition, and a latecomer to it. Given its importance as a subdiscipline, political sociology is also emblematic of sociology's blind spots regarding the various forms of terrorism, totalitarianism, dictatorship, revolutionary nationalism, anarchy, nihilism, genocide, and political messianism that have been among the most important driving forces in world politics for over a century. Ironically, through its own specialized "trained incapacity" to think about and address these issues, political sociology has all but ignored these antidemocratic threats and obstacles to freedom in the modern world. Because of this, political sociology has missed the opportunity to anticipate, evaluate, and give policymakers a framework to deal with these forces, which attack and threaten the most highly prized political values of Western Civilization.

For example, political sociology was unable to anticipate the pre-WWII rise of right-wing totalitarianism in Germany, Italy, and Japan. It also missed foreseeing the establishment of notable left-wing Communist dictatorships in Russia, China, Korea, Cuba, among other places, before and after WWII. Closer to our own day, political sociology missed the eventual downfall of Communism in Europe near the end of the twentieth century, and there has been no major article on terrorism in either the *American Journal of Sociology* or the *American Sociological Review* since 1989.

Equally remarkable has been the inability, or unwillingness, of political sociology to come to grips with the rise of nationalism in Third World countries, nor with the problem of terrorism, most especially among radical Islamic groups. The most unfortunate blind spot among political sociologists has been the greatest blot on humanity, namely the wide-ranging genocides that have taken the lives of tens of millions during the last century, and which continue today. This is not to say that there have been no political sociologists exploring the social landscape of genocide and terrorism, because there have been; notably Irving Louis Horowitz, Jack P. Gibbs, and Zygmunt Bauman, among a few others, come to mind here. The problem is that these areas of the social landscape need to be visited and mapped regularly, and while all roads—real, imagined, and intellectual—may once have led to Rome, the intellectual pathways leading to totalitarianism, genocide, dictatorship, and the like are seldom trod by political sociologists.

Indeed, it seems as if political sociology, especially in America, has built a wall of partial relevance around itself. Within its confines, political sociology concentrates heavily on race, class, and gender issues in terms of voting, political participation, resource-mobilization efforts, and the like, often relying on hackneyed and tired tropes concerning these variables. At the same time, it has virtually ignored the very real threats to the freedoms made possible by democracy, which are under attack by various forms of barbarism. Ironically, while ignoring threats to freedom on the world stage, its own conventional wisdom seems to have prevented political sociology from seeing that America was ready to elect a black man as President of the United States in the 2008 election. While this intellectual myopia has limited sociology's relevance, it also raises the question of why this should be so in the first place. Since the origins of these blind spots are to be found in the history of political sociology itself, the main purpose of this chapter is to explore why America produced virtually no political sociology during its founding years. Secondarily, my purpose here is to trace why political sociology has become so myopic regarding important events and threats to democratic values.

The founding of sociology, as we know the discipline today, and more particularly, the origin of political sociology, is both institutionally and intellectually enigmatic. There are no givens here. In terms of intellectual and theoretical content, we know that sociology emerged after a number of fits and starts in the nineteenth century, but there was no eureka moment of discovery. Instead there emerged from the tide pools of economics, history, political science, and philosophy pre-and proto-sociological ideas by individuals who were writing beyond the established boundaries of their disciplines, and collectively they established a body of work that can be recognized, with hindsight, as sociology.

Thus, Auguste Comte's *System of Positive Polity* (1851–1854), Henri de Saint-Simon's *New Christianity* (1825), Jeremy Bentham's *Introduction to Principles of Morals and Legislation* (1789), John Stuart Mill's *A System of Logic* (1843), *The Principles of Political Economy* (1848), and *On Liberty* (1859), and G. W. F. Hegel's *Phenomenology of Mind* (1807) and *Elements of the Philosophy of Right* (1821) are examples of pre-sociological works and ideas. While we cannot coax a full-fledged sociology from these writings, they are foundational, and hence essential to the development of the discipline. The ideas contained in these and other works filled the tide pools in which there evolved more advanced, but, here too, not quite really sociological concepts and theories.

Some thinkers, such as Karl Marx and Alexis de Tocqueville, came asymptotically close to true sociology, even though they never quite got there. Thus, the bulk of Karl Marx's work, from the early essays on *The Jewish Question* (1843) and alienation in the *Philosophical and Economic Manuscripts* (1844) to the first volume of *Capital* (1867) and the *Critique of the Gotha Program* (1875), brought forth proto-sociological ideas about social class, state and society, and alienation that would eventually lead others to produce solid sociological theory and studies in these areas. The same is true of Alexis de Tocqueville, whose *Democracy in America* (1835–1840) and *The Ancient Regime and the French Revolution* (1856) were filled with proto-sociological ideas about social stratification, power and authority, civil society, and revolution that would influence the course of modern sociology. Along with Marx and Tocqueville, other proto-sociologists such as Jacob Burckhardt and Herbert Spencer also contributed to the birth of modern sociology with their studies of alienation, social class, power and authority, and the organization of society. The proto-sociological writings of Marx, Tocqueville, and others were primordial to the discipline. They were sociology in essence, but not in form.

By the late nineteenth century, formal sociology as we know it had emerged from these pools of pre-and proto-sociological ideas, and it soon evolved, bursting with energy, into a wide variety of very different concepts and theories. In many cases, the evolutionary descent from Comte to Mill to Durkheim, or from Hegel to Marx to Weber, or from Mill to Tocqueville to Cooley is so seamless as to blur the lines of demarcation from merely pre-sociological to proto-sociological to what we accept as founding sociological ideas.

Nevertheless, from many of the tide pools from which sociology emerged came forth intellectual efforts that failed to contribute to the mainstream of sociology and ultimately dried up before coming to fruition. Thus, the earliest sociological efforts in America were Henry Hughes's *Treatise on Sociology* and George Fitzhugh's *Sociology for the South*, both published in 1854. The influence of Comte and Spencer is direct and prodigious. Neither of these early proto-sociological works had a lasting influence on the discipline, but, as Daniel Boorstin suggests, they are emblematic of American sociology's concentration on the institutional and associational life, rather than on politics and the separation of state and society. These works are remarkable in their neglect of the political background and implications of slavery (which is the main sociological variable in defense of which both books are written). In many ways, however, they reflect the preoccupation with civil society and the propensity to ignore politics that would mark the emergence of modern American sociology fifty years later.

The institutional history of sociology is easier to trace than the tipping point at which the accumulation of proto-sociological ideas becomes sociology per se. Thus, if we wish to speak about the institutional history of this discipline, we can begin with the *de novo* creation of sociology courses within already established departments of economics, education, or philosophy during the late nineteenth and early twentieth centuries. The next critical stage is the founding of professional sociological journals in one country after another, and then of professional sociological societies in America, Germany, France, Great Britain, and other countries in Europe. Finally, all of this leads to the creation of entirely new college and university departments of sociology. All these institutional events can be traced as to time, place, and personnel.

Institutional histories of the founding generation of sociology lead to some interesting, although often pedantic, questions regarding who among the founders were really sociologists. While the answers to such questions may have narrow antiquarian value in terms of disciplinary ancestry, they are not very useful categorizations when we consider that virtually none of the founders had or could have had a PhD in sociology. All the founders took degrees, wrote, and taught in other fields before adding their stamps to the new discipline, so institutional questions of disciplinary pedigree are much less important to understanding the nature of the new discipline of sociology than are questions of intellectual ancestry.

Far more vital here is the "history of ideas" approach. Who among the founders were called "sociologists," or who called themselves "sociologists," is pleasant to know, but in the end, this is nothing but a fruitless parlor game. Those tidal pools of pre- and proto-sociological ideas, out of which the discipline finally emerged, are the places we need to look for its origins. These intellectual tide pools contained sets of ideas that in themselves were not sociological in the exact sense of the term. For instance, philosophically based ideas about alienation were already extant in the works of Marx, Hegel, Nietzsche, Kant, and Kierkegaard before they were hammered into sociological concepts by Weber, Simmel, and Ferdinand Tönnies. Other than the social philosophers and quasi-social scientists already mentioned above, the indirect influence of thinkers such as John Locke, Thomas Hobbes, Jean-Jacques Rousseau, Adam Smith, Adam Ferguson, and Edmund Burke, whose ideas were sloshing about in those tidal pools out of which modern sociology emerged, would be profound.

That emergence of modern sociology itself raises categorical questions within the history of ideas. Was Max Weber a legal scholar or an economist or a sociologist? Was Werner Sombart an economist or a sociologist? What about Emile Durkheim, whose degree was in philosophy, and who taught pedagogy to future teachers? Was he a sociologist? The same might be asked about Georg Simmel, who was clearly trained and taught in philosophy. Was he also a sociologist? William Graham Sumner was trained and took a degree in theology, as did Albion Small, who took another degree in history. Were they sociologists? Answers to these questions and others like them may contribute footnotes to sociology's institutional history, but nothing more than that. Whether Weber's writings (those published posthumously, as well as those published during his lifetime) were sociology per se or still merely proto-sociological is a more difficult question to answer. Compound this question to include all the important founders—Weber, Tönnies, Sombart, Simmel, Michels, Durkheim, Cooley, Thomas, Park, Mosca, and Pareto, among others—and you have the answer to the question of when sociology, as we know it as an academic discipline today, actually began. The scope of such an enterprise is well beyond anything possible here. My purpose in the rest of this chapter is to examine the ideas that emerged from one particularly rich and fertile intellectual tide pool to form what we know of as political sociology. Why that emergence took place almost exclusively within European sociology, and hardly at all in America during the founding generation, is the springboard for this inquiry.

The reasons for the basic and original manifestation of political sociology in late nineteenth- and early twentieth-century Germany, Italy, France, and Russia, and the undeveloped state of that subdiscipline in America at that time, can be traced to the very different intellectual paths taken in Europe, on the one hand, and in America on the other. Furthermore, the relationship of the state to civil society, which is, of course, the point of demarcation for political sociology, differed dramatically from one continent to the other.

Generally speaking, during the nineteenth century, Germany, France, Italy, and Russia experienced the powerful tripartite forces of nationalization, centralization, and bureaucratization full bore as politics came to dominate civil society. In America, these forces were also experienced, but politics never overwhelmed the democratic institutions and culture of civil society. Even slavery, secession, and the Civil War were contests that played out in civil society, rather than as centralizing political events. Local, state, and sectional identities were more important in nineteenth-century America than was nationalism. Questions about the relationships of the state to civil society were always resolved in favor of the latter in America, but mostly in favor of the former in Europe.

The underlying premise of political sociology is that state and society, or perhaps more accurately, civil society, are separate entities that occupy the same social time and space, competing for priority and precedence.

In nineteenth- and early twentieth-century America, politics was absorbed into civil society as just another powerful associational influence. It is therefore not surprising that American sociology developed pragmatic concepts about community, consensus, and symbolic interaction, rather than political sociology. In Europe, politics vied with civil society, and even began to absorb it, thus creating the need to explain the relationship between these two spheres of life, hence the need for political sociology with its emphasis on state, conflict, elites, power, and revolution.

During the late nineteenth century and the early part of the twentieth century, there were often violent political upheavals in Europe. This stands in comparison to the relative political peacefulness on the American scene during this period. Thus, it is not hard to imagine that Weber, Sombart, Michels, and others who forged the new political sociology were jolted from any complacency about the social meaning of politics, while the American founders of sociology from Ward and Giddings to Cooley and Ross could see politics as a mere backdrop to the associational life. These differences in social context can be illustrated in the following two anecdotes.

In the mid-1880s John Dewey, then a professor of philosophy at the University of Michigan, and Charles Horton Cooley, one of the well-known founders of sociology, and their wives were members of the Samovar Club, which provided a meeting place for university staff to discuss great Russian literature while drinking tea or hot chocolate brewed in a metal urn called a samovar. Members of the Samovar met at the club, located on South State Street, which is now the home of Michigan's LSA Building and its sociology department. Photographs in the University of Michigan Library show peaceful gatherings in which Dewey and Cooley, among others, gathered on cold nights to discuss Tolstoy and Turgenev. Nothing could be more exemplary of civil society among American academics.

If we fast-forward to Munich, Germany when Max Weber gave two monumentally important addresses that were eventually published as "Politics as a Vocation" and "Science as a Vocation," we see a very different social context. When Weber addressed the hundreds of students of the Freistudentischen Bund gathered at the University of Munich late in 1918, the surrounding streets were pockmarked by machine-gun fire, and photographs from this time show machine-gun crews of soldiers and revolutionaries fighting in the German Revolution, a socialist revolt centered in Munich. Here the state was far more prominent than civil society, and Weber could not have missed the immediacy of politics all around him.

From 1871, when the unification of the thirty-nine Germanic states into the newly formed German Empire was completed by Otto von Bismarck, to Germany's instigation of WWI and the German Revolution of 1918–1919, Germany was the world's most politically active state. The centralization of government led to a highly bureaucratized state that exceeded the French bureaucracy under Napoleon and beyond. Consequently, German political authority multiplied in scope, and state power over the lives of citizens became the focal point for a myriad of political parties and party struggles. Two socialist parties, one founded by the Hegelian, Ferdinand Lassalle, and the other by August Bebel and Wilhelm Liebknecht, merged to form the Social Democratic Party, which curried favor with trade unions and drove home the divisive wedges of class interests and class struggles. Two other major parties vied for political power with the socialists after unification: the conservative Centre Party, which took up the cause of Catholic interests, and the National Liberal Party serving Bismarck's domestic and foreign policy interests. These parties represented radically different points of view, and they even split among themselves over ideological differences. Thus, even before WWI the Social Democratic Party was rocked by dissenting factions, some of which pushed for the party to become less Marxist and increasingly reformist, while other factions led by Rosa Luxemburg and Karl Liebknecht hived off to become the Spartacist League, and eventually the Communist party of Germany. All this political activity acted as a backdrop to the founding of sociology in Germany. Social problems and policy problems tended to merge together as one and the same thing. Indeed, to think about society and community, social class and power, or any other essential sociological concept was almost impossible without taking the political situation into account, in one way or another.

Contrasting this feverish and pervasive political activity in Germany with politics and society in the United States, we see a world of difference.

From the end of the Civil War in 1865, American politics was stabilized and mostly confined to the two-party system of Democrats and Republicans. There were, and still are, other small parties that were locally active, and which sometimes entered the national consciousness, but these never had the decisive and divisive impact of the major parties in Germany. Thus, some parties, such as the Greenback Party, which wielded some power from the late 1870s through the 1880s, and the Populist Party, which was active among western farmers from the late 1880s to about 1900, represented agrarian interests on specific matters concerning the form of currency in the United States. Unlike the immensely successful and powerful German Social Democratic Party, the Socialist party of America, formed in 1901, was never a powerful force in American politics. While Eugene V. Debs ran for President in 1904 and 1908 and got 6% of the popular vote in the election of 1912, the party was more of a diversion than a preoccupation in the political life of the nation. Politics contributed to the regular workings of American life, but unlike Germany, government was small at the local, state, and federal levels. American life, even in the period of immense industrialization and urbanization following the Civil War, was more dominated by the associational and communal life we call "civil society" than by big government. It is not surprising therefore that American sociology keyed in upon elements of civil society rather than on a sociology of politics during the founding period.

While it is remarkable that there is no body of nineteenth- or early twentieth-century American pre- or proto-political sociology, at least as interesting, and certainly ironic, is the fact that some of the most important works of European proto-political sociology and political sociology were written about America, even if they were written by Europeans. Two of the great proto-sociological cornerstones of modern political sociology are Tocqueville's *Democracy in America*, and James Bryce's *American Commonwealth*. When we get to modern political sociology, we have Werner Sombart's *Why Is there No Socialism in the United States?*

If American sociologists were not interested in creating political sociology, what were their interests? The American founders of sociology were most definitely interested in something akin to politics, indeed, something often associated with it, namely democracy. From Jane Addams' *Democracy and Social Ethics* (1902), *The Spirit of Youth and the*

City Streets (1909), and *Twenty Years at Hull House* (1910) to Charles Horton Cooley's *Human Nature and the Social Order* (1902), *Social Organization* (1909), and *Social Process* (1918), a democratic social order supported by a democratic culture, indeed, a common primary culture for democracy, as Cooley called it, was the undergirding for sociological analysis. Add to these Franklin Giddings' *Democracy and Empire* (1900) and *The Responsible State* (1918), Robert Park's dissertation on *The Crowd and the Public* as well as his enduring essays on the city, Lester Ward's *Psychic Factors of Civilization* (1906), and William Isaac Thomas' *Old World Traits Transplanted* (1921), and *The Polish Peasant in Europe and America*, written with Florian Znaniecki, and you have a representative sample of how committed early sociology in America was to understanding the relationship of society and culture to democracy. The problem from the standpoint of understanding why they produced no robust political sociology, is that democracy did not mean, first and foremost, political activity for these American founders. It meant civil society: in other words, the structure and function of voluntary associations, primary groups, and secondary powers. This makes sense from a sociology of knowledge perspective because social problems in America were more likely to have been addressed by voluntary associations than by government and political activity. Anti-saloon leagues were more likely to be productive of action than were political parties. This is in stark contrast to the power of government at every level in the highly centralized states of France and Germany.

As the immediate successors to the founding generation took their PhDs in sociology, they too lacked interest in a genuine sociology of politics, and they reproduced their mentors' primary emphasis on civil society. *Fields and Methods of Sociology* (1934), edited by L. L. Bernard, is a solid example of the paucity of interest in political sociology in America before WWII. Bernard was President of the American Sociological Society in 1932 when it held its annual meeting in Cincinnati, Ohio. Based on the program and papers of the meeting, Bernard chose the subdivisions of sociology that were deemed most representative of the research efforts of the association. The resulting book, *Fields and Methods of Sociology*, included chapters by many of the most active and well-known figures in the discipline, including "Historical Sociology" by Howard Becker,

"Biological Sociology" by Read Bain, "Urban Sociology" by Maurice Davie, "Social Psychology" by Emory Bogardus, and on "Social Work" by James Bossard. Other areas covered were the "Sociology of Religion," "Criminology," "Family Studies," "Folk Sociology," "Educational Sociology," "Rural Sociology," and "Statistics." Political Sociology was mentioned a few times in passing. Thus, pre-WWII political sociology was hardly worth mentioning in what was virtually an official compendium of the discipline in 1934. But the situation was about to begin changing dramatically.

Many institutional histories of political sociology in America place its origins in the post-WWII period, and it is true that this is the period in which political sociology becomes a very visible subfield of sociology. Nevertheless, what seems to be both an institutional and intellectual awakening, especially in America, is really an intellectual re-awakening to a body of work that was at the creative core of sociology during the founding period. What is most interesting about the revival of political sociology as a subdiscipline in the wake of WWII is that almost all the important work done in political sociology during the founding generation was done in Europe. America produced no political sociology to speak of during the founding years presided over by the likes of Cooley, Ross, Giddings, Sumner, and Small. When American sociology took the lead in political sociological studies after WWII, these studies were based on sociological theories of politics generated by the two great proto-founders of the field, Tocqueville and Marx, and by the early true political sociologists: Max Weber, Robert Michels, Joseph Schumpeter, Georg Simmel, Emile Durkheim, Moisey Ostrogorsky, Gaetano Mosca, and Vilfredo Pareto, among others.

Despite the fact that *Fields and Methods of Sociology* ignored political sociology, we can see in the 1930s a foreshadowing of the golden age of political sociology that would emerge just after WWII. It began with Harold Lasswell's *Psychopathology and Politics* (1930), *World Politics and Personal Insecurity* (1935), and his *Politics: Who Gets What, When, How* (1935). While Lasswell's doctorate from the University of Chicago was in political science, these works integrate Lasswell's broad sociological interests, and his studies of European social science at the Universities of London, Geneva, Paris, and Berlin. For instance, Max Weber's influence on Lasswell is evident in *Psychopathology and Politics,* and in his other works. The other great influence on the emergence of a European-centered political sociology in America was Talcott Parsons, whose seminal work, *The Structure of Social Action,* appeared in 1937. Parsons assured Weber's place in American sociology as one of the most important sociological theorists. Because so much of Weber's work could be called political sociology, his introduction to the larger field of sociology ensured that the subfield would be Weberian to the core.

Other than the emerging trickle of political sociology started by Lasswell and Parsons in the 1930s, other pools of political sociological thought were forming during this period, or even a bit before it. For example, Robert MacIver, who had taken over for Franklin Giddings at Columbia, published *Community: A Sociological Study* (1917), *The Modern State* (1926), and his influential textbook, *Society: Its Structure and Changes* (1931). Influenced by Durkheim, Simmel, Tönnies, and other European founders of sociology, MacIver's work stressed the reciprocal but separate relationships of politics and the state, on the one hand, to community and society, on the other hand. While the work of Lasswell, MacIver, and Parsons didn't add up to political sociology as a subdiscipline, it helped establish a base for this field to be built on during the post-war years.

One of the idiosyncrasies of these foundational efforts for political sociology is the overall boundary maintenance problem of American sociology from beginning to end. Under the metaphysical influence of Immanuel Kant, Georg Friederich Hegel, and other such philosophers, the major founders of sociology in France and Germany tended to hammer out general theories of society that marked off a definite conceptual language and field of study that could be called "sociology." Durkheim, Mauss, and other French sociologists were such general theorists, and so were the German founders, such as Weber, Tönnies, Simmel, and Sombart. At the same time, American sociological founders were molded by the pragmatic ideas of John Dewey and William James. This influence was profound and obvious in the case of Cooley, Park, and Thomas, all of whom had direct contact with the great pragmatist philosophers. Under the pragmatist influence, American sociology was more interested in problem-solving than in general theory. For the great European generalizers, such as Weber, politics was a central problem to be understood in sociologically relevant theoretical terms. For the pragmatist American sociologists, politics was no more than a means to fulfill other ends. It simply wasn't problematic enough to generate interest in hiving off a subdiscipline for political sociological studies.

Out of these transitional efforts in the 1930s, the post-WWII generation of sociologists created a period of efflorescence in political sociology that mirrored the founding period of political sociology in Europe at the end of the nineteenth and the beginning of the twentieth centuries. From the outset, it is important to mention the work of C. Wright Mills and his influence upon post-war American political sociology. Possibly the single most important publication for American political sociology was Hans Gerth and C. Wright Mills' edited and translated volume *From Max Weber* (1946). This volume contains Weber's indispensable essays "Politics as a Vocation" and "Class, Status and Party." Because of Weber's centrality and importance to modern political sociology, and because *From Max Weber* introduced Weber's political sociology to American scholars, its publication was a pivotal point in the development of the field. Besides *From Max Weber*, Mills left his mark on political sociology with the publication of *White Collar* (1951) and *The Power Elite* (1956).

Two other very prominent post-war political sociologists were Seymour Martin Lipset and Reinhard Bendix. With Lipset's *Agrarian Socialism* (1950), *Union Democracy* (1956), and *Political Man: The Social Bases of Politics* (1960), we have the importation and integration of the ideas of such founders as Weber, Michels, Durkheim, and Ostrogorski into American political sociology. Another prime example of the post-war burst of energy in political sociology was Reinhard Bendix, who collaborated with Lipset on *Social Mobility in Industrial Society* (1959). Bendix also was heavily influenced by Max Weber and Georg Simmel, as we can see in his *Work and Authority in Industry* (1956), *Max Weber: An Intellectual Portrait* (1960), and *Nation-Building & Citizenship: Studies of Our Changing Social Order* (1964).

Just as prominent, and influential in forging a solid Weberian and classical sociological foundation for political sociology in America during this period, is the following sample: Daniel Bell's *The End of Ideology* (1960), Edward Shils' *Torment of Secrecy* (1956), Irving Louis Horowitz's *Idea of War and Peace in Contemporary Philosophy* (1956) and *Radicalism and the*

Revolt against Reason, James Coleman's *Union Democracy* (with Lipset, 1956), Peter Blau's *The Dynamics of Bureaucracy* (1955), and *Exchange and Power in Social Life* (1964), Alvin Gouldner's *Patterns of Industrial Bureaucracy* (1954), Morris Janowitz's *The Professional Soldier: A Social and Political Portrait* (1960), Philip Selznick's *TVA and the Grass Roots* (1953), David Riesman's *The Lonely Crowd* (1950), Leo Löwenthal's *Prophets of Deceit* (written with Norbert Guterman in 1949), and Samuel Stouffer's *The American Soldier* (1949) and *Communism, Conformity & Civil Liberties* (1955). While this list could be expanded ten-fold or more, it gives a sense of the creative and prodigious activity going on in American political sociology in the post-war years.

The absence of a healthy political sociology in America during the founding generation, and up to WWII, is only surprising at first glance. Politics is an integral part of American social life, and has been from the beginning, but it has always been a handmaiden to the associational life at the heart of civil society. Few nations come close to America for having such a long-lived, stable, yet vibrant political system, but it is its very stability, and its supporting, rather than leading role, that made political sociology irrelevant until the period between the two World Wars, and especially after WWII. The fact that most of the founders of American sociology all but ignored politics as an area of study is not as much of a conundrum as it might seem. If civil society created the context and the backdrop for politics in America, just the opposite was true in Europe. Because politics was so instrumental to determining civil society in European societies it became the springboard for placing political sociology at the core of the vibrant and interesting writings of the founders.

Although there is no founding text for political sociology in Europe, early sociologists were so immersed and interested in politics that a sociology of politics was inevitable. Among the French sociologists, Emile Durkheim anticipated and analyzed Germany's participation in WWI in "*Germany Above All*": *German Mentality and War* (1914) and in *Who Wanted War? The Origin of the War According to Diplomatic Documents* (1915). Durkheim's lectures on the state and politics presented between 1890 and 1900 were published in 1922 as *Professional Ethics and Civic Morals.*

In Germany Max Weber almost single handedly founded political sociology through his studies of the Russian Revolution, socialism, and of parliament and government in Germany. Weber's "Politics as a Vocation" (1918) remains indispensable to political sociology today. Among Weber's German contemporaries, Robert Michels wrote *Political Parties* (1911) and Werner Sombart wrote *Socialism and the Social Movement* (1896) and *Why Is There No Socialism in the United States?* (1906). Franz Oppenheimer published *The State* in 1914.

Since virtually none of the original founders of sociology were sociologists to start, and many never identified themselves fully as such anyway, it is proper to include James Bryce's *American Commonwealth* (1889), *Modern Democracies* (1921), and *Essays on History and Jurisprudence* (1901) as basic to the beginning of political sociology. The notable influence of Bryce on Max Weber adds to his importance to political sociology. Add to this Walter Bagehot's proto-sociological works, *The British Constitution* (1867) and *Physics and Politics* (1872) and we see the seeds of political sociology being sown in Great Britain.

The Italian sociologist Gaetano Mosca wrote *The Ruling Class* (1896) and Vilfredo Pareto wrote *The Mind and Society* (1916), establishing the seedbed of political sociology in Italy. Moisey Ostrogorsky wrote *Democracy and the Organization of Political Parties* in 1902, establishing a beachhead for political sociology in Russia.

But a mere list of publications here can do no more than point to the fact that some of the most well-known and influential works in early sociology were also works that established political sociology at the heart of the discipline in Europe during the founding generation. So why was political sociology so important in Europe and so unimportant, to the point of non-existence, in America during the founding era of sociology?

To answer this, we need to ask first, what is political sociology? Today, as it developed since WWII, political sociology covers a lot of intellectual territory, so much so that it may be too inclusive to be easily defined by its subject matter alone. Clearly, among the usual topics covered by political sociology today are political parties, voting behavior, political interest groups, political opinion polling, citizenship, political leadership, authority, power, legitimacy, elites, democracy, the nation state, war, revolution, nation building, and comparative political systems. Political sociology is less interested in political formalities and institutions per se, but rather it looks for the relationship of class to politics, and the relationship of ideologies and group behavior to institutional development.

Furthermore, there is the amorphousness of politics itself, which begins with disagreement, and ends when agreement is achieved. But, as we have seen, politics may be central to the formation and maintenance of civil society, as it was in late nineteenth-century Europe, or it may be peripheral to such formations, and merely one of the mechanisms of maintenance, as it was in nineteenth-century America. Ultimately politics is a method for resolving conflicts among individuals and groups with opposing interests. When politics, as a method, becomes institutionalized within parties, an electoral process, legislative bodies, lobbying groups, and the like, rational political processes may make peaceful resolution of value conflicts possible, as they did in America.

On the contrary, politics may contribute to a heightening of conflict if it is the main mechanism of control, as it was in Europe. Where political institutions are essential to social order, as they were in Europe, and they are weak, or fail, two alternatives come to the fore within a society. On the one hand, we find anarchy, revolution, or civil war; on the other hand, we may find dictatorship, totalitarianism, or military takeover. It is not hard to see that politics as a means of resolving conflicts is also, therefore, a means to maximize freedom. This is most likely where politics is aligned with a strong civil society, including a strong associational life, and permeable class structures that allow for the distinct possibility of social mobility. Most other methods of conflict resolution tend to restrict freedom, sometimes to the point of extinguishing it.

Politics as a means of resolving conflicts and of achieving freedom comes to the fore during the same time frame as the centralizing and democratizing movements of the nineteenth and twentieth centuries, and the birth of the modern social sciences. It is striking to note that many of the most important members of the founding generation of sociologists in Europe placed political sociology at the core of their work. Equally striking is the fact that in America there was virtually no political sociology being done at all before the end of WWI, but that individualism, social organization, social control, social order, and forms of community were examined from every angle other than politics.

"Today's sociology is still struggling with the preposterous initial fact of the individual. He is the only possible social unit, and he is no longer a thinkable possibility. He is the only real presence, and he is never present" (Small, 1905, p. 113). In *General Sociology,* one of the earliest American sociology textbooks, Albion Small laid the ground for American sociology's initial dilemma: to see the place of the individual in civil society. Would sociology in America emphasize the individual over and above society, or diminish the importance of the individual in contrast to that of society?

This tactical and structural theoretical dilemma was resolved differently by American sociologists than it was by their European counterparts. In *Origins of Sociology* (1924), Small, looking back to the disciplinary beginnings, characterized the archetypical German sociological question of social progress in the relationship of community to the individual as following this form: "Without disturbing public order, what additions are possible to individual freedom?" He contrasted this to the American sociological question: "Without diminishing individual freedom, what additions are possible to social order" (Small, 1924, p. 114).

American sociology presumed, in Small's words, that "individual liberty is the fundamental and paramount factor in a rational human condition." On the other hand, according to Small, German sociology began from the premise that "the welfare of the state must always have precedence over the liberty of individuals" (Small, 1924, p. 114). Herein Small may have helped answer the question of why there was no political sociology in America during the founding period. A brief look at the relationship of civic voluntarism to proto-political sociological ideas is called for here.

The question of the importance of civic voluntarism and voluntary associations to American democracy can be traced back to *The Federalist Papers* and before, but while it is hardly new, the question is still fresh and fascinating. The most famous proto-sociological analysis of the place of civic voluntarism and the secondary associations through which it is effected is found in Tocqueville's two great nineteenth-century classics, *Democracy in America* and *The Ancient Regime and the French Revolution*, but social scientists have never been satisfied to allow Tocqueville to have the last word on this subject. As political sociology adapted Tocqueville's insights, one of the main thrusts is directed toward understanding the pattern of voluntary political activity.

One of the most important facts of political life in America is that, except for moments during highly contested elections, more Americans are involved in nonpolitical activities than in political ones. Indeed, this melding of politics into civil society is what Daniel Boorstin once called "the genius of American politics." By this, Boorstin meant that Americans rarely tried to create big changes through ideological movements. The sense that civil society could solve problems communally rather than politically meant that politics could be kept civil. Political sociology has confirmed this in many ways. Thus, it has found that more time and money is spent on religion-related and philanthropic activities than on exercising political influence, even in most presidential years, when political interest and activity are usually highest.

This is neither surprising, nor particularly bad news. Indeed Tocqueville, who, on his visit to America in the early 1830s was perhaps the first to notice this pattern, said that

> In all the countries where political associations are prohibited, civil associations are rare. It is hardly probable that this is the result of accident; the inference should be rather that there is a natural and perhaps a necessary connection between these two kinds of association.

Tocqueville understood that the more a government "stands in the place of associations, the more will individuals losing the notion of combining together, require its assistance: these are causes and effects that unceasingly create each other" (Tocqueville, 1945, p. 123). That Americans devote more time to nonpolitical activities than political ones indicates that individuals are well-buffered from direct contact with the state by a vibrant and healthy civil society. Besides, all this primarily nonpolitical activity ends up secondarily generating a considerable amount of political activity; this is especially evident if Americans are compared to citizens of other nations.

Political sociologists have also concluded that much, if not most, civic participation and activity in America involves the welfare of both local communities and the nation, rather than that of individual citizens. Here too, proto-political sociologists from Tocqueville through Bryce to Lippmann saw these same things in nineteenth- and early twentieth-century America, and they understood that the high value placed on individualism was directly related to the even higher value placed on equality. Thus, Tocqueville wrote that

> Men being no longer attached to one another by any tie of caste, of class, of corporation, of family, are only too much inclined to be preoccupied only with their private interests, ever too much drawn to think only of themselves and to retire into a narrow individualism, in which every public virtue is stifled.
> (Tocqueville, 1945)

The true genius of American politics has been to keep individualism balanced by a commitment to the larger community.

Clearly, the most famous description and definition of individualism is found in Tocqueville's *Democracy in America*:

> Individualism is a mature and calm feeling, which disposes each member of the community to sever himself from the mass of his fellows and to draw apart with his family and friends, so that after he has thus formed a little circle of his own, he willingly leaves society at large to itself.
> (Tocqueville, 1945, p. 104)

It is still commonplace to read commentaries suggesting that individualism is the driving force in American life today, but Tocqueville's work also shows that Americans combat the effects of individualism through their participation in voluntary associations. This insight has been a mainstay of political sociology ever since it was rediscovered by the post-WWII generation, especially in the work of Lipset, Bendix, and Shils.

A premise that we often see and hear in American politics today, especially during the 2008 election, is that democracy is meaningful only if democratic participation is equal. This sort of naïve commentary shows the flaw in much of contemporary political sociology, which lacks a theory of politics and its relationship to freedom and equality. Ideological thinking aside, the public's participation in politics implies inequalities of power. As Hannah Arendt and others have demonstrated in the case of totalitarian power, if everyone is equally powerful, and thus, *eo ipso*, equally powerless, there can be no politics, democratic or otherwise—nor any freedom.

In the sociological tradition built upon the work of Tocqueville, Weber, Durkheim and others of similar mind, democracy is a complex and flawed form of power which bears the weight of two conflicting and contradictory tendencies. On the one hand, democracy encourages the growth of politics, which in turn leads to both inequality and freedom; and on the other hand, it idealizes equality, which leads to individualism, and then to the centralization of power. These contradictory tendencies are constantly clashing. The compromises that keep democracy from pulling itself apart are found in what we call civil society, and it is here that civic voluntarism and political participation come into play, balancing the democratizing values of equality against the political tendencies toward stratification and inequality. In other words, the sociology of politics understands that democracy as a system of power is perpetually at odds with itself, with politics pulling in one direction, and equality in the other.

Any political premise about meaningful democratic participation being possible only when there is equal participation is contradicted by a considerable body of proto-sociological theory from Aristotle to Tocqueville to Arendt, which sees equality in hard-nosed and pragmatic terms, rather than in more utopian ways.

It should not be surprising to any political sociologist that there are differences in the rates of political and civic participation based on demographic categories. On this point, however, political sociology must bang heads with ideology, because these *differences* in participation are often interpreted as representational and participatory biases. Differences, a descriptive term, however, are not necessarily biases, a normative one. While differences may be easily discovered, biases—which imply prejudice and predisposition for or against individuals or groups—are much harder to prove.

The relationships of democracy, politics, and equality have a proto-sociological history that has related them to each other, in both theory and practice, for a long time. But taking our political ideas and beliefs for granted as we do in America, we may have become tender-minded about them, in a way that earlier thinkers were not.

Tocqueville, and others from Cooley to Lippmann to Arendt, understood individualism and equality to be intimately related to each other, with equality being the preceding and driving force behind individualism. In fact, Tocqueville saw in equality the root and stem of individualism, as well as of democratic despotism, and he feared that democracy would lead to a centralization of power. In Tocqueville's proto-political sociology, private intermediate associations provide a bulwark against concentrating too much power in the hands of the state. In line with this way of thinking about non-governmental power, Tocqueville applauded the inevitable fact of social stratification—inequality in terms of wealth and private property—as a countervailing force to the concentration of power in the public sphere of the state. This was because he feared egalitarianism. For him, equality of conditions, social mobility, and individualism almost inevitably lead to political alienation and tyranny. Tocqueville saw that political stability and freedom emanated from social hierarchies, and from tight-knit community structures, such as families and voluntary associations.

Post-WWII political sociology in America has been very good at describing who, how, and why certain types of people participate in American democratic politics and political associations. And, although democracy is a sponge word, with all too many meanings, one thing about it is clear: Democracy is a form of power that flows from the bottom up, rather than from the top down. From the golden age of democratic theory in the eighteenth century onward, a school of thought represented by theorists as diverse as Montesquieu, Kant, and the authors of the *Federalist Papers* has seen democracy in political terms, as a form of power in which the citizens themselves decide issues by electing representatives who make political decisions through which the common good is realized.

Democracy is also often described as a system of freedom, rather than as a form of power, but it is politics, the handmaiden of democracy, not democracy itself, which is the basis of freedom. As a form of power, democracy provides the most fertile environment for politics, which can be the least coercive, most meliorating method for solving the problems of distributing power in a society composed of divergent groups with diverse interests. This was Tocqueville's most important proto-sociological point for the eventual development of political sociology.

No one political sociologist has understood the relationship of politics to freedom better than Max Weber, who, in "Politics as a Vocation," defined politics as "striving to share power or striving to influence the distribution of power... among groups within a state" (Weber, 1946). A few things about Weber's definition are worth thinking about in terms of the value of political sociology today. First, Weber's notion of politics as "striving" places emphasis on it as a continuous process of struggle without any guarantees of winning or losing, but only that power *can* be shared or re-distributed through political struggle.

Second, Weber's definition of politics situates political struggle in and among groups, not individuals. Politics as striving and struggle implies freedom, while politics as a group activity implies that a secure and stable political democracy must not only allow for the existence of secondary groups and associations intermediate between the state and the individual. Political democracy as a cultural method of freedom—but not the state, as such—fosters and encourages the formation of such groups, no matter how unequal they may be.

Social disintegration leading to mass atomization, described and analyzed so brilliantly by early sociologists such as Durkheim—who saw that a society made up of unorganized individuals, no matter how equal they might be, "constitutes a veritable sociological monstrosity"—has implications for politics and, hence, freedom (Durkheim, 1965, p. liv). If group life deteriorates, exposing the individual to the unmitigated power of the state, there can be no politics in Weber's sense of the term, and following from this, no politics, no freedom.

But as Tocqueville observed, and as history has shown, political democracy in America is unlikely to degenerate into a full-fledged mass democracy because the associative principle is too deeply entrenched in the cultural and social structure to be easily obliterated. Here Tocqueville presents us with nothing less than an iron law of democratic political freedom:

> Among the laws that rule human societies there is one which seems to be more precise and clear than all others. If men are to remain civilized or to become so, the art of associating together must grow and improve in the same ratio in which the equality of conditions is increased.
>
> (Tocqueville, 1945, p. 598)

Thus, Tocqueville saw equality—not inequality—as a problem for American democracy.

Democracy is strangely and wonderfully paradoxical, pulling in two opposite directions at once. Democracy idealizes politics, as well as equality, but politics implies inequalities of power, albeit shifting inequalities. Equality taken to the extreme tends to level the groups that support politics, thus threatening it, but politics provides the basis for freedom within a democracy. American political sociology is itself part of the story of the shifting balance between politics and equality in civil society. That story is an old one. Indeed, just as political sociology was finding its legs in the late 1930s and early 1940s, a pair of philosophers, John Dewey, in America, and Bertrand Russell, in Great Britain, were coming very close to a sociology of knowledge approach to the question of how to balance individual freedom and social organization.

In a series of articles, most notable among them being "Authority and Resistance to Social Change," published in 1936, Dewey laid bare the inherent misunderstanding at the heart of civil society in America, namely, that authority is the enemy of freedom. He demonstrated that the important problem was to see that these two things are related to each other, and that one cannot exist without the other. In three influential books, *Freedom and Organization, 1814–1914* (1936), *Power: A New Social Analysis* (1938), and *Authority and the Individual* (1949), Russell reached many of the same conclusions as did Dewey.

Many American political sociologists still hold to the idea that freedom, or civil society, and authority, or the state, are antithetical, and this has allowed the discipline to drift away from analyses that would take their essential relationship into account. The first founders of political sociology made no such mistakes. Weber saw that politics was the mediating force between freedom and organization, and so did Bryce, Durkheim, Michels and Tönnies, among others. The civil society emphasis, a good starting point for analysis in itself, seems to have become an impediment to a more robust theory of the place of politics in today's world where barbaric forces of domination and force have challenged the values of democracy and freedom, at the expense of the civilizing tendencies of politics.

7

LIBERALISM AND THE DEMOCRATIC SPIRIT

The spectrum of contemporary political and intellectual life in America is composed of three ideologies: liberalism, radicalism, and conservatism. Since the beginning of the twentieth century, liberalism characterized the real center of both politics and the life of the mind. But while the liberal center still holds, by and large, in American politics, the center of gravity in the intellectual and academic world has shifted, since the late 1960s, towards the radical pole. The reaction to this normalization of radicalism, which has been most prominent in the humanities and the social sciences, played no small part in forming the moral career of Irving Louis Horowitz, who was one of our leading social scientists.

In this context, I relate the following anecdotes about my first contact with Horowitz, and about a conversation between Horowitz and a colleague in 1992 to which I was privy. The anecdotes are indicative of how Horowitz's reputation changed among his colleagues—what I call his moral career.

In 1971, I was a second-year graduate student in the Sociology Department at the University of Pennsylvania. Penn had developed one of the best graduate programs in sociology, with a teaching staff that included Digby Baltzell, Renee Fox, Erving Goffman, Edward Hutchinson, William Kephart, Richard Lambert, Otto Pollak, Philip Rieff, Vincent Whitney, Marvin Wolfgang, Charles Wright, and Samuel Klausner among other senior faculty members.

As part of the vibrant intellectual discourse in the department, a series of colloquia had been arranged for the Fall 1971 semester, featuring lectures by both departmental professors and outside guests, including Horowitz. Most of these colloquia were well attended by both students and faculty, but one, Horowitz's, stood out from the others because it attracted more than the usual number of graduate students, and far fewer than the usual number of senior faculty.

On March 5 at three o'clock, one of the larger rooms used by the Sociology Department in the McNeil Building was filled with graduate students waiting to hear Horowitz, who had the reputation of being in the vanguard of radical sociologists. He was to present a lecture titled "The Impact of Radical Thought on Social Science Research." Arriving a few minutes late, Horowitz noticed that there were almost no senior faculty in attendance; in fact, Digby Baltzell and Otto Pollak were the only ones I saw there. He seemed genuinely offended, and he chided his absent colleagues for not being there. For a moment, it looked as if he might leave without presenting his talk. He remained, however, and delivered a more reasonable and liberal, rather than radical, lecture than I expected to hear.

In the days after his presentation I asked a number of professors why Horowitz's lecture drew so few senior faculty, and the most common answer I got was that many of the older faculty saw him as a radical sociologist who had very little of interest to say to them.

As it turned out, at least to my mind, Horowitz was not nearly as radical as he was supposed to be, and what he said was powerfully interesting. My notes and diary entries concerning Horowitz's lecture confirm my suspicion that it was, by and large, drawn from a work then in progress, "Radical Politics and Social Research: Observations on Methodology and Ideology," an article co-authored with Howard Becker, and later published in the *American Journal of Sociology*, in July 1972. Perhaps it was the title or the subject of this presentation that helped foster the idea among the senior staff that Horowitz himself was an advocate of radicalism, but whatever the reason, this idea seems to have kept many of them away.

This first memory of meeting Horowitz is in sharp contrast to a conversation I heard Horowitz participate in after giving a public lecture in November 1992. By this time, I knew Horowitz well, having served on the editorial board of *SOCIETY*, and then as the book review editor.

After Horowitz's lecture on "Policy Research in a Post-Sociological Environment," given to a large audience of social scientists at the Woodrow Wilson School at Princeton University, he was approached by a well-known sociologist. After apologizing in advance for asking what seemed to be an impertinent question, he proceeded to ask, "What happened to the young radical who you were in the 1960s?" He then continued to ask Horowitz why he had become a conservative.

I was not at all surprised by the questions, for I often heard it said by colleagues that Horowitz, having started out as a left-leaning radical, had undergone a sea change and become a right-leaning conservative. Depending upon the ideological orientation of the person making such a statement, this supposed change was met with either approval or disapproval, leading me to think that it had less to do with the subject of the remark than with the politics of identity among social scientists, with Horowitz being an important focal point, or, perhaps better, a lightning rod.

This question of personal ideological transformation was addressed by Horowitz when he wrote that,

> Many times in recent years, I have been asked how I changed over the years. The question about 'change' comes to mean more than simple alteration in my point of view. It is often asked in a testy way, suggesting changes for the worse: the cardinal sin, a failure to keep pace with progressive tides, or still more awful, a turn away from first principles with which I have long been identified.
>
> (Horowitz, 1984, p. xiii)

If such an ideological transformation had actually taken place, it would probably be relatively uninteresting, except on a personal and psychological level; after all, individuals sometimes do experience huge transformations of character and belief, and these are hardly unprecedented.

Horowitz's answer to his critics, however, was that he didn't believe he had changed ideologically, and an examination of his writings from the early 1950s through his death in November 2012 confirms his point, and clearly shows that his ideas about society and politics had, by and large, changed very little. From the beginning of his career Horowitz had been a free-thinking, liberal, intellectual and so he remained. By liberal, however, I mean to emphasize liberality; liberalism as toleration rather than liberalism as centrism. Throughout his career, Horowitz emphasized the necessity for social science to get beyond the rituals and mantras of ideology, as well as the absurdity of radical doctrine, whether it be on the left or the right. After all, social science demands analysis, not adherence to political doctrine. Put another way, it is not right or left which counts in social science, but right and wrong in terms of truth.

Liberalism, democracy, and social science are intimately connected for Horowitz, as can be seen in the following passage from "The Pluralistic Bases of Modern American Liberalism," written in 1972. "Liberalism accepts the partiality of the world in a way that no other doctrine of the twentieth century does," he wrote, and

> ... what appears to critics as weakness is perhaps the ultimate strength of liberalism, for underneath the shibboleths and rhetoric of liberalism is something important. It is the assumption that one can live a life without knowing all the answers. The strength of liberalism is that it does not offer fanaticism, that it makes the assumption that the world is not always going to be fully known, and that men can yet act within a partial frame of reference.
> (Horowitz, 1977, p. 169)

As a believer in the pragmatic values needed to live in this world of partial knowledge, Horowitz was a strong advocate of social science knowledge to help guide us through the maze of choices we face in a free and democratic society.

The remainder of this chapter will examine the "moral career" of Horowitz's reputation within sociology. The term itself was first coined by Charles Horton Cooley (Cooley, 1896, p. 402), but was made famous by Erving Goffman, who used it in "The Moral Career of the Mental Patient," where he wrote the following:

> Traditionally the term career has been reserved for those who expect to enjoy the rises laid out within a respectable profession.

The term is coming to be used, however, in a broadened sense to refer to any social strand of any person's course through life.

Following from that was Horowitz's underlying liberal approach to the sociology of democracy and democratic politics. To understand Horowitz's place in contemporary sociology, however, I intend to use Goffman's concept in a different manner, by stressing instead the career aspects of moral symbolism, i.e., the sequence of changes that career entails, not in the person's self-conception, but in society's use of the person as a symbol to structure its framework of imagery for judging its range of actions and beliefs (Goffman, 1959).

Horowitz was one of our most prolific and widely published social science writers, and as editorial director of Transaction Publishers, he was also one of our most important gatekeepers for social science ideas. In consequence, he has been a highly influential and visible figure in sociology. It has been widely believed that Horowitz traversed the political and professional continuum from the radical left to the conservative right, but in fact, he remained an old-time liberal committed to reason and truth from the start. This belief is itself sociologically relevant, and raises the question of why so many social scientists have taken to thinking about Horowitz in this way.

In large measure this perception may be attributed to the professional sociological community's process of self-definition, which, in part, depends on the creation of collective representations of how sociology is "done," personified, sometimes totemically, in terms of "leading figures," or "big names." These leading figures, and I count Horowitz among them for at least the last thirty years of his life, come to have pattern-setting moral careers in the profession, and help shape a set of professional identities for its members.

In general terms, moral careers reflect the history of a culture's moral agreements and conflicts. Some "moral careers" serve as unifying symbols that pull the various elements of a society together behind a single moral identity, while others split society into antagonistic moral camps, each with its own particular moral identity, and each defining the other as a collective enemy held together by perverted or at least wrong-headed values. The latter category is certainly germane to sociology in recent years. Horowitz's symbolic life in the professional culture of sociology began in the 1960s, when he played a leading role in revamping the profession under the banner "the new sociology." He became a focal point in the soul-searching debate in the profession as to which is better: the "old" or the "new" sociology, the sociology of consensus or the sociology of conflict.

The radical image attributed to Horowitz may be traced back to 1964, when, in his introductory remarks to *The New Sociology: Essays in Social Science and Social Theory in Honor of C. Wright Mills*, Horowitz undertook a critical analysis of the state of his discipline which, given the context, might well have been taken as a radical gesture. "There can be little doubt," he wrote,

> that the prevailing tendency in American sociology during the past two decades between 1940 and 1960 has put this discipline into a *cul de sac*. This tendency has been to package sociology, its tendencies, its tangents, and its theorists, in an institutional setting that is more concerned with the presentation of a social image than with the forging of a sociological imagination.
> (Horowitz, 1964, p. 3)

Horowitz's main target in these remarks was sociological empiricism; his main goal was to infuse social science with a sense of social responsibility tied to social research. In 1964, such a critique of the status quo, combined with an advocacy of change, could easily be taken for radicalism, but was it really radical in any larger sense? I think not. A re-reading of *The New Sociology* shows its contributors to be far less radical, and far more liberal, than they were viewed at the time. Ultimately, Horowitz was advocating the uses of sociology in the context of a democratic society that needed the proper discovery and analysis of the facts of social life in order to provide the basis for responsible decision-making; or, as he put it, "the task of science is to lessen the pain of encountering the future by anticipating its problems" (Horowitz, 1964, p. 37). Nevertheless, *The New Sociology* helped win for Horowitz a radical reputation, which in 1964 meant something quite different than it would four or five years later when the intellectual left went berserk.

But there is a larger irony to the professional perception of Horowitz as a radical at this time. Even as *The New Sociology* was coming out in a paperback edition, in 1965, Horowitz was publishing "The Stalinization of Fidel Castro," a hard-hitting critique of the totalitarian tendencies to which the Communist revolutionaries in Cuba had succumbed. This was the first major Anglo assault on Castro's revolution and its aftermath, and a consequence was that Horowitz was called "the man who betrayed the legacy of C. Wright Mills" by some of his colleagues. He became almost persona non-grata in the Latin American Studies Association of which he had been a leading member (*New Politics*, 1965).

Horowitz had a complex view of the world. In terms of sociology, he leaned slightly to the left, and in terms of the larger issues of world politics, he leaned slightly to the right; but ultimately, he never moved very far from the classical liberal ethos. This apparent inconsistency never seemed to bother Horowitz, probably because consistency is the particular vanity of ideologues, among whom he has never been numbered. Indeed, from the beginning Horowitz idealized science and reason, and had an aversion to ideological correctness and ideological hatred of the enemy, which characterized radicals of both left and right. Looking back on the earliest phase of his career, Horowitz noted that for him "science was the harbinger of the open society, the source of democratic culture, the essence of a democratic style in which shared discourse rather than distilled hatred became the basis of policy" (Horowitz, 1984, p. 16).

If the radical label didn't really fit in 1964, when he published *The New Sociology*, it is even harder to imagine why it still stuck after the late 1960s, when Horowitz's criticism of the New Left became even sharper than had been his criticism of the old sociology. After all, whatever its shortcomings, the old sociology was itself couched in a genuinely liberal context. It never did drift towards conservatism, but just the opposite. Ultimately it was the radical temptation that threatened to undermine the positivistic and rational basis for sociology. The old left, among whom were many sociologists, believed in organization, i.e., "The Party," but the new left believed in spontaneity, i.e., "The Movement." In response to all this, Horowitz wrote the following:

> The purpose of revolution is to create a society which is better than existing society. On the other hand, given the fact that few warranties can be made that this will in effect come about,

the more proximate goal of revolution making is the therapeutic values instilled in the participants, the revolutionists themselves. Therefore, the true change, or the essential condition for dramatic change, comes not with the triumph of one class over another, or the victory of one nation over another, but rather the victory that each individual gains in the act of revolutionary performance.
(Horowitz, 1968, p. 9)

If Horowitz appeared to be changing, one wonders why. After all, his criticism of the radical left in the late 1960s emerged from the same democratic and liberal standpoint as had been his earlier criticism of sociology. The belief that Horowitz was changing, though he actually remained rock-steady and true to his basic liberal beliefs, may be attributed to the fact that the academic environment in general, and the social science environment in particular, were changing around him. Thus, in Horowitz, and in perceptions and judgments about the changing character of his work, we have a very interesting measure of social and cultural change, rather than a case of personal and psychological transformation.

It would be unwieldy in a single chapter to examine the transformation of our academic and social science cultures as reflected in Horowitz's work; his work includes more than 600 published items including books, articles, and book reviews covering a remarkably wide range of subjects. I have chosen to concentrate upon Horowitz's writings about the relationship of sociology to politics, and more specifically upon his unwavering liberal faith in reason and the search for truth (especially as these apply to the enterprise of social science theory and research) as factors that might strengthen democracy and foster freedom. That this view was once considered radical, or at least liberal, and is now labeled conservative speaks volumes, not only about Horowitz, but, even more importantly, about academic social science—where it once stood, where it stands today, and where it might be headed in the future.

When Horowitz began his career in the early 1950s, America was in the midst of what, in political terms, many have described as a somewhat "conservative age;" although we might do well to remember with Louis Hartz that the liberal tradition was really the only political tradition in America. Interestingly, at about the same time that Hartz was publishing his great book, *The Liberal Tradition in America*, Horowitz was saying much the same thing in a brilliant critique of the new conservatism: "The liberal belief is so profoundly rooted that the interesting question is how the triumph of liberalism took place so thoroughly" (Horowitz, 1977, p. 139). During this time, the field of sociology was, as I have suggested above, profoundly liberal, even if it was dominated by the functionalist approach that seemed to many young Turks to promote the social status quo.

By the early 1960s, however, as Horowitz's career progressed, we were becoming an increasingly liberal society; and, within an already liberal sociology, functionalism was being further challenged by other approaches less likely to advocate stasis. In both American society and sociology, the liberalizing trend became the norm by the late 1960s and early 1970s, and then actually tipped over into advocacy of radicalism among a large and well-educated portion of American society as well as among many, if not most, sociologists.

During this period, the movement towards radicalism among social science intellectuals far outpaced that of most other segments of American society, academia in particular. Many old-time liberals saw this radical movement as disastrous for both the university and the larger society for which the university provided future leaders. Sticking to liberal principles, these intellectuals were quickly and pejoratively labeled as "neoconservatives" by the more left-leaning radical elements of the intelligentsia for whom liberalism was too cautious, too compromising, too democratic, and too conservative.

By the late 1960s, Horowitz was already established as one of our most prominent social scientists. Although he leaned slightly left in his sympathies, and was associated with radicalism because of his conflict perspective, his criticism of the war in Vietnam, his support for some elements of the student movement, and his exposure of Project Camelot, Horowitz could easily be counted among those strong-willed liberals who refused to betray their democratic and rational principles to the anarchic and antinomian forms of radicalism vying for supremacy in the academy and in American political circles.

In this context, it is notable that the positive values expressed throughout Horowitz's work and career—democracy, freedom, rationality, autonomy, and decentralization of power and authority—are liberal values. Horowitz's work also reflects his aversion to absolutism, authoritarianism, Communism, Fascism, Utopianism, terrorism, violence, secrecy, populism, war, civil disobedience, anarchism, and alienation. He also portrays conflict as a more important and integral element of democracy than consensus; significantly, Horowitz's work clearly had a greater affinity to Simmel's liberal theory of conflict than to the more radical Marxian conflict theory. Indeed, of all the values that underlie his work, Horowitz's deep and abiding belief in the tenets and practices of liberal democracy, especially its constitutive elements of political conflict and freedom, are most characteristic of his thought, and best sum up the man and his ideas.

What then do we understand by the term "liberal democracy?" Although liberalism is essentially a nineteenth- and twentieth-century philosophy, it can justifiably be said to have its origins in the writings of John Locke in the seventeenth century. The hallmark of liberalism has always been its insistence that in and through politics, and the conflict of values undergirding politics, citizens should strive to "make their society rational, just, and capable of affording opportunities for everyone to develop his own potentialities" (Minogue, 1963, p. 2). As such, liberalism was well suited to become the prevailing theory of democratic politics, for democracy, associated as it is with the ideas that governments should function with majority consent but protect the rights of minorities, that they should insure the right of political parties to exist and to oppose each other, that they should not hamper the workings of a free press, nor the freedoms of speech, assembly, and movement, is really the only form of government suited to liberal doctrine.

All of these liberal democratic values inform Horowitz's work, but most of all Horowitz's political sociology is predicated on a belief in the liberal insistence on rationality as the basis for purposive political action, and as the basis of decision-making in which the anticipatable consequences of political action are taken into account. In retrospect, it is hard to imagine why Horowitz was ever thought to be a radical, or why radicals would want to call him one of their own.

But such is the course of moral careers that advocates and opportunists who think that they can use a particular person as a symbolic collective representation of their group will appropriate whomever they see fit to play this role. Thus, many saw Horowitz in this light despite the fact that he criticized the new radicalism from the standpoint of an old-time liberalism:

> This is the first generation in American society, at least in this century, to combine radicalism with irrationalism. As in the age of Sorel, reason has been displaced by passion...
> The current style of radicalism is abrasive, physical, impatient, and eclectic. It reflects a concern with the exercise of will over those objective forces which may exist in the world...
> The assertion of the priority of individual will assumes a strongly moralistic tone. The wills of individuals become objects to be mobilized into one total will. This moralistic style is a ready handmaiden to the "totalitarian democracy" that the historian Jacob Talmon spoke of. It is a fantastic attempt to impose a new social order upon the world, rather than to await the verdict of consensus building formulae among disparate individuals as well as the historical Muses.
> (Horowitz, 1968, p. 6)

These are hardly the words of "a radical authority on revolutionary thought," they are the words of a liberal authority on radical thought. Oddly, Horowitz was being referred to as a "radical authority on revolutionary thought" at about the same time as he was putting forth the following hard-hitting analysis of radicalism (Lipset, 1971, p. 116). Horowitz, an admirer of Max Weber, the most important liberal democrat among the founders of modern sociology, certainly would have found Weber's distinction between those politicians who follow an "ethic of ultimate ends" as opposed to an "ethic of responsibility," in accordance with his own view of 1960s radicalism (Weber, 1946, pp. 120–126).

Extremists—utopians, revolutionaries, and radicals—of the left and right—tend to follow some variant or other of the ethic of ultimate ends. They believe so strongly in the value of their cause that they will do whatever they can to further it, no matter what the consequences. "If", as Weber said of those following this ethos, "an action of good intent leads to bad results, then, in the actor's eyes, not he but the world, or the stupidity of other men, or God's will who made them thus, is responsible for the evil" (Weber, 1946, p. 121). Such an ethic has little to do with the liberal democratic imagination, nor of Horowitz's understanding of it.

In fact, it is the association of liberalism with what Weber called the ethic of responsibility that soured it in the eyes of Sixties' radicals. As Horowitz noted,

> … the modern Left movement…is not so much an attack on the world of ideas as it is an attack on the idea that reason is the only model of knowing. The suspicion is that reason is an ideology that teaches us to stand between two extremes, unable to act. This identification of liberalism with the spirit of judiciousness and prudence is precisely why liberalism, at the psychological level, continues to be the main target for radical jibes.
> (Horowitz, 1984, p. 14)

Liberalism is perfectly at home with an ethic of responsibility because those who follow such an ethic must take into account the predictable results of their actions, and ultimately compromise their consciences to decide on action that produces the least evil. Liberalism tends to balance reason and passion, while extremists on the left and right tend to allow passion to outweigh reason at every turn. "Fiat iustitia, et pereat mundus," let there be justice though the world may perish, was, said Kant, the catchphrase of the extremist imagination (Kant, 1949, p. 467). Hannah Arendt, whose name very appropriately graced the university chair Horowitz occupied at Rutgers University, saw the same sentiment as the banner for extremists of a different stripe, but with regard to truth rather than justice: "Fiat veritas, et pereat mundus" (Arendt, 1968, p. 228).

Although Horowitz was obviously a staunch advocate of rationality, it is often unclear whether reason in itself is of more importance to him than simply minimizing irrationality, which he sees as a constant threat not only to democracy but to all forms of social order.

Even before *The New Sociology*, Horowitz proved himself to be more of a critic of radicalism than a friend. In *Radicalism and the Revolt Against Reason: The Social Theories of Georges Sorel*, Horowitz's fifth book, published in 1961, he analyzes the European roots of irrationalist radicalism and concludes that

> ... our century bears firm witness to the fact that a radicalism founded upon irrationalism cuts two ways: it might serve as a decisive antiseptic to the infections caused by our inherited rational middle class civilization, but no less a poison which cures the infection by destroying the patient—civilization itself. ...
> (Horowitz, 1984, p. 195)

In other words, in 1961, Horowitz, as a liberal, was of two minds about middle-class civilization. On the one hand, he was left-minded enough to critique it, on the other hand, he was right-minded enough to warn against its destruction by irrationalist radicalism.

An objective reading of *Radicalism and the Revolt Against Reason*, however, should make it plain that Horowitz himself was clearly no radical. In fact, this book is an enormously important historical critique of radicalism, or at least the type of radicalism advocated by Sorel—one which glorifies violence, personalism, mysticism, and antinomianism. Nevertheless, it is interesting to note that during this time Horowitz was developing a reputation as a radical sociologist. Perhaps in a relatively conservative age, even within a liberal culture, such as our own, any criticism of the faults of middle-class civilization is considered radical, even when accompanied by a defense of its virtues.

In an insightful and analytical passage about Sorelian irrationalism, Horowitz presented both a critique and defense of democracy. "The appeal of Sorel's position," he wrote,

> is evident to all who have been disconcerted by the division between liberal democratic pledges and practices. He made it clear that power is at the basis of political change. The force of democracy can be essentially conservative particularly when it obstructs the desire for change behind a veil of electoral procedures...
> (Horowitz, 1968, p. 76)

But Horowitz went on to defend democracy in the face of the Sorelian radical critique:

> ... surely the growth of civilization and the worth of democracy itself rests not so much on how it obfuscates conflict, but on how it points to a resolution of conflict within commonly accepted rules. Too often, critics of democracy call any non-violent resolution of differences obfuscation; this because they start with a definition of society as lawless. But democracy, in providing the rules of procedure offers a method of channeling and directing behavior, despite the contentions of critics. Democracy can clarify the relative strength of contending forces in a conscious way. *Democracy therefore is perhaps the most reasonable expression through which the issues dividing men can be resolved.* [italics added]
> (Horowitz, 1968, pp. 76–77)

Democracy and reason are therefore intimately linked for Horowitz, as they are for all liberals. But Horowitz is also a consummate realist as well as a liberal. From the beginning of his career as a social scientist he realized that democracy and reason are merely utopian concepts unless one understands them in terms of power and politics to which they are always linked in reality. Having lauded democracy as the most reasonable form of government, Horowitz contends with power:

> The fact that power remains basic political capital in all existing societies is no serious critique against the employment of democratic procedures. Quite the contrary. The abuse of democracy is perhaps the soundest argument for broadening the scope of human involvement in political processes...What is needed at this juncture in history is not the overthrow of democratic procedures, nor the substitution of Sorel's method of direct violence, but a stipulation of the contents of democracy in functional rather than normative terms: that is, into terms which have utility and relevance for the masses of men in a scientific and technological civilization.
> (Horowitz, 1968, p. 77)

It is evident that Horowitz is saying that 1) while Sorel's utopian, or better still, anti-utopian, critique of democracy falls short of its mark, namely the subversion of democratic procedure, some sort of reevaluation of democracy is needed, perhaps constantly, and 2) that reason dictates that the social sciences are best poised to deliver such a thoroughgoing critique.

I have quoted at length from *Radicalism and the Revolt Against Reason* because it demonstrates my thesis about Horowitz, namely that, in his more youthful writings, he was never the radical he was said to have been, but merely a democrat and a liberal in a relatively conservative age within a historically liberal culture and a historically liberal social science environment. And, despite the popular perception among some intellectuals that he became a conservative, Horowitz's later writings show that he merely remained a democrat and a liberal in what is now a relatively radical age, and an infinitely more radical social science environment.

So why did Horowitz's reputation change? Although there are great complexities involved in answering such a question, the most telling reason is his publication of *C. Wright Mills: An American Utopian*, in 1983. Mills was, and to some extent still is, one of the great iconic figures of the New Left. That Horowitz was his literary executor after Mills' death in 1962 only enhanced, perhaps through the laws of charismatic succession, Horowitz's radical reputation.

But *C. Wright Mills: An American Utopian* was not an uncritical biography; in fact, it was a penetrating liberal critique of Mills and his work. This was obviously too much for some of the most pronounced guardians of the radical spirit. A powerfully placed review of the Mills biography, by Lewis Coser in *The American Journal of Sociology*, stated,

> ...had Irving Louis Horowitz written *C. Wright Mills: An American Utopian* in the years immediately following Mills's death in 1962 when he considered himself Mills's disciple and wished to emulate him, it would probably have been an uncritical hagiography. As it is, Horowitz has moved in the interim from a radical to a fairly conservative position and, as result, has gained critical distance from his subject...
>
> (Coser, 1984, pp. 657–658)

Likewise, Dan Wakefield, reviewing *C. Wright Mills: An American Utopian* in *The Nation*, said,

> Horowitz's opinion of Mills has shifted drastically. After Mills's death in 1962, Horowitz considered him 'the greatest sociologist the United States ever produced,' and in 1964, he described him as 'the man whose spirit and zest for life inform the current political struggle for a better world.' But the present volume calls him 'a prophet and fanatic' whose 'quite personal style led to a near-unanimous negative consensus about him.'
> (Wakefield, 1984, pp. 212–213)

Although the Mills book received many glowing mainstream reviews, the pied pipers of the New Left played a different tune when reviewing it, and, parenthetically, its author. Adding to Coser's view of Horowitz as a conservative, Mark Naison's review of the Mills biography for *Commonweal* suggested that Horowitz had integrated Mills's theoretical legacy "into a skeptical liberalism (or embittered neoconservatism)" (Naison, 1984, pp. 252–253).

The New Left reception of Horowitz's biography of Mills necessitates that we confront the fact that the terms "radical," "liberal," and "conservative," which once covered almost the entire political and social spectrum, have now been reduced to two: "liberal" and "conservative." Horowitz realized the formerly tripartite nature of the political spectrum when he wrote that liberalism "offers a middle range between whatever is at one extreme end and whatever is said to be necessary at the other" (Horowitz, 1977, p. 169). That Horowitz himself saw and understood that the compression of the political spectrum was underway decades ago can be seen in his 1965 essay, "Radicalism and Contemporary American Society," where he remarked that "Classical Liberalism has no future," by which he meant that it was being forced out of the political and social picture by both the radical and conservative movements (Horowitz, 1970, p. 563). Horowitz came back to the same point, this time from a different angle, in 1992 in "Morris Raphael Cohen and the End of the Classic Liberal Tradition," where, with the hindsight of more than two decades, he recognized that what he had predicted had come to pass, namely that liberalism had had no future. Before the 1960s, liberalism had been, in Horowitz's words "positioned *between* fascism and communism, or if one prefers, between the political right and left." But by now "liberalism has become part of the polarity" (Horowitz, 1992, p. 15).

Another way to look at this process of terminological and philosophical compression is to realize that, in terms of politics, up to the 1960s most Americans could have been called, and probably would have called themselves, liberals. Relatively few would have fallen into the two polar categories, radical and conservative. Thus, Horowitz could write, in 1956, that "Everybody is a liberal. Everybody believes in the free exchange of ideas. Everybody believes in restricted planning, but not national planning. Everybody believes that democracy is a good thing, but not at the expense of social order" (Horowitz, 1977, p. 139). Not surprisingly, the inherently liberal nature of American society was understood perfectly by Franklin Delano Roosevelt in the 1932 presidential campaign:

> Say that civilization is a tree which, as it grows, continually produces rot and dead wood. The radical says: 'Cut it down.' The conservative says: 'Don't touch it.' The liberal compromises: 'Lets prune, so that we lose neither the old trunk nor the new branches.' This campaign is waged to teach the country to march upon its appointed course, the way of change, in an orderly march, avoiding alike the revolution of radicalism and the revolution of conservatism.
> (Schlesinger, 1960, pp. 648–649)

In many ways Roosevelt, the epitome of American liberalism, struck a chord among a majority of Americans, who responded by electing him to four terms in office.

But, as Horowitz reminded us, since FDR's day we have drifted from this tripartite rhetorical structure. Today Americans talk about themselves in terms of being either liberals or conservatives, with the term "liberal" having taken on the meaning which the term "radical" used to have—at least when it is used by conservatives to characterize those they call liberal. The effect of this change has been to confuse people, most of whom still fall into what would have been the old liberal category, which no longer exists, and who no longer know how to characterize themselves politically and socially since they consider themselves neither new liberals, i.e. old radicals, nor conservatives.

The rhetorical compression has lumped together those who had been radically left of center with the vast majority who had previously been properly characterized as liberals, and who were at the center. The conservative category now encompasses not only traditional conservatives, but also many who had previously been cast as liberals, but who shunned the new more radical connotation of the term. These were dubbed "neoconservatives" by the left.

It is significant that Horowitz is not among those usually listed as neoconservatives, and that *The Neo-Conservatives* by Peter Steinfels, a prominent book about neoconservatives, places *Society* outside this camp. The overall result of this rhetorical compression was not merely to eliminate the old liberal category, which most Americans fit into, but to normalize the radical and conservative extremes, thus leaving the majority of Americans with no political and social category with which to identify. To counter this recent rhetorical revolution I suggest we return, with some modification, to the Rooseveltian trichotomy: radical, liberal, conservative. The major modification here would be to add a fourth term, neoconservative. This would allow us to recognize that the right has its left, and the left its right. Put another way, conservatism, viewed as a continuum, can be seen as having a right wing—traditional conservatives—and a left wing—neoconservatives; the same applies, *eo ipso*, for liberalism, which also can be thought of as having a continuum, with a left wing—radicals—and a right wing—liberals. The advantage of viewing the spectrum of political and social sentiments in this way is that we can see that neoconservatives and liberals are really part of a third way of looking at the world, a middle category, with liberals on the left and neoconservatives on the right.

This brings us back to the nature of politics, and ultimately, at least for sociologists, back to Max Weber. In "Max Weber and the Spirit of American Sociology," Horowitz got to the bottom of the Weber puzzle, by showing how differently Weber had been interpreted by the three prevailing icons of sociology in the 1950s and early 1960s, namely, Talcott Parsons, Robert K. Merton, and C. Wright Mills. "Weber became in

American sociological history," wrote Horowitz, "the form of legitimation for the conservatism of a Parsons, but no less for the liberalism of a Merton and the radicalism of a Mills" (Horowitz, 1968, p. 194). One might add, with hindsight, as well, that Weber became a form of legitimation for the liberalism of Horowitz.

What Horowitz, following Weber, has stood for as a political sociologist is the primacy of politics and political conflict, for the creation and maintenance of freedom in a democracy. While politics is synonymous with conflict, both of these are equally synonymous with freedom. No politics, no freedom; no freedom, no conflict; no conflict, no politics.

The work of Horowitz, as well as that of Weber, is at once democratic, anti-utopian, and anti-totalitarian; it is predicated upon the idea that through political conflict a rational and informed citizenry can create a good society, or at least a tolerable one. The place of social science in a democracy is then clear: to help inform politicians and other policymakers, as well as the citizenry, about the problems their society faces, and the possible consequences of making policies to solve those problems. If it does this well, sociology affirms the main Weberian lesson, which is, according to Horowitz, "that sociology is a human science and not merely a social science" (Horowitz, 1968, p. 194).

In a way, this Weberian lesson is also Horowitz's lesson as well, and it sums up his place in the moral economy of American democracy. In every democracy decisions must be made, and they are regularly and necessarily more difficult to make than in totalitarian societies, or indeed, than in any non-democratic society. The majority decisions in a democracy cast a long moral shadow because they are made against the will of a minority which opposes them, but which must live under them as well as must the majority which supported them. Hence, democracies operate under the conditions of a free market moral economy more so than any other form of government.

By advocating sociology with a human face, and through his place in social science publishing, Horowitz helped make social science research an integral part of the policymaking process in America. He has proved himself to be an exemplary citizen, and a liberal democratic voice among his social science contemporaries, and this, rather than speculation about his ideological stability, should be the essence of his reputation and moral career.

8
TALENT, WEALTH, AND POWER

Like the French nobility of the eighteenth century described by Alexis de Tocqueville, the American upper class, during the latter half of the twentieth, and into the twenty-first centuries has become less a ruling aristocracy, and more and more a caste. This decline in upper-class authority has been the focus of the sociological and historical works of E. Digby Baltzell, as it had been for Tocqueville. A member of this class himself, Baltzell's criticism of decreasing contribution to national leadership by the WASP (White, Anglo-Saxon, Protestant) upper class has earned him the epithet "WASP with a sting," from the *Wall Street Journal*. In *The Protestant Establishment*, he set forth a much cited, but often misunderstood theory of the structure and function of the upper class as not only necessary, but also as a desirable part of the process of securing responsible leaders in a democratic society, or what he calls an establishment.

Who was E. Digby Baltzell? What is his theory of the establishment? And why is it important? Baltzell came from an upper-class family which would today best be characterized as "WASP," a term which he himself made fashionable. Descended from an old stock English family, Baltzell's father, Edward Digby Baltzell, Sr, was born on a family estate called "Digby" in northeast Philadelphia. His mother, Caroline Duhring, came from a family of German professionals (see Friedrich Engels' *Anti-Dühring*) who had come to Philadelphia in the 1840s. Her grandfather was a physician, and her father an Episcopal clergyman who headed the City Mission to the poor. Baltzell Jr, himself was born at 1915 Rittenhouse Street, right off Rittenhouse Square, one of Philadelphia's most fashionable addresses, but grew up in Chestnut Hill, one of the city's old-family neighborhoods, just a cut above the famed Main Line.

Privilege, however, is no insulator against hardship, or marginality. Baltzell, the eldest of three sons, was born "dead"—his infant's heart started beating only after the doctor grabbed him by the feet and whirled him around in the air to revive him. Thus, his life was from the start not always easy. Although his family was an old one, they had come somewhat down in the world in his parents' generation—"impecuniously genteel," as Baltzell has described it. He was raised by a determined and domineering mother who, among other oddities, was fascinated with all sorts of Ouija boards and fortune-tellers. His father was an alcoholic. But they managed to send Baltzell to Chestnut Hill Academy, a private day school, and then to St. Paul's Academy, an exclusive boarding school in New Hampshire. During Baltzell's last year at St. Paul's his father lost his job in an insurance company due his drinking, and eventually died of a heart attack. After graduating from St. Paul's, Baltzell enrolled in the University of Pennsylvania, where he obtained a half-tuition scholarship and paid the rest himself with the proceeds of a summer job running a tennis club in Maine, and by working at odd jobs supported by the New Deal's National Youth Administration.

The connection between Baltzell's childhood experiences and his eventual turn toward the academic life is worth noting. Although raised within the relatively sheltered upper-class world of Chestnut Hill, which he called "the golden ghetto," the combination of difficult parents and lack of money made Baltzell something of an outsider among his rich friends. His mother's belief in Ouija boards and fortune-tellers became well known locally, and rumors spread among neighborhood children that she was a witch and that the Baltzell house was haunted. But it was his father's alcoholism that more than anything made Baltzell's early life difficult. He once said, "I was always on the outside looking in" (Baltzell & Schneiderman, 1991, p. xi).

Although he belonged to a heavy-drinking fraternity, he never drank while he was in college. In fact, his scholarship stipulated that the recipient not indulge in alcoholic beverages. Baltzell often compared his own life to that of the novelist J. P. Marquand, whose family was much like his own, poor but proud. As a marginal upper-class insider, Baltzell, like Marquand, saw through a great many things his class took for granted.

Even his attending the University of Pennsylvania was indicative of Baltzell's marginal status. While all but two or three of his graduating class at St. Paul's went on to Harvard, Yale, or Princeton, financial circumstances following his father's loss of his job dictated that he stay closer to home and attend the local university. He started out in the School of Architecture, but was forced to drop out after his first year for financial reasons. He was rescued from a sales job at Wanamaker's department store by a friend who lent him the money for one term's tuition ($200), allowing him to return to Penn. He abandoned his dream of becoming an architect and instead majored in insurance at the Wharton School. As he said later, "I was worried to death about getting a good job" (Baltzell & Schneiderman, 1991, p. xii). Odd as it might seem for someone born to privilege, Baltzell worked as a parking lot attendant, a chauffeur, and a ticket-taker and usher at football games at Franklin Field to pay his expenses while at Penn.

Graduating with a bachelor's degree in economics in 1939, he became an underwriter with an insurance company. Within a year, however, he left for a job at twice the salary and with Saturdays off, at Smith, Kline, and French Laboratories, then a pharmaceutical company in Philadelphia. In this new position Baltzell was to learn the techniques of social research first hand, as he helped conduct attitude surveys in many cities.

Baltzell's career in business ended with the Japanese bombing of Pearl Harbor. Like many patriotic Americans, Baltzell volunteered for the Armed Forces, joining the Navy in 1942. While earning his wings as a Navy pilot he made friends with young men from backgrounds far different from his own; among them were "Meathead" from Brooklyn, a group of "Flying Hawkeyes" from the University of Iowa, and a truck driver from Minneapolis. While serving in the South Pacific, as pilot and Air Combat Intelligence Officer, his circle of acquaintances expanded yet further.

For Baltzell, as for countless others, war was a great equalizer, breaking down peacetime class barriers. His experiences in the Navy stimulated his curiosity about the nature of society. For the first time in his life he was outside of his own privileged circle of family, friends, and business associates; and he began to question his inherited class biases. This, of course, might never have occurred without the war.

As he became increasingly self-reflective, Baltzell also became a voracious reader. While stationed in Hawaii, he wandered one day into the public library in Honolulu, and browsed through several issues of *The American Journal of Sociology*. This odd and fortuitous event, along with the discovery in the same library of a book on race relations by the then-famous sociologist E. B. Reuther, moved Baltzell to leave the business world, and taking advantage of the G.I. Bill, to begin graduate studies in sociology.

In *The Protestant Establishment Revisited*, he wrote: "The Bomb was dropped on Hiroshima in August 1945. As I had enough points to get out of the Navy almost immediately, I was able to enroll in the PhD program in Sociology at Columbia University, in September" (Baltzell & Schneiderman, 1991, p. 25). The war had changed him, and as he has said, "I decided I didn't want to work in business. I wanted to write and teach" (Baltzell & Schneiderman, 1991, p. xiii). In the flux of a world at war, a conventional business career ended, and an intellectual career was born.

Unknown to Baltzell at the time he enrolled, the sociology department at Columbia in 1945 was becoming the best in America. He was entering a department made up of Robert K. Merton, Paul Lazarsfeld, Robert Lynd, C. Wright Mills, and Robert MacIver, among others. Never having heard of Max Weber, to say nothing of Karl Marx, Baltzell recalled having to take stomach-settling medicine every Friday after listening to Gardner Murphy lecture in class. "I watched him over a cup of tea," Baltzell remembers of Murphy, "jot down three lines on a scrap of paper before class and then proceed to talk for two hours without stopping. It was all new to me, and extremely exhausting" (Baltzell & Schneiderman, 1991, p. xiii).

Exhausting, maybe, but Columbia provided a heady intellectual atmosphere. If Gardner Murphy was taxing, what must MacIver, Mills, Lynd, Lazarsfeld, and Merton have been like? At any rate, it used to be said that Lynd was the "heart" and Merton the "mind" of the department, and Baltzell later wrote in the preface to *Philadelphia Gentlemen*, that "above all, I should like to thank Robert S. Lynd, without whose constant faith and encouragement at critical periods in my early academic career, this book would never have been completed." He also thanked Merton, and wrote, in the same preface, that "all who have studied under Professor Merton will appreciate my large debt to him" (Baltzell, 1958 b, p. xx).

In his first year at Columbia, Baltzell read with great care Lynd's two famous *Middletown* studies, co-authored with Helen Lynd, and W. Lloyd Warner's equally well-known Yankee City studies. These helped him begin to formulate his ideas about the upper class and the elite. Among the best-known community studies ever done, the Lynds' *Middletown* and Warner's Yankee City studies presented two different points of view about social class in America. *Middletown* was about the distribution of power and economic position in a new and changing society in the Middle West.

Warner's Yankee City series, in contrast, was concerned with the distribution of lifestyles and social status in an old, traditional New England community. Impressed with both these emphases—of Warner's concentration on the *subjective* (status) elements of social class, and the Lynds' analysis of the *objective* economic aspects of class—Baltzell felt that a synthesis of both approaches was needed. He also recognized the influence of studies of "tribal cultures" on both the Lynds and Warner in their choice of small towns for their studies. He himself felt the need for studies of urban areas, leading eventually to *Philadelphia Gentlemen*. Baltzell also studied anthropology with Ruth Benedict. Her *Patterns of Culture* became central to his view of class leadership in Boston (Kwakiutl) and Philadelphia (Zuni), in *Puritan Boston and Quaker Philadelphia*, his most ambitious book on class leadership in the two cities.

Baltzell's ideas about social class were further clarified when he read a brilliant article-length review by C. Wright Mills of Warner's first Yankee City volume, *The Social Life of a Modern Community*. He was particularly struck by a series of question Mills posed in the book:

> Are the intermarriage chances, the flow of prestige, influenced by what happens in banks? What is the distribution of legal skill, by family, by firm? Are there overlaps between the boards of banks, the elders of churches, and the prestige of ministers? Are 'social

circles' and the religious affiliations subtly interwoven with financial interests? How do 'clubs' mark one's financial arrival? Are the chances to arrive financially enhanced by affiliation with clubs?

And Mills suggested that "it is to be regretted that such mechanics of interaction between the economic, social, and religious affiliations (not to mention 'political' spheres) as may exist were not systematically examined in the case of Yankee City." What Mills, a student of Weber, was saying is that one needs to divide the "sponge word 'class'" into "status"—or social class, and "class"—or what Marxists would call economic class. Comparing Warner's study to the Lynds', Mills said of the Lynds that they "presented a far superior picture of the composition and mechanics of a modern community" (Baltzell & Schneiderman, 1991, p. xv).

Unlike the warm memories he had of the personally helpful Lynd, Baltzell's memories of Mills are somewhat cooler. "Mills was a prophet in life-styles as well as in Sociology, as he roared up to Fayerweather Hall on a motorcycle," wrote Baltzell, who later saw Mills as "very much in the anti-institutional and egalitarian tradition of the seventeenth century sectarians" (Baltzell & Schneiderman, 1991, p. xv). Although they were contemporaries, both having been born in 1915, Mills, a tough, self-made intellectual and sociologist of the iconoclastic type, hardly won Baltzell's admiration. As Baltzell remembers, this was especially so after Mills included in his book *White Collar* parts of a long interview from a paper he had submitted to him without attributing any credit whatsoever to him.

He nevertheless agreed with Mills that the Lynds' studies were far superior to Warner's. He came to see the significance of the fact that while *Middletown* in the first study was dominated by elite businessmen at the top of the functional class hierarchy, the families of some of these individuals eventually formed an upper class at the top of the social class hierarchy by the time the Lynds came back to write *Middletown in Transition*. Lynd's course at Columbia was an important, and serendipitous, component of Baltzell's early development as a theoretician of status and power.

While Lynd and Mills stimulated Baltzell's thinking about class, status, and power, it was Robert K. Merton, a fellow native Philadelphian like himself, who impressed Baltzell more than any other professor at Columbia and sparked his enthusiasm for the field of sociology. Born in a South Philadelphia slum in 1910 to first-generation immigrant parents, Merton was an academic prodigy throughout his student years. He came to Columbia as an assistant professor in 1941. It is interesting that these two Philadelphians from opposite ends of the social structure should have had, contrary to the Marxist canon, such an affinity in ideas and values. "I learned everything from Bob Merton," Baltzell has said, "and while I have never looked back at my notes from his classes, I have never lectured about anything, nor written anything, that wasn't related to those notes" (Baltzell & Schneiderman, 1991, p. xvi).

The subject that fascinated Baltzell most—social class and leadership—was however, a deeply personal matter and had much to do with his family's marginal financial position. Moreover, as an athlete rather than an intellectual in his youth, Baltzell valued personal ability far more than background. He was a catcher on St. Paul's baseball team, and captain of the tennis team at Penn. As he has written, talk of social class was considered "effeminate" in his circle of friends. When he came to Columbia, however, he found that his peers were obsessed by status distinctions. His own ambivalence about thinking in terms of social stratification, combined with his insider's heart and outsider's mind, made Baltzell uniquely qualified to study American elites and upper classes. It was sheer good luck for him that two of the works most influential to his career were published during his first year of graduate studies.

Although Tocqueville's name was mentioned only once in his courses during his two years at Columbia, while browsing in the Columbia bookstore in December 1945 Baltzell found and bought the last boxed copy of a newly published two-volume set of *Democracy in America* and read it eagerly. During the next summer, he bought and read a copy of Hans Gerth and C. Wright Mills' just published edition of *From Max Weber: Essays in Sociology*, containing, among others, the famous essay "Class, Status, and Party," which had the most profound and lasting effect upon his thinking.

He heard Tocqueville's name first mentioned in a guest lecture by Albert Salomon, a sociologist from the New School for Social Research, who said that "the greatest book in the social sciences is Tocqueville's *The*

Ancient Regime and the French Revolution." This was before the paperback revolution, and before many people read Tocqueville. Unable to find a copy in New York, Baltzell eventually bought a secondhand copy from Blackwell's in Oxford. The works of Tocqueville and Weber, along with the writings and teaching of Merton, formed the core of his thinking for the next forty years, and the *Ancient Regime* was the direct model for Baltzell's analysis of the rise and fall of the Protestant establishment in America.

Just as Tocqueville concentrated on analyzing the fate of his aristocratic class before and after the French Revolution, so Baltzell devoted himself to analyzing the more or less similar fate of his own class in the years before and after the Second World War. He was now on his way to becoming a unique American intellectual, a social historian and sociologist, who would construct a theory of the establishment which tied social status to responsibility.

Baltzell left Columbia in 1947, having started work on his doctoral thesis, and began his teaching career at the University of Pennsylvania, as an instructor of sociology. He completed his doctoral thesis in 1952. Although many opportunities presented themselves at other institutions, Baltzell loyally taught at Penn until his retirement in 1986—fifty years after first entering as a student. In his thirty-nine years on the Penn faculty, Baltzell taught over 20,000 undergraduate students, and was a major influence on a dozen or so graduate students. For years after retiring from Penn he still taught his legendary social stratification course once a year, during the spring terms.

Baltzell wrote four contemporary classics of social analysis: *Philadelphia Gentlemen*, *The Protestant Establishment*, *Puritan Boston and Quaker Philadelphia*, and *Sporting Gentlemen*. He also wrote numerous essays and articles, many of which are collected in two volumes: *The Protestant Establishment Revisited* and *Judgment and Sensibility*.

Philadelphia Gentlemen: The Making of a National Upper Class, published in 1958, evolved from his doctoral dissertation. He used Philadelphia's social structure as an example of how a national upper class was formed in American cities in the latter part of the nineteenth century. In a detailed analysis Baltzell demonstrated how successful moneymakers— businessmen, bankers, lawyers, and physicians—many of whom came from lower social class backgrounds, founded families whose individual members through marriage, private school and college education, and club membership associated themselves with old money families, generation after generation, thus constituting an upper class with a distinctive set of traditional values. The subject matter of *Philadelphia Gentlemen* also provided, in Baltzell's words, "an excellent example of a business aristocracy which has too often placed the desire for material comfort and security above the duties of political and intellectual leadership" (Baltzell, 1958, p. 5). Nevertheless, as Baltzell showed, up to the Second World War upper-class Philadelphia families dominated the business and cultural life of the city. This organic upper class, almost an extended family with a sense of communal solidarity, stabilized the elite of leaders in the city before the Second World War. It was this class domination by an elite that Baltzell conceptualized as an "establishment," a concept he defined further in later works.

Baltzell ended *Philadelphia Gentlemen* with the question, "What is the future function of a predominantly Anglo-Saxon and Protestant upper class in an ethnically and religiously heterogeneous democracy?" He noted that "the American upper class has been from the beginning open to new men of talent and power and their families" (Baltzell, 1958, p. xiii). But at the time of his writing, at mid-century, a caste situation had developed, and upper-class status appeared to be limited to old and new families of Anglo-Saxon Protestant origin only.

His next book, *The Protestant Establishment: Aristocracy and Caste in America*, published in 1964, examined the problems of privilege and authority. Introducing the acronym "WASP," Baltzell showed that the white, Anglo-Saxon, and Protestant upper class had become, by and large, a privileged caste rather than a ruling and authoritative class. As he states: "[T]his book has been an attempt to analyze the decline of authority in America." Here Baltzell follows Tocqueville, who showed, in *The Ancient Regime and the French Revolution,* that when new men of talent, wealth, and power were refused membership in the French aristocracy by noblemen who drew a caste line, class authority failed and set the stage for the French Revolution. A similar crisis of leadership had developed in America, says Baltzell, because the WASP upper class was becoming increasingly caste-like. It excluded from its ranks talented individuals and their families from different ethnic or minority backgrounds, especially Jews, who had already become vital members of the elites of Philadelphia and other cities before and after the Second World War.

Baltzell's third book, *Puritan Boston and Quaker Philadelphia: Two Protestant Ethics and the Spirit of Class Authority and Leadership*, published in 1979, contrasts the upper class in Puritan Boston—which had exercised authority over the elite from the beginning—with the Quaker-turned-Episcopal upper class in Philadelphia, which had never produced an authoritative leadership in the state or nation. Boston, in other words, was a deferential, Philadelphia was a defiant one.

Baltzell often said that he was less interested in Boston and Philadelphia in a concrete sense, than as lessons about America—which was more like Boston until the Second World War and very much like Philadelphia since. For this book Baltzell was presented the prestigious Sorokin Award of the American Sociological Association.

In his 1995 book, *Sporting Gentlemen, Men's Tennis from the Age of Honor to the Cult of the Superstar*, Baltzell traced the decline of upper-class authority through the game of tennis. In this book, he showed that lawn tennis was once by and large an upper-class and amateur game which was played according to a gentlemanly code, but that it had become a classless sport, played by professionals under a mass of increasingly bureaucratic rules. In tracing the decline of manners in tennis, Baltzell demonstrated a correlation with the decline of Western civilization, especially since the 1960s.

Baltzell's work on leadership emphasized the interrelationship of five concepts: upper class, elite, establishment, authority, and community. All societies are led by elite individuals (political leaders, economic leaders, and leaders in art, law, medicine, religion, and other professions). Elites are made up of successful, but morally neutral, individuals. Over the generations any stable society will produce families descended from past elite members. These families buttressed by upper-class institutions, such as schools, colleges, and clubs, form a community that inevitably develops moral and social norms of its own. "Lady" and "gentleman" are class terms; "lawyer," or "doctor," or "governor," are elite terms.

As Baltzell has shown in his writings, traditional authority is class authority in Weber's sense of the term. Classless elites gain cohesion from charismatic or bureaucratic manipulators of authority. Finally, for Baltzell, class and authority are at the very core of communal leadership. Contrary to contemporary wisdom, egalitarian individualism will always run counter to community. He writes in *The Protestant Establishment*,

> The idea of equality lies at the very heart of the American Dream and has become the basis of the various secular faiths of our time. While the socialist faiths, on the one hand, have centered on the vision of equality of condition in a classless society, our own best traditions have stressed equality of opportunity in a hierarchical and open-class, as opposed to a classless, society. Karl Marx well understood the strengths of the Anglo-Saxon version of democracy when he wrote in *Das Kapital*, that 'the more a ruling class is able to assimilate the most prominent men of the dominated classes, the more stable and dangerous its rule.' I have written this book because I believe that our traditions of mobility and equal opportunity, so dangerous to the Marxian dreams of revolution, are infinitely superior to the leveling ideals of socialism.
>
> (Baltzell, 1958b, p. 3)

Despite popular recognition for introducing the term WASP into everyday usage, Baltzell's really important intellectual contribution is his theory of the establishment. The establishment concept, as Baltzell uses it, implies an elite influenced and dominated by upper-class members and their values and norms. Those few members of any upper class who form an establishment stand in contrast to the majority who are satisfied to have high status but little or no authority, in other words, those who form a caste. The aristocratic ethos of an establishment emphasizes the upper-class members' duty to lead, while the snobbish ethos of caste emphasizes only the right to privilege. While Boston's Brahmins stress *noblige*, Philadelphia's Gentlemen stress *nobless*.

Baltzell's theory of the establishment, as well as his other contributions to sociology, respond to a basic paradox of democracy in America, that John Adams and the Federalist founders of our nation saw sociology. Social classes as well as power and authority violate the egalitarian values at the core of modern American culture while at the same time being indispensable to democracy's survival. Baltzell recognized this paradox when he wrote,

> Every civilized society in history has been faced with the twin problems of creating and preserving communal order on the one hand and answering legitimate demands for social justice on the other. As the social forces for order, hierarchy and authority tend to be antithetical to those for equality and social justice, all societies are actually only relatively orderly and always unjust.
> (Baltzell & Schneiderman, 1991, p. 35)

Such Whiggish insight into one of the great paradoxes of modern society allowed Baltzell to chart a theoretical course between the ideological Scylla of Marxism and the equally perilous Charybdis of "right-wing" authoritarianism. In his preface to the *Ancient Regime* Tocqueville wrote: "I hope that I have written the present book without prejudice, but I do not pretend to have written it without passion" (Tocqueville, 1856, p. vii). Baltzell quoted those very words in the preface to *The Protestant Establishment*. Like Tocqueville, he blended passion and enthusiasm with cold factual examples to produce masterpieces of social analysis.

That his writing is marked by a personal point of view and by personal involvement is not to say, however, that he is not objective. Baltzell often used means of objective analysis (especially the comparative method). But he has never fallen under the seductive sway of objectivism. Many sociologists, of course, are objectivists. This perhaps explains the allure of objectivist ideologies such as Marxism, which, as wrote Michael Polanyi, "enables the modern mind, tortured by moral self-doubt, to indulge its moral passions in terms which also satisfy its passion for ruthless objectivity" (Polanyi, 1958, p. 242). Baltzell's writings betray no hint of moral self-doubt, nor passion for ruthless objectivity. Baltzell's books and essays demonstrate that understanding does not come from facts alone, but from an emotional involvement as well.

For over forty years Baltzell thought and wrote about the interrelations of class, status, and authority, always approaching his topic from a different angle. His ideal has been to rewrite the same problem in an endless variety of ways, much as Cezanne painted and re-painted the same mountain outside of Aix-en-Provence, in seemingly endless variations.

Methodological ingenuity and theoretical perspective are hallmarks of Baltzell's work. His theoretical design makes clear that, contrary to conventional views, aristocracy and representative democracy are not incompatible. This combination may even be preferable to those who value freedom, to democratically chosen, but autocratically ruled regimes.

The idea in Baltzell's work that evokes his emotional involvement more than any other is that "Americans have been trained to succeed rather than to lead" (Baltzell & Schneiderman, 1991, p. xxvii). This is the animus behind his theory of the establishment. Like William James he despised the "Bitch Goddess of Success." Caste ideals, wherever they are found, emphasize success and the protection of privilege at the expense of authority and leadership. An establishment exists only when an upper class emphasizes aristocratic ideals, favoring power and leadership over success and the protection of privilege. Baltzell examines this powerful theme in his essay, "The Protestant Establishment Revisited," written in 1976, when he reflects on "the national consequences of the fact that our society has no secure upper class which is able to dominate our leadership and see that it remains rooted in some kind of tradition or institutional continuity" (Baltzell & Schneiderman, 1991, p. 80).

That Baltzell's work was well received over the years is interesting when one considers that his emphasis on the need for an authoritative and responsible establishment has always run counter to unquestioned assumptions of most American social scientists. Despite the respect he has received, Baltzell has often been pigeonholed as an elitist. But while there is some truth in this categorization, the same would have to be said about the two intellectual giants whose work has influenced him most, Weber and Tocqueville. Both would probably have agreed with Baltzell that "while social justice definitely has improved in the last fifty years, social order has just as definitely declined," and that this has not necessarily been a good thing, at least not unqualifiedly so (Baltzell & Schneiderman, 1991, p. 35).

Baltzell's research on, and musings about, class, status, and power show how he explored these themes in ways no other sociologists have. He is one of the first of what was an expanding circle of colleagues who saw the importance of authority, establishments, classes, and hierarchy for the preservation of freedom in modern societies. It is interesting to note that this circle is to be found in the midst of a discipline in which class hierarchies are often regarded as evils to be eliminated or at least controlled. But the waves of "political correctness" beginning in the 1980s may have begun to drown out what Baltzell has to say. Thus, it may not be surprising to read what Harold Bershady, Baltzell's friend and colleague, reports hearing from a Penn graduate student in 1980: "As I was walking unnoticed behind two of the new sociology graduate students, one turned to the other and said in hissing anger," Baltzell is a fascist, presumably because he "thinks the upper class should rule" (Bershady, 2014).

Like many sociologists of his generation Baltzell's thinking had been influenced by his reaction to the upheavals of the 1960s. "I think the 60's were a tragic disaster," he has said, "and we're still paying for it. It was a very great revolt against civilization. ... People identified downward instead of upward. It was a very sad time" (Baltzell & Schneiderman, 1991, p. xxxi). His essays and books reflect this sense of tragedy and despair, which continued to animate his work from the Sixties on. In spite of the ideologies which developed since the Sixties labeling elitism an evil and upholding the equality of everything, Baltzell continued throughout his work to press the claim that what is needed in American society is *more* authority not less. If we really are in the process of wrecking Western civilization, Baltzell's books and essays need to be taken very seriously now, lest in some future time they are looked back at as merely brilliant analyses which warned of the dangers of destroying class distinctions and established authority, but which went unheeded.

9
SUCCESS AND LEADERSHIP

For over century and a half, sociological observers from Alexis de Tocqueville through James Bryce, and from the first generation of American sociologists through those writing today, have noted that Americans place an unambiguously high value on wealth and monetary success, but have mixed feelings about exercising authority and leadership. And, while American children are fed a steady diet of monetary success stories, and want to succeed in life, most of them seem to have been inoculated with what John W. Gardner once called "the anti-leadership vaccine," by which he meant that negative attitudes about leadership outweigh the positive ones.

Contrary to what popular opinion, if not common sense, might suggest, success, as in striving for wealth, and leadership, as in exercising authority, haven't necessarily gone hand in hand, in America. The first to see this was Tocqueville. In a powerful chapter in *Democracy in America*, "Why So Many Ambitious Men and So Little Lofty Ambition Are to Be Found in the United States," Tocqueville said that

> ... ambitious men in democracies are less engrossed than any others with the interests and the judgment of posterity; the present moment alone engages and absorbs them ... and they care much more for success than for glory ... I confess that I apprehend much less for democratic society from the boldness than

for the mediocrity of desires. What appears to me most dreaded is that in the midst of the small, incessant occupations of private life, ambition should lose its vigor and its greatness.

(Tocqueville, 1945, p. 3)

What Tocqueville meant by "glory" here has been analyzed brilliantly by Albert O. Hirschman in *The Passions and the Interests*. Showing that there is a long and direct philosophical line from St. Augustine to Blaise Pascal to Tocqueville, Hirschman helps us to understand that over the course of centuries, Western Civilization transformed passions that had once been considered personal vices—pride, ferociousness, lust, and others—into the virtuous pursuit of honor and glory. Before the Renaissance was over, honor and glory had become the defining aristocratic values of civic virtue. By the time that Tocqueville wrote that Americans care more for success than for glory, success had become the prevailing meaning of "interests," and as Hirschman wrote, "Interests' of persons and groups eventually came to be centered on economic advantage as its core meaning" (Hirschman, 2013, p. 32). If we extrapolate from Hirschman's analysis we see that passions for honor and glory tend to be caste values, while economic self-interests tend to be associated with class.

While Tocqueville was among the first, he was hardly alone in seeing American culture as fertile ground for success seekers, but as inhospitable to authority and leadership. Though he may still be regarded as the best analyst of the inner meaning of American society, but surely James Bryce rivals his insights. In his much-neglected chapter on "The Politicians" in his master work, *The American Commonwealth*—from which Max Weber derived without attribution his famous dualism about "living for" and "living off" of politics—Bryce wrote about the pecuniary independence needed for politicians to make political leadership their lives' work, thus setting up the arguments he made in his two most famous chapters: "Why Great Men Are Not Chosen President," and "Why the Best Men Do Not Go Into Politics." Without getting too deeply into the extensive arguments made by Bryce, it is clear that the attractiveness of more lucrative endeavors in business that Bryce noted in 1888 still keeps many of the most talented Americans out of seeking honorable leadership positions in local, state, and national government, and politics.

Beyond the observations of Tocqueville and Bryce, from the beginning, social scientists in America were interested in this dichotomy between the quest for monetary success and the aversion to exercise authority and leadership. At the same time, they were interested in that other set of twin-born tendencies: caste and competition.

Thus, discussing hero-worship in America in 1902, Charles Horton Cooley wrote in *Human Nature and the Social Order* that,

> Intellectual initiative, high and persistent idealism, are rare. The great majority of able men are ambitious, without having intrinsic traits that definitely direct their ambition to any particular object. They feel their way about among the careers which their time, their country, their early surroundings and training make accessible to them, and selecting one which seems to promise them the best chance of success, they throw themselves into the pursuit of the things that conduce to that success… they strive to gain wealth and prestige…
>
> (Cooley, 1902, p. 277)

Cooley kept thinking and writing about the distinction between success and leadership in his second book, *Social Organization*, published in 1909. He was certain, with Tocqueville before him, that democracy created a "generous contempt for distinction," and that Americans would rather strive for success than distinction. Thus, for Cooley, "success means possessions, and possessions are apt to imprison the spirit. It has always been held that worldly goods, which of course include reputation as well as wealth, make the highest life of the mind difficult if not impossible" (Cooley, 1909, p. 138). But Cooley didn't stop here. *Social Organization*, notable for introducing the indispensable primary group concept, and the remarkable section on public opinion and democracy, also contains, in chapter after chapter, one of the earliest and best discussions of the hereditary caste tendencies and the open-class competitive ones in American society.

Anticipating Linton's rediscovery of this dualism between ascribed and achieved status decades later, Cooley said that "fundamental to the study of all classes are the two principles, of inheritance and of competition, according to which their membership is determined" (Cooley, 1909, p. 210). With unmatched wisdom Cooley also noted that after ascribed and achieved status is accounted for, the element of chance—sheer luck—accounts for a large part of the stratification system in our society.

Chance aside, however, Cooley is blunt about the subject of caste:

> ... on every side we see that differences arise, and that these tend to be perpetuated through inherited associations, opportunities and culture. The endeavor to secure for one's children whatever desirable thing one has gained for oneself is a perennial source of caste...
>
> (Cooley, 1909, p. 211)

Among the early sociologists who understood the difference between success and leadership, Cooley devoted many chapters of his last book, *Social Process*, to the question of success in America. Following Tocqueville's distinction between success and glory, Cooley categorized success into a higher and lower type:

> Ordinary success—wealth, power, or standing coming as the prompt reward of endeavor—is, after all, for second-rate men, those who do a little better than the jobs offered by the ruling institutions. The notably wise, good, or original are in some measure protestants against these institutions, and must expect their antagonism. The higher success has always been and must always be attained at more or less sacrifice of the lower.
>
> (Cooley, 1918, p. 108)

Cooley was not alone among the founders of sociology in America in thinking about the difference between success and distinction. His contemporary, Edward A. Ross, had much to say about this as well. Ross was much more of a reformer than Cooley, and he was more likely to see personal success-seeking in pejorative terms than his colleague in Michigan. For example, in *Sin and Society*, written in 1907, Ross said that corrupt bankers, builders, labor leaders, and corporate directors "want nothing more than we all want—money, power, consideration—in a word, success; but they are in a hurry, and not particular as to the means" (Ross, 1907, p. 51). Indeed, Ross seems to critique success-seeking in almost all his books, including his most enduring effort, *Social Control*, in which he wrote the following:

> Or take that wonder of our age, the growth of cities. The modern commercial or industrial city, with its lack of neighborliness, its mutual indifference, its mingling without fellowship and its contact without intercourse, its absence of communal opinion, its machinal charities, its vicarious philanthropy, its dismal contrasts of wealth and poverty, its *wolfish struggle for personal success*, its crimes, frauds, exploitations, and parasitism—surely this strange agglomeration is the work of the economic man, not the social man! (italics mine)
>
> (Ross, 1916, p. 19)

But if Cooley and Ross were among the most relentless in rooting out the differences between seeking success and seeking honor, their contemporary, Thorstein Veblen, was the most brilliant. Published in 1899, *The Theory of the Leisure Class* is without equal in its dissection of success-seeking. Although Veblen was an economist, his influence was greatest among sociologists who mined his work for concepts that would help them to research and to understand social stratification in America. A sampling of chapter titles from the book indicates how much Veblen saw success-seeking as the driving force in American social structure: "Pecuniary Emulation," "Conspicuous Leisure," "Conspicuous Consumption," "The Pecuniary Standard of living," and "Pecuniary Canons of Taste," among others. For Veblen, success does not only mean being able to afford and consume costly things, it is to be able to affirm and reaffirm having arrived. The symbols of success become at least as important as success itself, for as Veblen wrote, "In any community where an invidious comparison of persons is habitually made, visible success becomes an end sought for its own utility as a basis of esteem" (Veblen, 1899, p. 16).

Beyond the founding generation of sociologists, others noted the same tendency of Americans to value wealth over leadership. Thus, in 1929, the year of the great crash, Walter Lippmann, one of our most sociologically astute journalistic commentators, wrote the following in *A Preface to Morals*:

> Our rulers today consist of random collections of successful men and their wives. They are to be found in the inner circles of banks and corporations, in the best clubs, in the dominant cliques of trade unions, among the political churchmen, the higher manipulation bosses, the leading professional Catholics, Baptists, Methodists, Irish, Germans, Jews, and the grand panjandrums of the secret societies. They give orders. They have to be consulted. They can more or less effectively speak for, and lead some part of the population. But none of them is seated on a certain throne, and all of them are forever concerned as to how they may keep from being toppled off. They do not know how they happen to be where they are, although they often explain what are the secrets of success. *They have been educated to achieve success; few of them have been educated to exercise power.* Nor do they count with any confidence upon retaining their power, nor in handing it on to their sons. They live therefore from day to day, and govern by ear. Their impromptu statements of policy may be obeyed, but nobody seriously regards them as having authority.
> (Lippmann, 1929, p. 66)

Lippmann picked up on this theme again and again, and much like Tocqueville, Cooley, and others before him, he understood that while success is well established as a high priority in American life, exercising authority and leadership is not.

Not even the Great Depression could derail social science's critique of the American quest for wealth, in itself, and as a symbol of achievement. Thus, in 1933, Elton Mayo published *The Human Problems of an Industrial Civilization*, in which he parodied R. H. Tawney's *Acquisitive Society*: "the problem is not that of the sickness of an acquisitive society; it is that of the acquisitiveness of a sick society" (Mayo, 1933, p. 153). Here again, we see the social science critique of success-seeking, the implication being that a healthy society would not value acquisitiveness so highly.

Perhaps the most astute social science observations about the emphasis on wealth accumulation in America were Robert K. Merton's, especially in his remarkable 1938 article, "Social Structure and Anomie." Anchoring his analysis directly to Georg Simmel's groundbreaking book about the meaning of money in modern societies, Merton wrote that "the extreme emphasis on the accumulation of wealth as a symbol of success in our society militates against the completely effective controls of institutionally regulated modes of acquiring a fortune" (Merton, 1938, pp. 672–682).

This theme was also central to David Riesman's *Lonely Crowd*, one of our most widely read social science books. Writing in 1950, Riesman suggested that Americans could be divided into a few character types, among which were inner-directed and other-directed individuals. Riesman's understanding of the inner-directed character type was that a person's goals were instilled within him by strict and disciplinary parents, and that the individual strived to achieve these internalized goals, relatively unaffected by the opinion of others. The contrasting character type of the other-directed individual finds that his peers are his major source of goals, and that these might fluctuate far more than those of the inner-directed type. But Riesman saw that Americans were less and less likely to be inner-directed, and more and more likely to be other-directed. The consequences of this shift from inner-to other-directedness were that young people want

> ... security, not great achievements ... [and] approval, not fame. They are not eager for talents that might bring them into conflict; whereas the inner-directed young person tended to push himself to the limit of his talents and beyond... [The other-directed youth] learns to conform to the group almost as soon as he learns anything. While the inner-directed youth wanted to set the world on fire, the other-directed person prefers love to glory. As Tocqueville saw, he willingly takes up with low desires without daring to embark on lofty enterprises, of which he scarcely dreams.
> (Riesman, 1950, p. 260)

With Riesman's Tocquevillian critique, we return to the relationship of caste and class to success and honor. The dichotomy of monetary success and the exercise of authority and leadership came up again and again during the 1950s and 1960s, notably in the work of C. Wright Mills, Daniel Bell, and Seymour Martin Lipset, but it reached a deeper level of analysis in E. Digby Baltzell's theory of class authority, which was rooted in his observation that the pursuit of monetary success and affluence, on the one hand, and the persistence of a closed caste-like establishment monopolizing prestige and power, on the other, has often prevented capable men and women in America from taking the lead in the public life of the nation. This idea, that the ideal of success as measured in terms of making money has somehow been opposed to the ideals of exercising authority and taking the lead in civic affairs, runs through almost all of Baltzell's work. For example, in 1964 Baltzell wrote in *The Protestant Establishment* that,

> whereas generations of British gentlemen had proudly, and sometimes smugly, assumed it was their natural right and duty to rule the world, there is something uncharacteristic in America's assuming such leadership. But, then, we Americans have been trained to succeed rather than to lead, and all too many of us would gladly forgo the need for greatness which has been so suddenly thrust upon us.

Baltzell picks up on this theme time and again in *The Protestant Establishment*, thus he also wrote that

> ... the postwar years have witnessed an unprecedented democratization of plutocracy. Millionaires are multiplying, and most Americans are now driven by materialistic dreams of ever greater affluence and comfort ... but unfortunately success is not synonymous with leadership, and affluence without authority breeds alienation.
>
> (Baltzell, 1964)

In his 1979 book, *Puritan Boston and Quaker Philadelphia*, Baltzell again returned to this theme. Thus, he asked,

> could it be true that deep down in their collective unconscious the American people mistrust excellence and fear superiority? ...

many of our most thoughtful citizens, have called attention to the fact that although we both understand and admire success, we seem far less than eager to devote ourselves to the pursuit of fame and leadership.

(Baltzell, 1979)

What is it about the quest for monetary success (as well as security and comfort) that leads observers such as Tocqueville, Bryce, Lippmann, Merton, Mills, Riesman, and Baltzell to distinguish it from the exercise of authority, and leadership? The beginning of an answer to this question may be formulated by comparing success terms and glory (or accomplishment) terms as defined by some of our most definitive dictionaries, from *Webster's Second New International* to the *Oxford English Dictionary*.

Success and glory are most often associated with the following words and terms:

Success	Glory
Prosperity	Distinction
Thriving	Notability
Making good	Importance
Achieving success	Consequence
Making a success of oneself	Significance
Making one's mark	Prominence
Getting ahead	Greatness
Giving a good account of oneself	Lasting fame
Prospering	Recognition
Faring well	Coming to the front
Rising in the world	Outstanding achievement
Arriving	Honor
Coming out on top	Praiseworthiness
Making one's fortune	Meritoriousness
Well-being	Laudability
Comfortable circumstances	Exemplary accomplishment
Comfort	Admirability
Ease or a life of ease	Superiority
A high standard of living	Pre-eminence
Booming	Excellence
Flourishing	First-rateness

In one way or another all of the "success" terms are connected to monetary success and personal well-being, and all the "glory" terms are about distinction and taking the lead.

This comparison of "success" terms to "glory" terms is reminiscent of what is discussed in Chapter 11, "Class and Authority in the Oval Office." There is a high correlation between upper-class backgrounds and greatness in the presidency.

In a way, the American obsession with success and with getting a better job is intimately related to our socially mobile society; only a relatively few Americans have ever had the luxury of bypassing the scramble up the ladders of success, thus being able to concentrate on doing a better job, as prescribed by class codes and traditions.

While monetary success may be linked *in the long run* to glory and achievement, they are not necessarily related in the short term. Tocqueville, Bryce, Cooley, Merton, Lippmann, Riesman, and Baltzell used these as relative terms, that is not in an either/or sense, but as tendencies that show that Americans value one more than the other, not necessarily one in place of the other. Much more than success and comfort, achievement and glory are terms likely to be associated with leadership and authority. As for leadership itself, the problem is not to persuade most Americans to be led, but to persuade the relatively few who are really capable of it to take the lead. As Bryce suggested, as a rule, the masses don't desire to govern themselves; they desire to be well governed.

One of the main problems in terms of securing capable and stable leadership in America is tied directly to the high value placed on monetary success: both success-seeking and leadership avoidance are consequences of something lacking in our highly mobile and anxiety ridden other-directed society, namely confidence in a secure future.

Confidence has always been one of the main ingredients in successful leadership, and is no less important for the few who lead as for the many who are governed by them. Only a few weeks before the presidential election of 1996, Lee Iacocca, one of the most important businessmen of our times, spoke at Lehigh University. One thing he said seems essentially, but, not fully, true. Iacocca said that leadership means *making someone do* something that he otherwise doesn't want to do—this, of course, is a lot like how Max Weber defined "power." Perhaps it would be truer to say that leadership means making someone *want to do*, or at least think he *ought* to do, something that he otherwise doesn't want to do, which is a lot like how Weber defined "authority."

One way or the other, however, one might well concede that all leadership consists of convincing people to do something now that will only come to fruition later. Any type of leadership, whether it is political, military, economic, religious, or moral, involves some sacrifice now for advantages in the future.

To persuade others to make sacrifices here and now for future gains means that a leader must show intense confidence in that future. Indeed, instilling confidence in the future is the essence of all leadership. If potential leaders, that is, those with the capacity to take the lead, are not optimistic about the future, and if they are not secure in their vision for future achievement, they are more likely to expend their energies protecting themselves *against* the future, than in attempting to shape it through their leadership.

If our society is insecure about its values and its direction, and if potential leaders are convinced that the future is bound to be worse than the present, instead of setting goals and convincing others to work towards achieving them, they will lose interest in trying to influence coming events. In other words, they will not act as leaders at all. Instead they will do whatever it takes to secure a comfortable life here and now.

Are Americans confident in the future, let alone secure in the present? Since 1973, the National Opinion Research Center (NORC) at the University of Chicago has surveyed Americans attitudes about many aspects of life in the United States. One of the things that NORC has been interested in is confidence in a wide variety of American institutions. As the following table demonstrates, the proportion of Americans surveyed who expressed a great deal of confidence in major areas of American life such as the U.S. Congress, television, major corporations, organized religion, and the press has declined significantly since 1973, and is worrisomely low in many cases. Faith in the military, medicine, and science remains relatively high, with over a third of Americans having confidence in them.

Confidence in American Institutions

	Percent Confident				
	1973	1983	1993	2004	2014
Major Corporations	29	24	21	17	18
Organized Religion	35	28	23	24	19
Education	37	29	22	28	25
Executive Branch of Gov.	29	13	12	21	11
Organized Labor	15	8	8	12	12
Press	23	13	11	9	7
Medicine	54	52	39	36	38
Television	19	12	12	10	10
Supreme Court	31	27	31	30	23
Scientific Community	37	41	37	41	41
Congress	23	10	7	13	5
Military	32	29	42	57	55

Lack in faith in American institutional life must make for lack of faith in the future, as well. If faith in the future, among leaders as well as those they lead, is essential for leadership, widespread lack of confidence in American institutions makes it difficult to convince capable people to take the lead, as well as to follow the lead of others. Instead, such conditions might well drive everyone to try to successfully pad themselves *against* the future, rather than to help form and reform it.

It is against such a backdrop of pessimism that the value of a secure class authority and of an establishment is best seen, because the aristocratic and inner-directed emphasis on leadership can stand beyond the slippery slopes of optimism and pessimism.

The establishment concept as Baltzell used it implies an elite influenced and dominated by upper-class members and their values and norms. Those relatively few members of any upper class who form an establishment stand in contrast to the majority who are satisfied to have high status but little or no authority, in other words, with those who form a caste. As Baltzell said repeatedly, the aristocratic ethos of an establishment emphasizes the duty to lead, while the snobbish ethos of caste emphasizes only the right to privilege. Here we see that privilege that is too secure, as in caste, is as problematic as privilege that is too insecure, as in a power elite, when it comes to taking the lead.

Baltzell was fond of quoting Karl Marx's *Das Kapital*, which stated that "the more a ruling class is able to assimilate the most prominent men of the dominated classes, the more stable and dangerous its rule" (Marx, 1909, p. 706). Baltzell agreed with Marx's assessment, except that where Marx saw danger, he saw desirability. One important element of a strong establishment is its ability to assimilate men and women of great ability as well as their children into the upper class. In an open-class democratic society, we will always need to have a circulation of elites, as talented men and women rise into positions of power and leadership only to pass on their newly achieved statuses to their children.

When caste becomes stronger than the establishment as the operative upper-class principle, leadership positions will be open to a highly mobile power elite. As Baltzell's work demonstrates, this has been the case in America for many decades. This viewpoint is bolstered by Ralph Linton, the noted anthropologist who wrote *The Study of Man*, in which he wrote that,

> The lack of a definite aristocratic culture [in America] which provides the members of this ruling group with common ideals and standards of behavior and thus integrates them into a conscious society is perhaps the most distinctive aspect of the modern condition. Exploiters and exploited have existed since the dawn of history, but the only parallel to the modern situation is that of Rome in the days of the late Republic. Here also power came to be vested in the hands of a group of self-made men who had no common standards and no feeling of responsibility to each other or to the state.
>
> (Linton, 1936, p. 129)

All viewpoints, such as Baltzell's and Linton's, about the sociological functions of an establishment can ultimately be traced back to Tocqueville, who suggested that "a powerful aristocracy does not merely shape the course of public affairs, it also guides opinion, sets the tone for writers, and lends authority to new ideas." In other words, an establishment has an overarching authority over society, which is necessary to the well-being of society.

Sociologists today often debunk authority as mere manipulation, and leadership as nothing but refined, or sometimes raw, self-interest. A number of social scientists, some of whom I have mentioned above, from Tocqueville on, have thought about leadership and success without cynicism.

What are the underlying elements of leadership? First, all leadership involves optimism about the future, meaning the possibility of achieving something important. Second, a society that has lost confidence in its values will very likely also lose confidence in its institutions. Under such conditions it is tough to convince those who have talent and ability to become leaders, because optimism will be at a premium. Why should these potential leaders care much for a future that seems so much out of their control? Third, a society that has lost confidence in its values is likely to seek immediate comfort today as a more enticing activity than striving to shape the future tomorrow. Since the possibility of formulating goals and persuading others to follow them to fruition requires a solid set of agreed-upon values to begin with, leadership may seem futile.

These last few points lead to a brief consideration of three types of privilege in America today. There is the privilege of an ever-changing upwardly mobile elite that is too insecure; the privilege of a caste of often wealthy, certainly high-status individuals that is much too secure; and there is the privilege that is just secure enough to allow its holders to be optimistic about the future, and to think that they owe something to society that can be paid back in terms of leadership.

Privilege that is too secure is likely to promote selfish indulgence, class snobbery, and arrogant complacency. Privilege that is too insecure cannot spur excellence, because status anxiety has the effect of lowering standards to heighten one's sense of security. Once the standards are lowered beyond a certain point, the whole idea of achievement loses its meaning, and of course so does leadership, which, after all, is nothing if it is not about setting goals for the future.

An establishment means that talented, basically secure, and generally inner-directed leaders in many walks of life from politics and business to religion and education are secure enough to have shared visions for shaping the future, and which they hope to persuade others to follow to fruition.

The first two decades of our presidency, under Washington, Adams, and Jefferson, were probably the greatest in our history. The second greatest was arguably the two decades after 1901 when Theodore Roosevelt, Taft, and Wilson were in office, and a third great twenty-year period under Franklin Roosevelt and Harry Truman. There is no doubt that "public purpose" dominated over "private interest" under the secure class-bound leadership of the presidents in these three periods.

Thus, while boundless leadership opportunities are dispersed throughout American society and its seemingly endless groups and voluntary associations, there is no simple and easy blueprint for achieving class leadership. Unless those who have the ability to take the lead are encouraged to do so, and to be confident about their chances of exerting their authority and achieving something, and hence to be optimistic about the future, and allowed to be adequately secure in status, they simply will not lead. Under these conditions look for far more success-driven individuals than leaders with visions for shaping and reshaping the future of our country.

10

CLASS AND AUTHORITY IN THE OVAL OFFICE

In this election year, two very rich, upper-middle-class candidates for president ran what may be long remembered as among the nastiest campaigns in history. The tone was low, and the stakes were high, as Hillary Clinton and Donald Trump kept squaring off against each other. When Digby Baltzell and I first published this chapter in 1988, we were witnessing what may have been the last presidential campaign featuring a candidate representing what was left of the Protestant Establishment, when the upper-class George H. W. Bush ran against Michael Dukakis, a wealthy, upper-middle-class son of immigrants. Unlike the election of 2016, where wealth was openly discussed, social status but not wealth was on display in 1988, and Governor Dukakis made repeated references to his social origins, while Vice President Bush seemed to be trying to hide his high-status background. The "log-cabin" myth, which had been around for over a hundred years, was having its latest, and perhaps its last incarnation.

Because of intense interest in the log-cabin myth in 1988, Baltzell and I made our own examinations of historical records and polls of American historians, and we came to an unpopular conclusion, which goes against the conventional wisdom: Presidents from high-social class backgrounds have performed better in office and been ranked as more effective than presidents from lower-class origins. Our point was not that upper-class candidates should be preferred, but that their privileged social origins should not automatically be used as a basis for dismissal of their ability to govern a nation of many economic and social levels.

Franklin D. Roosevelt once described the presidency of the United States as "preeminently a place of moral leadership" (Burns, 1979, p. 34). During the Watergate affair, Arthur M. Schlesinger, Jr, paraphrasing Clark Clifford, a distinguished presidential advisor, wrote that the government of the United States "was like a chameleon, taking its colors from the character and personality of the President" (Baltzell & Schneiderman, 1991, p. 241). At about the same time, the *London Spectator* noted that two centuries of American history had come full circle "from George Washington, who could not tell a lie, to Richard Nixon, who cannot tell the truth" (Westley, 1973, p. 705). In January 1988, the *Washington Post* summed up 1987, the year in which we celebrated the 200th anniversary of the writing of our Constitution, as "The Year of Lying Dangerously," and then went on to note that "66 percent of Americans believe that Ronald Reagan is an honest man—at the same time 65 percent of Americans believe he was lying about the Iran-Contra affair" (Harrington, 1987). Perhaps James Bryce was right just a century ago, in 1888, when he wrote in the famous chapter "Why Great Men Are Not Chosen Presidents" in his classic book, *The American Commonwealth*, that the best men in America do not go into public life nor do they seek the presidency, at least not since the aristocratic generation that made a revolution, wrote the Constitution, and founded the new nation.

In 1948, when we were the most powerful and respected nation in the world and American authority reigned supreme, Professor Arthur M. Schlesinger, Sr, of Harvard, took issue with Bryce and asked a group of leading American historians to rank our presidents from Washington through Franklin Roosevelt in terms of their performances in office. The twenty-nine presidents (W. H. Harrison and Garfield were left out as they had spent less than a year in office) were ranked by the fifty-five men who responded as follows:

Great 1) Lincoln 2) Washington 3) Franklin Roosevelt 4) Wilson 5) Jefferson 6) Jackson
Near-Great 7) T. Roosevelt 8) Cleveland 9) John Adams 10) Polk

Average 11) J. Q. Adams 12) Monroe 13) Hayes 14) Madison 15) Van Buren 16) Taft 17) Arthur 18) McKinley 19) A. Johnson 20) Hoover 21) Benjamin Harrison
Below Average 22) Tyler 23) Coolidge 24) Fillmore 25) Taylor 26) Buchanan 27) Pierce
Failure 28) Grant 29) Harding

In the 156 years between Washington's inauguration and Franklin Roosevelt's death in office, moreover, the ten presidents of "Great" and "Near-Great" ranking were in office for seventy-two years, or 45% of the time. Professor Schlesinger considered this "a creditable showing for any system of government." And he was backed by the British expert on the American presidency, Harold Laski, who wrote in *Parliamentary Affairs* (Laski, 1949), that the seven leading British Prime Ministers between the American Revolution and the New Deal—Pitt, Peel, Palmerston, Disraeli, Gladstone, Lloyd George, and Churchill—were easily matched in distinction by Washington, Jefferson, Jackson, Lincoln, Theodore Roosevelt, Wilson, and Franklin Roosevelt.

Schlesinger's 1948 article had great popular appeal when it was published in *Life magazine*. In 1962, during the optimistic Kennedy presidency, he published a second article on presidential ranking in the *New York Times Magazine* which was not too different from the first: the top five presidents ranked "Great" remained in the same order; Jackson was moved down to "Near-Great" among other minor changes; and Truman (Near-Great) and Eisenhower (Average) were added.

Since the Kennedy assassination, the American presidency has passed through increasingly debilitating times of trouble. Lyndon Johnson, after a brilliant period of social reform, was finally defeated by the Vietnam War and almost revolutionary unrest at home. Richard Nixon was utterly disgraced by Watergate, when he was forced to resign, as was his vice president before him. Jimmy Carter floundered and finally failed to free the American hostages in Iran. And, after the most successful and popular first term since Franklin Roosevelt's, Ronald Reagan lost much of his authority in the Iran-Contra affair. The authority of the presidency has surely reached one of its lowest points in our history.

All the while, scholarly research on the presidency has steadily increased; books and articles have not only continued to rank the presidents but also have employed all sorts of scientific methods in attempting to fathom the causes of presidential greatness in order to better predict performance in office. As an index of this new interest, a learned journal, *Presidential Studies Quarterly*, was founded in 1970 and is still thriving.

The latest scientific attempt to rank the presidents was undertaken in 1981 by Robert K. Murray, Senior Research Fellow at Pennsylvania State University, and his graduate student, Tim H. Blessing. While Professor Schlesinger had been rather informal and elitist in methodology (his two panels included Felix Frankfurter of the U.S. Supreme Court, five past presidents of the American Historical Association and a dozen Pulitzer Prize winners), Murray and Blessing, in keeping with our more egalitarian and quantitative age, were far more systematic and scientific. In November 1981, they sent out 1,997 19-page questionnaires to all PhD holding American historians who were teaching full-time at the assistant professor level and above. "By March 1982," they wrote in their article published in the December 1983 issue of *The Journal of American History*,

> 846 completed questionnaires were in hand and coding of the information for the computer was begun. While the coding was being undertaken, 107 additional completed questionnaires were received... The reply rate of 48.6 percent, representing almost one-half of the total mailed, was a response beyond our rosiest expectations.
> (Murray & Blessing, 1983, p. 538)

The presidents ranked by the Murray–Blessing respondents were as follows:

Great 1) Lincoln 2) Franklin D. Roosevelt 3) Washington 4) Jefferson
Near-Great 5) Theodore Roosevelt 6) Wilson 7) Jackson 8) Truman

Above Average 9) John Adams 10) Lyndon Johnson 11) Eisenhower 12) Polk 13) Kennedy 14) Madison 15) Monroe 16) J. Q. Adams 17) Cleveland

Average 18) McKinley 19) Taft 20) Van Buren 21) Hoover 22) Hayes 23) Arthur 24) Ford 25) Carter 26) Benjamin Harrison

Below Average 27) Taylor 28) Tyler 29) Fillmore 30) Coolidge 31) Pierce

Failures 32) A. Johnson 33) Buchanan 34) Nixon 35) Grant 36) Harding

The rankings of the Murray–Blessing respondents did not vary greatly from those of the two Schlesinger panels. They of course added Kennedy, L. B. Johnson, Nixon, Ford, and Carter (and left out W. H. Harrison and Garfield as did Schlesinger). Among the important changes in ranking were the movement of Franklin Roosevelt to second place, ahead of George Washington, placing Theodore Roosevelt ahead of both Wilson and Jackson, and, most interestingly, moving Eisenhower from the low average rank of twenty-second to a high above-average rank of eleventh. Finally, A. Johnson, just below Eisenhower in 1962, was moved down to the top of the list of failures.

While Schlesinger listed the seventy-five distinguished participants in his 1962 poll by name and function at the end of his article in the *New York Times Magazine*, Murray and Blessing made an exhaustive quantitative analysis of their anonymous respondents by age, sex, birthplace, field of specialization, where they had obtained their PhDs and so forth. A large part of the article was devoted to a fascinating discussion of how the different categories of respondents ranked the presidents. Two examples seem to nicely reveal the changing climate of opinion in America since the 1962 Schlesinger poll.

First, the authors separated out the seventy-five most distinguished historians in the panel and compared their rankings with the rest. This elite group happened to be predominantly male and over forty-five years of age, yet their rankings were quite similar to the rest, except for their more traditional placing of Washington, rather than Franklin Roosevelt, in second place. On the other hand, the fifty-nine women in the panel, on the whole much harsher on presidential performance than their male colleagues, were particularly severe in their treatment of Washington, ranking him almost a half-category lower than the males did. As might be expected, Jimmy Carter, surely the least sexy and most egalitarian of recent presidents (in style at least), was ranked "significantly" higher by females than by males. In this connection, the fifteen women's-history specialists rated Washington "lower by as much as two-thirds of a category than any of the others" (Murray & Blessing, 1983). They also downgraded Teddy Roosevelt, the Rough Rider, while the respondents as a whole elevated him above Woodrow Wilson and Andrew Jackson. At the moment, the Murray–Blessing study is widely recognized as state of the art in presidential-ranking research.

In addition to ranking, there is another problem of equal importance. That is the problem of what biographical factors are the best predictors of success or greatness in office. A large literature has been produced in this field since Schlesinger's day. Political psychologists, historians, sociologists, and others have analyzed the presidents in terms of birth order, family size, education, age at time of election, occupation, political career before entering office, and such slippery psychological factors as the need for power, the need for achievement, the need for social approval. None have proved highly significant as predictive variables. Dean Keith Simonton, a psychologist at the University of California, Davis, has published profusely in this field. In his latest book, *Why Presidents Succeed* (1987), he writes that "it must be acknowledged that there really may not be many direct biographical predictors" (Simonton, 1987, p. 292).

Evidence of this difficulty is the hardly useful fact that one of the best predictors of greatness in office has proved to be the ascriptive factor of height: Of the four great presidents, Lincoln was 6'4" and Franklin Roosevelt, Washington, and Jefferson were 6'2" or more. Strangely enough, having had a college education, which we Americans so value in our day, seems not to have been a very good predictor at all. The ten presidents rated below average or as failures were more likely to have graduated from college than the eight men of great and near-great stature: college graduates among the "Great" numbered 50%, "Near-Great" 50%, "Above Average" 78%, "Average" 78%, "Below Average" 60%, and "Failures" 60%.

Although not remarked on by any studies we have seen, by far the best (100%) predictor of high performance in office has been the possession of a Harvard undergraduate degree. The two Roosevelts, the two Adamses, and John Fitzgerald Kennedy were all rated "above average" as presidents. Up until Kennedy's time at least, Harvard was known as a snobbish college where the sons of the rich and well-born had always set the tone; and the Harvard Yard had always been a long distance socially from the mythical log cabin on the ever-moving American frontier.

Curiously, in all the thousands of tedious hours devoted to analyzing the biographical factors which most contribute to success in the Oval Office, nobody has ever considered the ascribed social class origins of our presidents as significant for explaining their performance in office. Soon after the publication of the Murray–Blessing article, however, this problem was first attacked systematically by Edward Pessen, in *The Log Cabin Myth: The Social Backgrounds of the Presidents*.

Pessen is a prolific writer on a wide variety of subjects in American history. Among other things, he is thoroughly familiar with the sociological literature on social stratification. Knowing that American society has always been relatively fluid and classes have been difficult to define or identify, Pessen, nevertheless, followed the lead of an influential school of American sociologists and divided the social structure into six basic class levels—upper-upper, lower-upper, upper-middle, lower middle, upper lower, and lower lower. Even though he devotes a whole chapter to defining just what he means by these six levels, Pessen is well aware that all classifications or categories in the social sciences are ultimately arbitrary. They are useful and necessary tools of analysis at best.

At any rate, Pessen, rightly arguing that the family of origin is the basis of social class position, ranked the families of all the presidents from Washington through Reagan in the following hierarchy: in the upper-upper class he placed the families of Washington, Jefferson, Madison, John Quincy Adams, William Henry Harrison, Tyler, Taylor, Benjamin Harrison, Theodore Roosevelt, Taft, and Franklin Roosevelt; running into his first difficulty with his model, he ranked Polk and Kennedy in a category "straddling the upper-upper and lower-upper classes;" he ranked the families of John Adams, Monroe, and Wilson in the lower-upper class; "on a plateau between the lower-upper and the upper-middle class" he placed the families of Pierce, Hayes, Cleveland, Harding, Coolidge, and Truman; the upper-middle class families included those of Jackson, Van Buren,

Buchanan, Grant, Arthur, McKinley, Hoover, Lyndon Johnson, Ford, and Carter; "in the 'true' middle or between the upper and lower middle classes" he placed the families of Lincoln, Eisenhower, and Reagan; in the lower middle class, the families of Fillmore, Garfield, and Nixon; and alone in the lower class, upper lower at that, was the family of Andrew Johnson (Pessen, 1984, pp. 68–69). To summarize, Pessen ranked the families of the thirty-nine presidents: the top sixteen (41%) include eleven upper-upper, two middle-upper, and three lower-upper; the next sixteen (41%) include six lower-upper to upper-middle and ten upper-middle; the lowest seven (18%) include three true middle, three lower middle, and one upper lower.

Pessen was surprised to find that only seven of our presidents were born to middle-class status or below, and that the vast majority (82%) were born into families of privileged upper-middle-class status or better. Those who place their faith in the log-cabin myth have a hard time facing those facts. But Pessen had to agree with an economic historian who wrote that self-made men "have always been more conspicuous in American history books than in American history" (Miller, 1962, p. 79).

The very essence of the log-cabin myth is to be found in the legendary life of Abraham Lincoln: "Everybody in this world knows," Lincoln's son, Tad, once said, "that Pa used to split rails." Honest Abe carefully fostered and dramatized the self-made myth throughout his political career. "I am a living witness that any one of your children may look to come here as my father's child has," he once told some members of an Ohio regiment who were visiting the White House. "I presume you all know who I am," he said at another time, "I am humble Abraham Lincoln…" (Hofstadter, 1973, p. 111). And so it always went; no wonder his enemies resented this Uriah Heep style.

In reality, Lincoln's grandfather was an officer in the Revolution and the owner of a 200-acre farm in Virginia before he brought his family West. His father, Thomas Lincoln, "at the time of his great son's birth," to quote Pessen,

> …owned two farms of six hundred acres, several town lots, livestock, and horses, property that was quite close to the total owned by the wealthiest man in the area. Five years later he belonged to the richest fifteen percent of taxpaying property owners in his community.
>
> (Pessen, 1984, p. 25)

But the truth also is that it was a long way socially from Abraham Lincoln's birthplace in a small town in Hardin County, Kentucky, to the White House.

The log-cabin myth was born in the cynical campaign of 1840. The power-starved Whigs, led by Daniel Webster and the Eastern moneymen, chose the old hero of Tippecanoe, General William Henry Harrison, as their candidate. Picturing Martin Van Buren as a champagne-drinking aristocrat, they manipulatively portrayed Harrison as a hard-cider-drinking man of the people whose simple tastes nicely fitted the Midwestern, log-cabin stereotype. Although his campaign featured log-cabin songs, log-cabin clubs, and log-cabin badges, Old Tippecanoe was the son of Benjamin Harrison, acme of Virginia's patrician-planter class, signer of the Declaration of Independence, and one time Governor of his state (the first Harrison was elected to the Virginia House of Burgesses in 1642, and the family, like the Adamses and Roosevelts, produced two presidents).

Throughout history, great men have tended both to have had mothers who were socially, morally, or intellectually superior to their husbands and also to have chosen as wives women who were above them in one way or another. Pessen became well aware of this pattern in his study of the presidents' origins.

Abraham Lincoln's marriage was of course the classic example of a man-on-the-make marrying well. Such marriages were not always happy ones, and Mary Todd spent a miserable married life looking down socially on her great husband. Even ambitious young men of higher class origins have done the same. Thus, George Washington's grandfather, like other Washingtons after him, married "above himself" into what Pessen called "the crème de la crème of Virginia society." When George Washington married Martha Dandridge Custis, he moved into "another economic sphere." Similarly, with John Adams of Massachusetts, whose marriage to Abigail Smith brought a "strain of aristocracy… into the Adams line." Actually, the second president not only married above himself but his father before him had done the same: The president's mother was born Susanna Boylston, a member of one of the leading families of the entire commonwealth of Massachusetts. To round out the founding trio of presidents, Jefferson, at the age of twenty-five, was one of the five richest men in Virginia and also the best educated. His father had married Jane

Randolph, whose distinguished family was both wealthy and socially at the top of the "First Families of Virginia" hierarchy at the time. Two years after Jefferson married, his new wife inherited 135 slaves and some 11,000 acres of farmland (Pessen, 1984, pp. 148–149).

Of recent presidents, one great difference between Dwight Eisenhower and his vice president, Richard Nixon, was that the former married way above himself while the latter did not. Right after graduation from West Point, young Ike married Mamie Dowd, whose ancestors were evidently part of the British aristocracy when they came to Guilford, Connecticut in 1639. Both sides of the family had prospered and her father made a fortune. "Small wonder," writes Pessen, "that her parents pointed out that 'a second lieutenant's pay could not support her in the style to which she was accustomed'" (Pessen, 1984, p. 121). Of all the 39 presidents only Nixon, Ford, and Carter, according to Pessen, married beneath themselves.

This is not the place to go into the details of Pessen's rating of each president's social origins; although perhaps differing in some respects, most historians or sociologists would go along with the usefulness and accuracy of his overall model. It is our own view that he has leaned over backwards to be fair in his treatment of the log-cabin myth, by tending to rank a number of presidents lower than we would. Hayes and Cleveland, to take two examples, might very well have been placed in at least the lower-upper class. Hayes's grandfather was known as Rutherford Hayes, Esquire, before he moved from a small Vermont town to Delaware, Ohio, where he built the first brick house in town. Because his father died just before he was born, Hayes was brought up by his mother's brother who, even after the panic of 1830, was "independently wealthy for life," having accumulated a fortune in merchandising and land speculation. Hayes's uncle (whom he called "Father") was also reputed to enjoy "one of the widest circles of influential acquaintances in Ohio." Cleveland, though spending his happy early life as the son of a poor clergyman who held pulpits in various small towns in New Jersey and New York state came not from "poor and commonplace stock," as most superficial biographers have had it but, according to Allan Nevins, "from the truest aristocracy that America can boast…men who made themselves community leaders." And most of these leaders were Puritan clergymen, from his great-great-grandfather, Aaron Cleveland, a graduate of Harvard in 1735 and friend of Franklin, down to his father who graduated from Yale with honors and also trained at the Princeton Theological Seminary. After his father's death when he was but 16, moreover, young Grover went to live with his uncle, who was one of the wealthiest and most eminent men in the thriving young city of Buffalo. Thus, he began the way to eminence at the Buffalo bar with the best social and business connections, not only in Buffalo but in the whole northern part of the state. This brief look at Hayes and Cleveland, in other words, should emphasize that Pessen did not overestimate the number of presidents born to upper-class status (Pessen, 1984, p. 158).

Pessen is certainly not pleased with the fact that a majority of our presidents have been born to privilege. Although no Marxist himself, and in disagreement with "three well-known non-Marxist social scientists who could actually write that 'a person thinks, politically, as he is socially. Social characteristics determine political preference,'" Pessen ends his book with the following sentence:

> A decent respect to the opinion and needs of mankind requires that we seek in the future, as we have not sought in the past, to select candidates of commanding intelligence, learning, and above all patience, wisdom and humanity—traits all that are not necessarily revealed by high social standing and the ideological preferences that typically accompany such standing.

That is indeed a curious ending to this study. A reader would find that on an earlier page Pessen picked out the six most brilliant presidents—John Adams, Jefferson, Madison, J. Q. Adams, Taft, and Wilson—all of whom were bred to the highest levels of privilege; later on he noted, moreover, that the only four presidents who were political philosophers of any stature—John Adams, Jefferson, Madison, and perhaps Wilson—were of upper-class origins; and finally, one does not get the impression that Pessen prefers the "ideological preferences" of Dwight Eisenhower, Richard Nixon, or Ronald Reagan over those of Woodrow Wilson, Franklin Roosevelt, or John Kennedy (Pessen, 1984, p. 183).

Pessen also comes to another interesting conclusion about his book: "Although I have challenged James Bryce's observations that most presidents were men of humble or ordinary beginnings who rose to the nation's highest office primarily because of their own 'merits,'" he writes, "I have no quarrel with his equally famous dictum that few great men have been elected president." We should like to make two points about this statement. First, all of the 39 men who have reached the White House have gotten there by "their own merits;" no man ever got to the White House entirely because of his class origins, and many have gotten there in spite of their class origins, high or low as the case may be. Second, of course, we would have to disagree sharply with both Bryce and Pessen in their judgments as to the quality of our presidents. In this connection, it is revealing that nowhere in Professor Pessen's book does he mention the Schlesinger rankings or any of the other systematic efforts to rank presidential performance in office. But, of course, that was not what he set out to do (Pessen, 1984, p. 149).

All of this suggests that it should be fruitful to systematically compare the Pessen rankings of our presidents by social origins with the Schlesinger and Murray–Blessing rankings of them by accomplishments in office. In the long run, facts and theories in themselves are far less important than the relationships between them. For convenience of analysis, the thirty-six presidents shown in Table 10.2 (W. H. Harrison, Garfield and Reagan were not included, as of 1981, for lack of evidence of performance) may be divided into the fifteen men of upper-class origins and the twenty-one men born of less privileged families. That there is a positive correlation between high accomplishment and high social origins is clearly shown Table 10.1.

There has been, then, not only a high correlation between high social origins and getting to the presidency, as Pessen clearly has shown. Once elected to office, as we have just seen, men of privileged origins have performed far better than those of lower social status. This has been especially the case with the great presidents: of the eight great and near-great presidents, five were born of highly privileged families. On the other hand, men of low social origin have tended to be the least successful presidents. While Lincoln has been ranked number one in all the studies of

Table 10.1 Relationship Between Accomplishments and Social Origins

Accomplishments in Office	Social Class Origins	
	Upper Class	Below Upper Class
Above average	11%–73%	6%–29%
Average and below	4%–27%	15%–71%

accomplishment in office which we have seen, three of the other four men born of simple origins—Fillmore, A. Johnson, and Nixon—were ranked as below average, or as failures by the Murray–Blessing respondents. Fillmore was actually the only president to have been born in a log cabin. His father was a Vermont farmer who went west to Cayuga County, New York, where Millard was born, as he later wrote, "in a log house in the middle of a forest, having no neighbors nearer than four miles." Millard's mother, true to form, "was brought up in comfortable surroundings in Pittsfield, Massachusetts, where her father was a doctor." Although Fillmore had only a fitful formal education in his youth, he married a widely-read school teacher who later built the first library in the White House. Bitter about his grim youth on his father's farm, Millard began to read law at the age of nineteen under a judge in a small town near Buffalo, where he later moved and made a fortune at the bar. Pessen seems hardly to have admired this man of the soil, whose "adult lifestyle consisted of formal dinners, dances, recitals, and hobnobbing with celebrities," and whose political career was devoted "largely to pursuit of the main chance." Fillmore reached the presidency after Zachary Taylor's death at midterm. Both the Schlesinger and Murray–Blessing respondents agreed on ranking him as below average in performance (Pessen, 1984, pp. 87–88).

We have as much, or more, to learn from failure as from success. In this sense the careers of Andrew Johnson and Richard Nixon, both ranked as failures by the Murray–Blessing respondents, are of great interest. Both came of lowly origins and spent parts of their youths in bitter struggles with poverty; both married orphans of equally plebeian origins (Johnson, who had no schooling, was taught by his wife to write). In contrast to Lincoln and Eisenhower, who rose to become insiders, on the surface in Lincoln's case, through judicious marriages and flexible political and personal styles, both Johnson and Nixon resented their early struggles and remained outsiders and loners throughout their political careers, always mistrusting the establishment even after they became relatively affluent and moved in establishment circles.

Although similar in so many ways, both men were rated failures for almost opposite reasons. Thus, Richard Nixon, the first president to be driven from office, was finally defeated because of his inability to tell the truth in the Watergate affair. Johnson, a man of absolute honesty and great courage, was impeached by the Senate, although acquitted by one vote, because, following Lincoln, he fervently believed in the Union (he was the only southern Senator to remain loyal during the Civil War) and stood for sectional reconciliation and constitutional rights as against the vindictive Radical Republicans and predatory northern business interests bent on consolidating their power and wartime gains. His tactless honesty almost caused his downfall. This is the view of those who followed the classic interpretation of Reconstruction and saw it as a "tragic era." Thus, Clinton Rossiter in *The American Presidency* (1956) gave Johnson a near-great ranking, finding him to be a man of "much courage, whose protests against the ravages of the Radicals and Congress were a high rather than a low point in the progress of the presidency" (Rossiter, 1956, p. 106). Both the Schlesinger polls ranked him as average. The failure ranking given him by the Murray–Blessing respondents reflects a Revisionist view of Reconstruction, which came to the fore in the 1960s, and stressed the civil rights aspect of Reconstruction more than their predecessors had done. As Kenneth Stampp, a leading Revisionist historian, wrote in 1969: "What was crucial in the failure of Andrew Johnson was his refusal to demand even minimal civil rights for Negroes and a crystallization of Republican sentiment over this fundamental question" (Stampp, 1969, p. 59). But perhaps it is understandable that Johnson, who rose from "redneck" to slaveholder status in the years before the war, found it hard to change.

In 1949 Arthur Schlesinger, Sr, published an essay in which he outlined how American history had moved in cycles of alternating liberal and conservative periods. His son, following his father's theme, has conceptualized these cycles in terms of alternating emphases on "private interests" and "public purposes" (Schlesinger Jr, 1986, p. 254). It is our view that the ebb and flow of upper-class hegemony in the White House has followed a pattern not entirely unlike the Schlesinger cycles. This may be seen by breaking down the social class and accomplishment rankings of our presidents shown in Table 10.2 into four periods: (1) The Age of Aristocracy 1789–1850; (2) Middle Class Ascendancy 1851–1901; (3) WASP Hegemony 1901–1953; and (4) Ethnic Democracy 1953–1981.

During the first sixty years of the American presidency, the Age of Aristocracy, men of patrician or aristocratic background held office for all but twelve years. The stereotypical exception, Andrew Jackson, who held office for eight of those twelve years, was actually a frontier aristocrat

Table 10.2 Murray-Blessing's Ranking of Presidential Performance Related to Pessen's Ranking of Social-Class Origins

		UPPER CLASS	UPPER MIDDLE CLASS	MIDDLE AND LOWER CLASS
GREAT				
1.	Lincoln			Middle
2.	F. Roosevelt	Upper-Upper		
3.	Washington	Upper-Upper		
4.	Jefferson	Upper-Upper		
NEAR GREAT				
5.	T. Roosevelt	Upper-Upper		
6.	Wilson	Lower-Upper		
7.	Jackson		Upper-Middle	
8.	Truman		L. Upper/U.Middle	
ABOVE AVERAGE				
9.	J. Adams	Lower-Upper		
10.	L. Johnson		Upper-Middle	
11.	Eisenhower			Middle
12.	Polk	Middle-Upper		
13.	Kennedy	Middle-Upper		
14.	Madison	Upper-Upper		
15.	Monroe	Lower-Upper		
16.	J. Q. Adams	Upper-Upper		
17.	Cleveland	Upper-Upper		
AVERAGE				
18.	McKinley		Upper-Middle	
19.	Taft	Upper-Upper		
20.	Van Buren		Upper-Middle	
21.	Hoover		Upper-Middle	
22.	Hayes		L.Upper/U.Middle	
23.	Arthur		Upper-Middle	
24.	Ford		Upper-Middle	
25.	Carter		Upper-Middle	
26.	B. Harrison	Upper-Upper		
BELOW AVERGE				
27.	Taylor	Upper-Upper		
28.	Tyler	Upper-Upper		
29.	Fillmore			L.Middle
30.	Coolidge		L.Upper/U.Middle	
31.	Pierce		L.Upper/U.Middle	
FAILURE				
32.	A. Johnson			U.Lower
33.	Buchanan		Upper Middle	
34.	Nixon			L.Middle
35.	Grant		Upper Middle	
36.	Harding		L.Upper/U.Middle	

who inherited land and a substantial sum of money at an early age, was educated at a local Latin academy, and read the Declaration of Independence to thirty or forty adult neighbors when he was only eleven years of age. And Martin Van Buren, Jackson's handpicked successor in the White House, had a long established and upper-middle-class standing in Kinderhook, New York. In short, leaving Jackson and Van Buren as Pessen ranked them, 83% of the presidents in this aristocratic period originated in the upper classes and 73% were rated above average by the Murray–Blessing respondents.

The period of aristocratic presidential leadership came to an end with the death of Zachary Taylor in 1850, and we entered the period of Middle Class Ascendancy. For the next half-century, from Fillmore through McKinley, only Abraham Lincoln and Grover Cleveland were above average in performance; Fillmore and Pierce were below average and Buchanan was a failure. After the Lincoln presidency, Johnson and Grant were failures, while Hayes, Arthur, Harrison, and McKinley were only average. This period was not only the lowest of the four in performance, but also the lowest in social origins: only Harrison was a born aristocrat, and four men, including Lincoln, were born to middle- or lower-class families. Except for Lincoln's wartime presidency, moreover, in Arthur M. Schlesinger Jr's terms, "private interests" predominated over "public purpose," these private interests being the selfish slave-holding interests during the fifties and the selfish business interests from the times of Grant through McKinley. Small wonder Bryce held a low view of the presidency when he wrote *The American Commonwealth* during the 1880s.

After McKinley's assassination, Theodore Roosevelt came to power, beginning the third cycle of leadership, the period of WASP Hegemony. A Harvard man of impeccable patrician background, Roosevelt was extremely proud of, and self-conscious about, his class position and was determined to justify it by attaining leadership not only in government but also in molding the attitudes and values of the country as a whole; probably no president before or since has so dominated the imagination of the nation.

Following Roosevelt, Taft, who graduated second in his class at Yale, was a great and brilliant man from one of America's finest families whose members have been leaders in education, in religion, and in law and politics for several generations. Taft was only an average president; he was far more at home on the United States Supreme Court.

The next president during this period, Woodrow Wilson, a keen student of political science and history, was surely one of the best prepared men for the office, and he was one of our greatest presidents, even though the Murray–Blessing respondents demoted him to near-great status.

If the first two decades of our presidency, under Washington, Adams, and Jefferson, were the greatest in our history, these two decades after 1901, when T. Roosevelt, Taft, and Wilson were in office, were surely the second greatest. After the "private interest" Twenties when Harding (Failure), Coolidge (Below Average), and Hoover (Average) were in office, the presidency went through a third great twenty-year period under Franklin Roosevelt and Harry Truman. And "public purpose" surely dominated over "private interest" under the patrician leadership of the two Roosevelts and Taft, as well as under Wilson and Truman, both from only slightly less privileged backgrounds. Perhaps this high quality of performance and emphasis on public service has been partly due to the fact that our best aristocratic traditions have stressed doing a better job rather than the prevalent, middle-class ideology which has always stressed getting a better job.

The period since Truman's presidency, characterized by Ethnic Democracy, has come full circle since the 1850s. Just as the issues of slavery and the civil rights of Negroes greatly influenced politics in the thirty years after 1850, so the issue of civil rights for blacks became a major political issue during this fourth period, especially after May 1954 when the Supreme Court unanimously decided that public schools must be desegregated in *Brown v. Board of Education*. While the presidents after 1953 have been of higher caliber than their predecessors following 1850, their performances in office, as we have just seen, have been above average but flawed by unmanageable obstacles in the end, especially since Kennedy's assassination.

In social origins, the presidents during these two periods were much alike: Kennedy matched Harrison in privileged origin if not in lineage; Lincoln, though certainly superior to all presidents, was much like Eisenhower in origin and success in office; and of course, Nixon and Andrew Johnson were much alike in both origin and achievement. Finally, and most important of all, this last period is the only one of the four in which no great president occupied the Oval Office. Since

Kennedy's tragic assassination, this may be due partly to the anti-elitist ideology which was born in the middle Sixties and still dominates conventional wisdom today.

In 1938, for example, when we were a poor but proud and hopeful country under the leadership of Franklin Roosevelt, Mrs. Robert Alonzo Taft made a statement to the mineworkers of Ohio which the political pundits branded as political suicide. "My husband is not a simple man," she said during the senatorial race that year. "He did not start from humble beginnings. My husband is a very brilliant man. He had a fine education at Yale. He has been well trained for his job. Isn't that what you prefer when you pick leaders to work for you?" Taft won (Hess, 1966, p. 335).

Today the TV pundits would brand such a statement as suicidal nonsense with far more venom than their professional antecedents of New Deal days. But let us not forget that in that hopeful era, the administration was dominated by such "preppies," as they would be derisively called today, as Franklin D. Roosevelt, John G. Winant, who was chairman of the first Social Security Board, William C. Bullitt, our first ambassador to the Soviet Union, Attorney General Francis Biddle, and many others like them. But in every age, as this article suggests, the "truth" has a hard time when it runs counter to conventional wisdom.

In spite of, or maybe because of, the low moral tone of the election of 2016, our findings would suggest that the anti-elitist, conventional wisdom of our day may run counter to the traditional wisdom of our ancestors who repeatedly, although not unerringly, sought out the best men for the presidency, regardless of their social origins. We would do well to continue to build on our best democratic traditions by choosing the most talented available men and women to represent us in high positions of moral and political leadership, regardless of their class, religious, ethnic, or racial origins.

Some among these may be, like Louis Brandeis, John F. Kennedy, and Martin Luther King, Jr, before them, born into families which have already achieved high social standing, if not nationally, then at least in their own local, ethnic, or minority communities. Such privileged backgrounds of high social standing, however, should not stand in the way of our choosing them as leaders if they are among our "best and brightest" citizens. Indeed, the self-made candidates of 2016, make many of the privileged candidates of the past look very inviting today.

11

THE HORATIO ALGER MYTH AND THE SUPREME COURT

If Horatio Alger's "rags to riches" stories are a conservative's democratic daydream, the thought of an American aristocracy may be a liberal's nightmare. There is one American institution, however, where daydream and nightmare have come together to create, in a manner of which Horatio Alger would approve, an aristocracy arising from democratic origins. Thus, Tocqueville wrote,

> If I were asked where I placed the American aristocracy, I should reply without hesitation that it is not among the rich, who are united by no common tie, but that it occupies the judicial bench and bar. The more we reflect upon all that occurs in the United States, the more we shall be persuaded that the lawyers, as a body, form the most powerful, if not the only, counterpoise to the democratic element... to neutralize the vices inherent in popular government.
> (Tocqueville, 1945, p. 265)

A century later Professor John W. Burgess of Columbia University, the virtual founder of the academic discipline of political science in America, wrote, "I do not hesitate to declare that our form of government is an aristocracy of the robe, which I venture to regard as the best form of aristocracy in the world" (Burgess, 1890, p. 360).

At the top of the aristocracy of the robe are the justices of the United States Supreme Court, who are appointed for life by the president and who are responsible only to their own private and professional consciences. These justices, many of whom lived rags to *robes* stories, are uniquely qualified, as institutionalized aristocrats, to balance the leveling and all too often short-term values of democracy. This delicate balancing of the social forces of aristocracy and democracy lies at the core of our ever changing yet relatively stable political traditions.

As with much else in American life, the gentlemanly and aristocratic traditions of our legal profession originated in England, when in 1756 William Blackstone became the first Vinerian Professor of law at Oxford, and his lectures, revised and published in the 1760s as *Commentaries on the Laws of England*, became the most widely read of all Anglo-American law texts, before or since his day. "One of the delightful ironies of American history," Daniel J. Boorstin once wrote,

> ... is that a snobbish Tory barrister, who had polished his periods to suit the taste of young Oxford gentlemen, became the mentor of Abe Lincoln and thousands like him. By making legal ideas and legal jargon accessible to the backwoods, Blackstone did much to prepare self-made men for leadership in the New World.
> (Boorstin, 1958, p. 202)

Lawyers, of both haughty and humble origins, have played major roles in the history of American political leadership: thus twenty-five of the fifty-six signers of the Declaration of Independence were lawyers, as were thirty-one of the fifty-five members of the Constitutional Convention; in the first Congress, ten of the twenty-nine senators and seventeen of the sixty-five Representatives were trained in the law. While George Washington, Andrew Jackson, and Theodore Roosevelt were amateur and voluntary military heroes before entering the presidency, and William Henry Harrison, Zachary Taylor, Ulysses S. Grant, and Dwight Eisenhower were professional soldiers, twenty-four of the remaining twenty-nine presidents (John Adams through Nixon) were trained in the law (Jackson had been a lawyer and a judge as well as a military hero).

Nomination to the Supreme Court by the President of the United States, with the advice and consent of the Senate, is the highest honor available to the members of the American legal profession. The history of the political and personal relationships between the presidents and the justices is a fascinating one. A few days after John Marshall's death in 1835, John Quincy Adams wrote in his diary of his father's appointment of Marshall to the Chief Justiceship of the Supreme Court as follows:

> It was the last act of my father's administration, and one of the most important services rendered by him to his country…the office of Chief Justice is a station of the highest trust, of the deepest responsibility, and of influence far more extensive than that of the President of the United States.…Marshall cemented the Union which the crafty and quixotic democracy of Jefferson had a perpetual tendency to dissolve. Jefferson hated and dreaded him.
> (Warren, 1923, p. 276)

While all Federalists were pleased with Adams' appointment of Marshall, President Dwight Eisenhower and most conservative Republicans considered his appointments of Chief Justice Earl Warren and Associate Justice William J. Brennan, Jr, to the court a disaster. And of course, the Bork affair during the Reagan presidency and the recent resignation of Justice Brennan from the court, followed by President George H. W. Bush's nomination of Judge David Souter, of New Hampshire, to replace him, make this subject of timely interest.

This essay will show how the social class origins of the first ninety-six justices appointed to the Supreme Court (1789–1969) were related to their levels of performance on the bench. At the same time a comparison will be made between the justices and the presidents on the dimensions of class and performance. Offhand, one would expect the appointed and aloof aristocrats of the robe to have originated in more privileged families than the presidents who are elected by the people. After all, the Horatio Alger myth has always applied to the presidents rather than the justices who meet behind closed doors and are hardly known by the common man, who has no say in their appointments. John A. Schmidhauser, a student of the Supreme Court, once wrote,

> The political variation on the Horatio Alger theme—any boy, but preferably one of humble origins, might become President—has

long been one of the most satisfying of the myths of American political recruitment. This myth has been applied to national legislative and to other national executive offices. But it is hardly likely that many young men of humble origin have lost sleep contemplating their prospects for attaining a seat on the Supreme Court of the United States. Our highest judicial institution has always been veiled, in the public mind, in an aura of inaccessibility. (Schmidhauser, 1979, p. 41)

It seems that reality is much more complicated than myths or social and political theory. The chapter "Class and Authority in the Oval Office" shows that contrary to the "Log Cabin Myth," all but a handful of our presidents have come from upper or upper-middle class backgrounds. Perhaps more surprising, and certainly more irritating to egalitarian political theorists, we showed that presidents born with silver spoons in their mouths had far more distinguished careers in the Oval Office than did those of less advantaged backgrounds—Lincoln being the mythical exception proving the rule. This was shown by a comparison of the social class origins of the presidents, as set forth in Edward Pessen's 1984 book, *The Log Cabin Myth*, with two classic studies of presidential performance in office, in 1948 and again in 1962, by Arthur M. Schlesinger, Sr and especially with the 1981 study undertaken in 1981 by Robert K. Murray and Tim H. Blessing of Pennsylvania State University, which asked 846 professors of American history to rank the thirty-six presidents from Washington through Nixon.

Contrary to conventional thinking, the Horatio Alger story has been far more applicable to the appointed members of the aloof Supreme Court than to the popularly elected presidents. Although several rankings of the greatest Supreme Court justices have been made, only one study has systematically ranked, in the style of the Schlesinger and Murray-Blessing rankings of the presidents, all the justices in the history of the court up to 1990. In June 1970, Albert P. Blaustein of Rutgers University and Roy M. Mersky of the University of Texas asked a panel of sixty-five law school deans and professors of law, history, and political science to evaluate the performances of the first ninety-six justices, placing them within the categories of "great," "near-great," "average," "below average," and "failure."

Up to now there has been no systematic effort to identify the Supreme Court justices by their social-class origins as had been done with the presidents. Rating a person by social class origins is a difficult thing to do in an open-class society like ours. The difficulty is compounded in the case of many great men who so often derive their drive to success from their mothers, who are frequently their husbands' superiors in social class origins, and in moral and intellectual stature. For example, Pessen ranked Thomas Jefferson of upper-class origin, while many experts on the history of the Supreme Court have referred to John Marshall, who was born in an authentic log cabin on the Virginia frontier, as a self-made man. A glibly liberal professor at the Yale Law School, Fred Rodell, wrote in his history of the Supreme Court published in 1955 that Marshall's extremely conservative views were due to the fact that he "identified himself completely with the class to which he had climbed" (Rodell, 1955, p. 104).

But Jefferson, who belonged to the class into which Marshall supposedly "climbed," was Marshall's bitter political enemy. "The Republicans," Marshall once remarked, "are divided into speculative theorists and absolute terrorists. With the latter I am disposed to class Mr. Jefferson" (Rodell, 1955, p. 71). Actually, these famous political enemies were surprisingly similar in social origins. Through their mothers, both were descended from William Randolph and Mary Isham, both of British gentry stock and founders of one of the leading First Families of Virginia. At the same time, both men's fathers were of ordinary origins but leaders of their respective county communities, which they represented in the House of Burgesses, in Williamsburg. Both Marshall and Jefferson, like their fathers, married well, as great leaders have done for many centuries before them and since. So, we ranked them as of upper-class origins.

Marshall's father, Thomas—as schoolmate, professional surveying associate, and comrade-in-arms, from Valley Forge through Yorktown, of George Washington—had a far more distinguished career than Jefferson's father, Peter. Professor Julien Boyd once described these two kinsmen and political enemies felicitously as follows:

> Both were Virginians. Both had been born within the frontier, though far enough on the outskirts of settlement to feel the challenging winds from the vast wilderness to the westward.

> Both stemmed from the distant and progenitive Randolph, deriving from him a consanguinity that neither exhibited in outward expression. Both grew up in the same kind of sturdy, self-reliant home environment, each possessing at its head a stalwart, intelligent, respected leader of the county. Both had been bred to the law under the noble teacher, George Wythe, though his tutelage of Marshall was but a brief and tenuous relationship and that of Jefferson a profound and transforming influence. Both had eagerly embraced the principles of the Revolution and had served the American cause well, the one distinguishing himself in the field and the other in legislation. Yet out of this remarkable identity of background came one of the mighty opposites of American history. The explanation of this divergence arising from similarity is as baffling as the explanation of genius.
>
> (Boyd, 1950, pp. 243–247)

Yet, of course, genius above all is hardly ever explained by background and the two men were almost entire opposites in temperament: Marshall a humorous and gregarious lover of men of all kinds and conditions, Jefferson a humorless and lonely lover of mankind. Perhaps it is not entirely irrelevant to note here the little-known fact that the aristocratic beauty Rebecca Burwell, the one great passion of Jefferson's youth, jilted him to marry Jacquelin Ambler. The Amblers were one of the wealthiest families in the little village of Yorktown, when young Captain John Marshall first visited the battle site and met, and later married Rebecca's beautiful daughter, Mary. Both Marshall and Jefferson, like their fathers, married well, as great leaders of men had done for many centuries before them, and since. And so, we have ranked John Marshall as of upper-class origins.

Here we should note that, for purposes of this study, men ranked in both the upper (U) and the upper-middle (UM) classes are considered to be of *privileged* origins. On the other hand, the middle and lower (ML) ranking is an inclusive category of all those of *unprivileged* (but not necessarily underprivileged) backgrounds. About half (eighteen) of the thirty-two justices of ML ratings came from solid middle-class farming or small-town families, such as Justice Frank Murphy's. This pro-New Deal justice was born, in 1890, in a small farming community on the Michigan shore of Lake Huron. His biographer, J. Woodford Howard, Jr, writes of his origins in the American social class hierarchy as follows:

> Murphy's father was a country lawyer. Despite financial problems which seemed endless, he was able to educate his children beyond average expectations… Frank Murphy came from small town, middle-class and politically alert America. In class and values, he was indistinguishable from thousands of his generation.
> (Howard, 1968, p. 3)

While eighteen of the justices in this ML category had backgrounds similar to Frank Murphy's, the other fourteen justices were less privileged, ranging from the sons of poor farmers and lower-status small-town residents to the two most-deprived future justices, Abe Fortas and Thurgood Marshall. Fortas, the son of immigrant Orthodox Jews, grew up in the ghetto of Memphis, Tennessee. Although his father, a cabinetmaker, taught himself English, his mother died illiterate. Marshall grew up in a black ghetto in Baltimore. His father was a servant at the snobbish Gibson Island Club, and his mother taught at an all-black elementary school.

One further point of clarification: for comparative convenience we have included both "average" and "above average" presidents, as used by Schlesinger and Murray-Blessing, within the single category of "average" in the following table, where the social origins of both presidents and justices are divided into upper (U), UM, and ML class levels, and their performance ratings into great and near-great (G/NG), average (AVG), and below average and failure (BA/F).

The comparison of the social class origins of the presidents and justices in Figure 11.1 was immediately revealing, and at first surprising, to us and perhaps to many of our readers. Few good American democrats, especially hard-edge liberals, would expect that the Horatio Alger myth has been far more applicable to the aristocrats of the robe than to the popularly elected presidents. Yet the justices were more than twice as likely as the presidents to have originated in the ML origins (justices 33%, presidents 14%). Not only were the justices less privileged than the presidents, they were, at the same time, slightly more likely to have distinguished performance records (G/NG performance: justices 28%, presidents 22%) and definitely less likely to have poor performance records (BA/F performance: justices 15%, presidents 28%).

The performance differences by social class origins between the presidents and the justices are strikingly revealed in a quantitative comparison of the social origins of the great and near-great presidents (8) and justices (27), which we have listed below in Figure 11.2, by name, term in office, and social origins (U, UM, ML).

A quantitative comparison of the class origins of these great and near-great presidents and justices shows that five of the eight presidents (63%) as against only nine of the twenty-seven justices (33%) were of upper-class origins. Of even more importance to our Horatio Alger thesis is that while only one of the eight (12%) presidents, Lincoln, was born to an unprivileged family, thirteen (48%), or a clear plurality, of the twenty-seven justices were born to unprivileged families.

It is now time to ask ourselves why privileged origins are so much more important in determining high performance in the White House than on the Supreme Court. Moreover, how do we account for the fact that the justices of middle or lower-class origins have much higher performance ratings than the presidents of similar origins? Perhaps presidential performance depends to a greater extent on the subtleties of upper-class habits of authority, whereas professional competence and superior intelligence

Social Class Origins and Performance in Office

	Social Class Origins				Performance in Office		
	Pres.	Just.	C.J.*		Pres.	Just.	C.J.*
U	(15) 42%	(29) 31%	(8) 57%	G/NG	(8) 22%	(27) 28%	(8) 57%
UM	(16) 44%	(35) 36%	(2) 14%	AVG	(18) 50%	(55) 57%	(5) 36%
ML	(5) 14%	(32) 33%	(4) 29%	BA/F	(10) 28%	(14) 15%	(1) 7%
	(36) 100%	(96) 100%	(14) 100%		(36) 100%	(96) 100%	(14) 100%

* The Chief Justices will be discussed below and should be ignored until then.

Figure 11.1 Presidents, Justices, and Chief Justices

Great				Near Great		
			Presidents			
ABRAHAM LINCOLN	1861-1865	ML		THEODORE ROOSEVELT	1901-1909	U
FRANKLIN ROOSEVELT	1933-1945	U		WOODROW WILSON	1913-1921	U
GEORGE WASHINGTON	1789-1797	U		ANDREW JACKSON	1829-1837	UM
THOMAS JEFFERSON	1801-1809	U		HARRY TRUMAN	1945-1953	UM
			Justices			
*JOHN MARSHALL	1801-1835	U		WILLIAM JOHNSON	1804-1834	UM
JOSEPH STORY	1811-1845	U		BENJAMIN R. CURTIS	1851-1870	UM
*ROGER B. TANEY	1836-1864	U		SAMUEL F. MILLER	1862-1890	ML
JOHN M. HARLAN	1877-1911	U		STEPHEN J. FIELD	1863-1897	UM
OLIVER W. HOLMES	1902-1932	U		JOSEPH P. BRADLEY	1870-1892	ML
CHARLES E. HUGHES	1910-1916	ML		*MORRISON R. WAITE	1874-1888	U
*	1930-1941			EDWARD D. WHITE	1894-1910	U
LOUIS D. BRANDEIS	1916-1939	UM		*	1910-1921	
HARLAN F. STONE	1925-1941	ML		*WILLIAM H. TAFT	1921-1930	U
*	1941-1946			GEORGE SUTHERLAND	1922-1938	ML
BENJAMIN N. CARDOZO	1932-1938	UM		WILLIAM O. DOUGLAS	1939-1975	ML
HUGO L. BLACK	1937-1971	ML		ROBERT H. JACKSON	1941-1954	ML
FELIX FRANKFURTER	1938-1962	ML		WILEY B. RUTLEDGE	1943-1949	ML
*EARL WARREN	1953-1969	ML		JOHN M. HARLAN II	1955-1971	U
				WM. J. BRENNAN, JR	1956-1990	ML

*Connotes service as Chief Justice. J. Marshall, Taney, Waite, Taft, and Warren were appointed directly; White, Hughes, and Stone had previously sat as Associate Justices.

Figure 11.2 Great and Near-Great Presidents and Justices

are more essential for Supreme Court performance. Thus, thirty-one or more than one-third of the justices (35%), as opposed to only four (J. Q. Adams, Arthur, T. Roosevelt, and Taft), or about a tenth (11%) of the presidents, were members of Phi Beta Kappa in college. Further clues to this difference may be suggested by a look at the class origins of the eight great and near-great chief justices, whose professional competence must be augmented with the subtle qualities of leadership apparently possessed also by upper-class presidents. Thus five (63%) of the eight most distinguished chief justices were of upper-class origins, exactly the same proportion as among the eight most distinguished presidents.

Turning to the fourteen Chief Justices of the Supreme Court we see immediately, in Figure 11.1 above, that these few aristocrats of the robe were both more likely to come of upper-class backgrounds and have high performance ratings than either the thirty-six presidents or the whole group of ninety-six justices: upper-class origins of presidents 42%, justices 32%, and chief justices 57%; great and near-great performance of presidents 22%, justices 28% and chief justices 57%.

The history of the court has most often been looked at in terms of the chief justice's name, the Marshall, Taney, Hughes, or Warren courts for instance. In this study, the history will be discussed in terms of the four distinct historical periods described in Chapter 10 "Social Class and the Oval Office":

1 The Age of Aristocracy (1789–1850).
2 Middle Class Ascendancy (1850–1901).
3 WASP Hegemony (1901–1953).
4 Ethnic Democracy (1953–1981).

In terms of both social origins and levels of performance, these four periods were distinctive and different. Of the twelve presidents of the *Age of Aristocracy*, ten were of upper-class origins (William H. Harrison, who died in the first year in office, was not rated), while of the eleven who were rated, three—Washington, Jefferson, and Jackson—were rated great or near-great. During the years of *Middle Class Ascendancy* mediocrity was the rule; only Benjamin Harrison was upper-class born, and only Lincoln was distinguished in office (James A. Garfield, who was assassinated, was not rated).

Contrary to conventional wisdom and the views of some scholars, the half century of *WASP Hegemony* produced more distinguished presidents than any other. Of eight presidents, the two Roosevelts, William H. Taft, and Woodrow Wilson were all born to upper-class privileges, and Theodore Roosevelt, Wilson, and Harry Truman had near-great ratings while Franklin Roosevelt was ranked by the Murray-Blessing respondents as second only to Lincoln. Finally, as might be expected in our age of mediocrity, the era of Ethnic Democracy produced only one president, John F. Kennedy, of privileged origins and none of great or near-great stature.

The chief justices in each of these four periods are listed as follows in Figure 11.3, by name, dates, and number of years of service, class origins, performance rankings, and appointing presidents. As far as the Supreme Court is concerned, the *Age of Aristocracy* must be divided into two

AGE OF ARISTOCRACY (1789–1850)

John Jay	1789–1795	6	Upper	Average	Washington
John Rutledge	1795	1	Upper	Average	Washington
Oliver Ellsworth	1796–1799	3	Upper	Average	Washington
John Marshall	1801–1835	34	Upper	Great	John Adams
Roger B. Taney	1836–1864	28	Upper	Great	Jackson

MIDDLE CLASS ASCENDENCY (1850–1901)

Salmon Chase	1864–1873	11	U.Middle	Average	Lincoln
Morrison Waite	1874–1888	14	Upper	N. Great	Grant
Melville Fuller	1888–1910	22	U.Middle	Average	Cleveland

WASP HEGEMONY (1901–1953)

Edward D. White	1910–1921	11	Upper	N. Great	Taft
William H. Taft	1921–1930	9	Upper	N. Great	Harding
Charles E. Hughes	1930–1941	11	Mid/Lower	Great	Hoover
Harlan F. Stone	1941–1946	5	Mid/Lower	Great	F. Roosevelt
Fred M. Vinson	1946–1953	7	Mid/Lower	Failure	Truman

ETHNIC DEMOCRACY (1953–1980)

Earl Warren	1953–1969	16	Mid/Lower	Great	Eisenhower

Figure 11.3 Chief Justices of the Supreme Court in Four Historical Periods

parts—before and after John Marshall. The first three chief justices, Jay, Rutledge, and Ellsworth, were great aristocrats and great patriots who played major roles in the founding of the Republic. Their "average" performance ratings were largely due to the lack of the court's importance in that first, Federalist-dominated decade.

John Marshall, whose idol was George Washington, was the Father of the Supreme Court, which he dominated for thirty-four years, longer than any other chief justice. Liberty and freedom, Marshall was convinced, rested on the unfettered rights of private property rather than on democracy or equality; he despised the "leveling Jeffersonians." In many ways Marshall's Hamiltonian and Federalist views influenced the Supreme Court down to the Hughes Court, which finally, and wisely, compromised with the New Deal modifications of private property rights, which, in turn, began the era of leveling democracy that is still with us. As Holmes said so well: "Time has been on Marshall's side... the theory for which Hamilton argued, and he decided, and Webster spoke, and Grant fought, and Lincoln died, is now our corner-stone" (Holmes, 1989, p. 385). Both Marshall and Holmes were, in their very different ways, consummate aristocrats and undisputedly the two greatest justices in the court's history.

Marshall's successor, Roger Brooke Taney, was born and raised among the Catholic, planter aristocracy of Maryland. As a second son, he turned to the law. Nominated by Andrew Jackson, he served as chief justice longer than anyone except Marshall. Unfortunately, his name has forever been associated with the infamous Dred Scott decision (*Scott v. Sandford* 1857), which many in the North claimed brought on the Civil War. When he died at the age of 87, in 1864, he was scorned by the war-frenzied masses as well as the famous abolitionist senator, Charles Sumner. Taney's reputation improved during and after the 1930s and he was rightly rated "great" by the Blaustein–Mersky respondents.

All three chief justices of the period of *Middle Class Ascendancy* were born in New England and made their legal and political careers in the Middle West. All were raised in privileged circumstances. Salmon Chase, though born the son of a small-town tavern-keeper in New Hampshire, came of a well-connected family, one uncle being a U.S. Senator from Vermont and another, Philander Chase, the Episcopalian Bishop of Ohio, who raised young Salmon after his father died when he was nine. Hence Chase is rated of upper-middle class origins. Morrison R. Waite, son of a Chief Justice of Connecticut and a graduate of Yale, went west to Toledo, Ohio, where he became a leading member of the bar and a solid private citizen. Virtually unknown outside of Ohio when Grant nominated him, Waite turned out to be a very hard-working and respected chief justice, writing almost a thousand opinions during his fourteen years in office. Finally, Melville W. Fuller was born of an established upper-middle class family in Augusta, Maine. He graduated from Bowdoin, spent one year at the Harvard Law School, and began practice at the Augusta bar. After an unhappy love affair, he went west to Chicago where he married a prominent bank president's daughter, built a solid and lucrative law practice, and made wise investments, especially in real estate. Fuller was regarded as a God-fearing (Episcopalian) private citizen of little public renown in either Chicago or the state. He was virtually unknown politically when Cleveland finally picked him over several famous candidates. A dedicated

Social Darwinist, Fuller presided over a conservative court at the height of the age of enterprise. Holmes, who first sat on the Fuller Court, considered him somewhat of a judicial lightweight, and he deserved no better than an average rating.

The period of *WASP Hegemony* produced more distinguished presidents and Chief Justices of the Supreme Court than any other period in American history. The first two chief justices of this period, Edward D. White and William H. Taft, were upper-class patricians of near-great accomplishment on the bench. White's father had been a sugar planter, lawyer, and Governor of Louisiana; Taft's father, born on a Vermont farm, founded Cincinnati's undisputed First Family. Taft, a Unitarian, nominated White, a Catholic, for the chief justiceship. Taft, a great man from one of America's great families, was only an average president, but a near-great chief justice. Notably, Taft was responsible for the erection of the present imposing Supreme Court building in Washington.

All chief justices before Charles Evans Hughes were born of privileged families; Hughes and his successor Harlan Stone were of middle-class origins. Hughes had a rigidly religious upbringing. His father was a Welsh Methodist minister who immigrated to America after reading Benjamin Franklin's *Autobiography*, became a Baptist partly because of his pious, schoolteacher wife, and held several parishes in New York state. Young Hughes went to Brown University on a scholarship, where he was a great social and academic success, serving as president of one of the most prestigious fraternities at Brown and other New England colleges, as well as being elected to Phi Beta Kappa. After attending Columbia Law and passing his New York bar examinations with an unmatched 99.5 score, he became a successful Wall Street lawyer and Governor of New York before his first appointment to the court by Taft, in 1910. He resigned from the Court in 1916 to run unsuccessfully for president against Wilson, narrowly losing in the Electoral College by 4,000 votes in California. During the twenties, he made some $400,000 a year as a Wall Street lawyer (a huge sum for that time) before being nominated for the chief justiceship by Hoover, in 1930.

Harlan Stone came from a solid farming family in New Hampshire which eventually bought a farm outside Amherst, Massachusetts, in order to raise their son in a more intellectual atmosphere. Stone graduated from

Amherst—president of his class, Phi Beta Kappa, and right guard on one of the college's famous football teams. He was a successful Wall Street lawyer and Dean of Columbia Law School before being appointed to the Supreme Court by his college friend, Calvin Coolidge. Franklin Roosevelt elevated him to the chief justiceship during the war as a gesture towards bipartisanship; Stone was the only Republican on the Court. Stone had been a great associate justice, dissenting along with Oliver Wendell Holmes and Louis B. Brandeis and then with Benjamin N. Cardozo and Felix Frankfurter, but he was not a great chief justice. It was said that whereas Hughes would guide his Court to a decision in four hours, it would take four days for the Stone Court to accomplish the same thing.

Frederick M. Vinson and Earl Warren were both of lower-middle-class origins. Vinson, the son of the county jailor in a small hill town in Kentucky, was a mathematical wizard and a very good athlete, both talents helping him through Centre College where he graduated first in his class, and then obtained an LLB at its law school. As a statistically-minded lawyer he became a valuable bureaucrat under Roosevelt and Truman. He had fought along with Truman for Roosevelt's notorious court-packing plan in 1937. As president, Truman appointed Vinson as Secretary of the Treasury, in 1945, and nominated him for the chief justiceship the next year. Vinson was a fine public servant but a poor chief justice. Harry Truman, in fact, made the worst set of appointments in the history of the Supreme Court: Vinson, Harold H. Burton, and Sherman Minton were all failures and Tom Clark was barely average.

Earl Warren's is truly one of the great Horatio Alger stories in American history. His father emigrated from Norway to Minneapolis; after marriage to a Swedish girl, he moved to Los Angeles where he was a repairman on the Southern Pacific Railroad when Earl was born. When young Earl once asked his father why he had no middle name (which had produced a minor passport crisis) the answer was: "Son, when you were born, we were too poor to enjoy any luxury of that kind" (Weaver, 1967, p. 20). Earl Warren was a man of high moral character rather than intellectual or legal brilliance. He tenaciously worked his way through the University of California, at Berkeley, earning AB and JD degrees there. He then went on to serve as a local district attorney and attorney general of the State of California before becoming the state's first three-time Governor.

Warren was a solid but liberal Republican when Eisenhower nominated him for the chief justiceship. Just as Taney will forever be remembered for the infamous *Dred Scott* decision, so will Warren forever be remembered for engineering the unanimous vote in the *Brown v. Board of Education* case in 1954, which declared that separate schools for whites and blacks were inherently unequal. John Marshall was a dedicated anti-leveler, Earl Warren was a dedicated leveler, and Charles Evans Hughes was the diplomatic bridge-builder between the two philosophical positions; all three were great Americans and rank as the greatest chief justices.

How then does the Horatio Alger myth apply to all ninety-six of the Supreme Court justices? The proportion of justices of middle- and lower-class origins in each period is as follows:

Age of Aristocracy	5 of 31 or 16%
Middle Class Ascendancy	6 of 26 or 23%
WASP Hegemony	14 of 30 or 47%
Ethnic Democracy	7 of 9 or 78%
Total	32 of 96 or 33%

These figures show that the chances of bright, ambitious youths from the farms and small towns of America to become members of the bar and to being appointed to the Supreme Court have steadily increased in each of the four periods. Increasing opportunity for upward mobility in the legal profession in the twentieth century has been largely due to the growth of law schools, both the more ancient and prestigious such as Harvard, Yale, and Columbia as well as the lesser known schools, and especially the urban night law schools which made legal careers available to the lower levels of society.

Justice Joseph Story, Marshall's philosophical right-hand man, has often been called "the American Blackstone." In 1828, while still on the Court (which then sat for only brief periods) he was appointed to the Dane Professorship of Law at Harvard where he produced "a profound revolution in legal education," and became the father of the Harvard Law School, which has been, in many ways, America's leading elite-producing institution.

Oliver Wendell Holmes was the first justice to hold a modern university law degree when he came to the Supreme Court in 1902 (LLB,

Harvard 1869); and it was not until Charles Evans Whittaker, a poor farmer's son who earned his LLB at the night school of the University of Kansas City, replaced Stanley F. Reed on the Court in 1957, that all nine of its members had formal law school degrees.

While Reed, who had attended both the Columbia and University of Virginia Law Schools without taking a degree, had been securely bred to privilege, Whittaker's story was classic Horatio Alger. Born on a farm near Troy, Kansas, he trapped animals and sold their hides to help make family ends meet; his schooling was meager and he finally had to quit high school, after which he stepped up his trapping to save money for a legal education. In 1920, he attempted to enroll in the night program at the Kansas City Law School. At first, he was turned down due to not having a high school diploma but his persistence won out and he received an LLB there in 1924, having previously passed the bar examination in 1923. All through law school he worked a full day at a law firm which he joined upon graduation, became a partner in 1930, and went on to great success as a corporate lawyer and senior partner in his own firm. Appointed to the court by Eisenhower in 1957, he only served until 1962; this short length of service and the fact that he took a rather conservative position on civil liberties probably had a lot to do with his ranking as a failure by the Blaustein–Mersky respondents.

In our age of ethnic diversity, it is important to point out that not only has the Court given increasing opportunities to those of lower and middle-class backgrounds but, unlike the presidency, it has been accessible to religious minorities almost from its beginning. Five Catholics were appointed in the period before the Second World War—among them Joseph McKenna, the son of an Irish Catholic immigrant (1898), Pierce Butler, another son of an Irish Immigrant (1922), and Frank Murphy in 1940—and two, Roger B. Taney and Edward D. White, became chief justices long before the First World War, while the first Catholic president, John F. Kennedy, was elected a decade and a half after the Second World War. After the war, Eisenhower, in 1956, nominated as associate justice William J. Brennan, Jr, yet another Irish immigrant's son. This suggests that presidents and senators are less prejudiced than a majority of the electorate.

While there have been no Jewish presidents, five Jews have served on the Court. Wilson appointed Brandeis over bitter opposition in 1916, Hoover appointed Cardozo in 1932, Franklin Roosevelt appointed Frankfurter in 1938, Kennedy appointed Arthur Goldberg in 1962, and Lyndon Johnson appointed Abe Fortas in 1965. After Warren sent a letter to President Johnson in 1968 announcing his desire to resign from the Court, Johnson nominated Fortas as chief justice. The Senate refused to confirm the nomination because of Fortas' involvement in a complicated financial scandal. Fortas, the first justice to do so, resigned in disgrace in 1969.

Not all Catholic and Jewish justices qualify as Horatio Alger figures in terms of social class backgrounds. Brandeis, Cardozo, Taney, and White, were all born into privileged upper or upper-middle-class families. However, given the deep ethnic prejudices in American history, it is worth reiterating that the legal profession as well as the presidents and senators who appoint members of the Court have been less prejudiced than the voters. It is also worth noting that about two-thirds of all the Catholic and Jewish justices were rated as great or near-great.

Franklin D. Roosevelt appointed more justices to the Supreme Court than any other president except George Washington. A brief look at his appointments is, therefore, a fitting conclusion to a study of Horatio Alger and the Supreme Court.

A millionaire by inheritance, with a pronounced Groton and Harvard accent, Roosevelt was a privileged patrician to his fingertips; yet among the eight associate justices he appointed to the court, seven were of middle and lower-class origins. Roosevelt did not have an opportunity to make a Court appointment during his first term, which was marked by a bitter fight with the early Hughes Court. The Court was then dominated by four extreme conservatives, the "Four Horsemen"—Willis Van Devanter, James C. McReynolds, George Sutherland, and Pierce Butler. Three of these justices were ranked as failures by the Blaustein–Mersky panel, among them McReynolds, an anti-Semite who refused to speak with either Brandeis or Cardozo. The first opening on the Court occurred when Van Devanter, after finally losing his bitter battle against the New Deal, resigned in 1937. Often called a "traitor to his class," Roosevelt purposely infuriated his conservative enemies by nominating Hugo Lafayette Black, a fighting, left-wing Senator from Alabama.

When Cardozo died in 1938, Frankfurter was appointed to fill the "Jewish" seat. Born of middle-class Viennese parents, he was brought to

America at the age of twelve and spent his teens on New York's Lower East Side. After graduating with a Phi Beta Kappa key from the City College of New York, he entered the Harvard Law School, in Cambridge, which remained his spiritual home.

William O. Douglas, Roosevelt's next appointment to the Court, was the first-born son of an itinerant Presbyterian preacher in a small town in eastern Oregon. He had polio at the age of five and lost his father a year later. His determined and domineering mother, who called her favorite son "Treasure" during his early years, bravely raised him, and his younger brother and sister, on the wrong side of the Northern Pacific Railroad tracks in Yakima, Oregon. For the rest of his life, Douglas bitterly resented his early poverty and his snobbish schoolmates from the establishment on the other side of the tracks.

James F. Byrnes was also raised in difficult circumstances in a small South Carolina town. His father died before he was born and his doting mother took up dressmaking to earn a living. Byrnes left school at fourteen, but won a shorthand competition and got a job as a court reporter, all the time reading law and passing the state bar examinations by the time he was twenty-four. Finally, Frank Murphy and Harlan Stone, as we have already seen, as well as Robert Jackson and Wiley Rutledge, all grew up in comfortable but undistinguished middle-class families.

After James F. Byrnes resigned in 1942, the membership of the Stone Court was certainly the most brilliant in our history. Seven of the eight associate justices had been ardent New Dealers when appointed by Roosevelt, while Owen J. Roberts, a conservative Republican from Philadelphia, appointed by Hoover, was the critical swing man whose final break with the "Four Horsemen" allowed Chief Justice Hughes to preserve the Court, in 1937, by recognizing that the New Deal's egalitarian opposition to the absolute sacredness of private property was the inevitable wave of the future.

Stone, Black, and Frankfurter were rated among the twelve greatest justices ever to sit on the court, while Douglas, Robert Jackson, and Wiley Rutledge were all of near-great stature. Five of the nine members of the court (Stone, Frankfurter, Douglas, Rutledge, and Roberts) had been law school professors and four (Stone, Frankfurter, Douglas, and Roberts) were elected to Phi Beta Kappa in college.

Black, Frankfurter, and Douglas stayed on the Court right through the Warren era. Black, who had been the intellectual dean of the New Deal Court and a revered member of the Warren Court, was widely recognized as the greatest justice of his era when he resigned in 1971, at the age of eighty-five, after thirty-four years on the Court. Born the son of a redneck Confederate Army veteran, in a tiny cabin in a crossroads town in a red-dirt, cotton-chopping part of the state, Black was an entirely self-made man. With little formal schooling, he managed to earn an LLB from the small new law school at the University of Alabama by the age of twenty. An omnivorous reader, Black educated himself rigorously all his life.

Black, who had joined the Ku Klux Klan for a brief period in his early political career, then rose to become a member of the legal, political, and social establishment of Birmingham, Alabama, marrying a well-born "Society Girl" on the way. He was sent to the U.S. Senate in 1927 where he vigorously opposed the national business establishment whose members bitterly resented his views, but always respected him personally. His soft-spoken Southern manners concealed a steel-trap mind and an iron will; it was said in the Senate that he "spoke with the assurance of a Bourbon and the fiery passion of a populist" (Leahy, 1996, p. 115). Unlike his ideological colleague, William O. Douglas, who alienated everyone close to him, including his four wives, his children, his students at the Yale Law School, his law clerks and his colleagues, Hugo Black was a first rate and mature human being who had a blessed family life and never lost a friend, or the respect of an opponent, over ideological differences. While Black and Douglas belonged to the activist wing of both the New Deal and Warren courts, Frankfurter was the leading advocate of judicial restraint, in the style of his idol Holmes. Whereas Douglas refused to speak to Frankfurter for many years, personal relations were never broken between Black and Frankfurter; in 1957, during a conference, on the spur of the moment, Black passed Frankfurter a note saying, "I strongly hope nothing will happen that causes you to leave the court..." (Dunne, 1977, p. 463).

Hugo Black's Horatio Alger career has always been an inspiration to all who have ever known or heard of him. What better example of the leveling-up character of our Supreme Court as it functions as an open but authoritative aristocracy in the midst of our ever more democratic society? Perhaps, however, not all would agree. Thus, Roy L. Brooks, a law professor at the University of Minnesota, wrote in the *New York Times*,

> From all accounts, our society will become even more diverse as we enter the next century. Whites will be outnumbered by blacks, Hispanics, Asians, and other people of color. As our least democratic governmental institution, the Supreme Court can least afford to be managed by those from elites who have little feel for their social environment.
> (Brooks, 1990, p. 21)

Professor Brooks' concern may yet be unfounded. Given the Court's history, there is every reason to think that future presidents and senators will continue to appoint to the Supreme Court men and women of ever wider class, race, and ethnic origins. Or as Tocqueville wrote of the legal profession, at the top of which stands the Supreme Court: "Lawyers belong to the people by birth and interest, and to the aristocracy by habit and taste; they may be looked upon as the connecting link between the two great classes of society" (Tocqueville, 1945, p. 268).

12

LIFE AND DEATH OF THE PROTESTANT ESTABLISHMENT

At its height in the nineteenth and early twentieth century, the Protestant Establishment, dominated by a group of wealthy and powerful consanguine families of old-stock, white, Anglo-Saxon Protestants, or as they are now generally called, "WASPs," provided the nation with an authoritative core of important and influential leaders. These old-stock WASP families exercised national authority in the presidency, as well as the cabinet, in diplomatic circles, and in other governmental jobs. They took the lead in legal and juridical roles, and as heads of important corporations, banks, investment houses, and other commercial interests, not to mention churches and colleges throughout America. In short, they set the tone for American political, business, and cultural life. As such, WASPs were less an ethnic group than a high-status group. The Protestant Establishment's power and authority, as well as its social class and status, rather than its ethnicity, were driving forces in American history and contemporary society. Yet it must be said that the Protestant Establishment is now all but gone from the American scene; or as Robert C. Christopher, the author of *Crashing the Gates: The De-Wasping of America's Power Elite*, says, "relatively few members of the national social aristocracy have made truly major contributions to the political or economic development of the United States in the last four decades" (Christopher, 1989, pp. 267–268).

Taking the lead and setting the tone in a democracy is never easy, neither for individuals nor for a social class. Complex and imperfect, democracy has been called, by no less a judge than Winston Churchill, "the worst form of government—except for all the rest." The problem of leadership in America is particularly difficult to resolve because our democracy is beset with two special paradoxes not shared by more hierarchically oriented societies. The first paradox—the paradox of leadership itself—involves the ideal of egalitarianism and the reality of inequality of social class, status, power, and authority. These elements of inequality violate the egalitarian ethos at the core of American culture, while being indispensable to its survival—an uncomfortable fact of democratic life with which we must always live. The second paradox—the paradox of social mobility—also involves the ideals of egalitarianism, which stress the principle of an open-class system in which everyone has the opportunity to rise to positions of leadership and success based on merit. But this meritocratic principle of achievement often leads to a very different reality in which ascription as well as achievement come to bear on success. After all, successful men and women always want to pass on to their children whatever advantages they themselves have earned, in the form of enhanced and unequal opportunities for education and a leg up in their careers, thus violating the basic premises of our egalitarian values. Both of these paradoxes are always at play in American society. As we shall see, they are part of the story of how the Protestant Establishment was able to command deference and to exercise authority in America until the middle of this century.

The Protestant Establishment

Oddly, it was not when the Protestant Establishment was at the height of its authority, a period referred to by Joseph Alsop (1992) in his memoirs as the "WASP Ascendancy," and somewhat earlier by E. Digby Baltzell and me (1988, 1991) as the period of "WASP Hegemony," but only when it was declining, that the acronym "WASP" came into existence. The term "WASP" is now so much a part of our contemporary language that many readers may find it curious that it was nowhere to be found before the mid-1960s, even in the best and most definitive dictionaries. This is probably partly due to the fact that like many newly minted words, no standardized usage had been associated with it. The term has been in use since the 1950s, at least among intellectuals, but did not enter our general usage until it was made popular by sociologist E. Digby Baltzell in his widely-read book, *The Protestant Establishment: Aristocracy and Caste in America* (1964), which chronicled the decline of WASP authority in American society.

While lacking a standardized definition, the term is closely identified with the American upper class, as well as with various elites in the American system of political and social stratification. For instance, *Webster's Third International Dictionary* defines WASP as: "an American of northern European and especially British stock and of Protestant background; especially a member of the dominant and most privileged class of people in the U.S." Expanding on this same theme of stratification Christopher Hitchens, the author of *Blood, Class, and Nostalgia: Anglo-American Ironies*, wrote about WASPs that

> ... somewhere in the subtext of all this is the ticklish question of race and the awkward matter of class. Ethnic hierarchy in America actually confuses the two things in a revealing minor way, since the word WASP, which denotes a racial and religious group, is only ever applied to a certain social layer of it. (George H. W. Bush is a WASP. George Wallace may have been a white Protestant of Anglo-Saxon descent, and even rather vocal on all three points, but a WASP he was not.)
> (Hitchens, 1990, pp. 34–35)

To this last point we might add that while presidents such as Theodore Roosevelt, William Howard Taft, Woodrow Wilson, and Franklin Delano Roosevelt were definitely WASPs, Lyndon Johnson, Richard Nixon, Gerald Ford, Jimmy Carter, and William Jefferson Clinton are not; and although after his presidency Ronald Reagan was knighted by Queen Elizabeth, neither was he a WASP despite being wealthy, white, Protestant, and of Irish descent. But if only some Americans of Anglo-Saxon heritage are WASPs, how did they become so? How did a relatively small group of families become a national upper class, and how did a relatively small subgroup among these families come to have disproportionate power and authority in America from just after the Civil War to just after the Second World War?

A century and a half ago America was very different than it is today. The vast majority of Americans were white, of Anglo-Saxon origin, and Protestant. They lived in small towns, not large cities, or on farms, not in suburbs. Wealth, status, and power were diffused throughout these small communities in ways that are largely foreign to us now. For instance, Alexis de Tocqueville could easily write in 1835 that "in America there are but few wealthy persons; nearly all Americans have to take a profession" (Tocqueville, 1945, p. 52). And Tocqueville knew that these professions were sources of prestige and authority in the small communities of which America was composed. Not great wealth, but rather eminence as a minister in a local church, or as a lawyer or jurist, or merchant, or doctor commanded deference and authority. Thus, Henry Adams, the eminent author and historian, born in 1838, and scion of one of America's leading establishment families—son of Charles Francis Adams, the American Ambassador to Great Britain, grandson of President John Quincy Adams, and great-grandson of President John Adams—could look back upon his own childhood and remember that "down to 1850, and even later, New England society was still directed by the professions. Lawyers, physicians, professors, merchants were classes, and acted not as individuals, but as though they were clergymen, and each profession were a church" (Adams, 1931, p. 32). All of this is to say that authority in America until just after the Civil War was highly localized, as was deference, power, and leadership in general.

Emergence

Great changes were in store for America in the aftermath of the Civil War. Throughout the 1870s and 1880s urbanization and industrialization, coupled with the growth of railroads and large corporations, broke down small town ties of community, and in Richard Hofstadter's terms "transformed the old society and revolutionized the distribution of power and prestige" (Hofstadter, 1955, p. 136). This status revolution was accompanied by a significant shift in population from rural to urban America. In 1850, for instance, only 15% of Americans lived in cities, but by 1880 this percentage had just about doubled, and by 1890 about 35% lived in urban areas. The tidal waves of immigration which began during this period helped swell the urban population even further, and by 1920 more than half of all Americans lived in urban areas. The trend towards urbanization continues to our day. In 1870 only about one in four Americans lived in cities; since 1970 this percentage has been stood on its head, with only one in four Americans not living in cities or their immediate vicinity.

Immigration has also changed the ethnic makeup of America. In 1790 over 80% of the population was white, and between 60% and 70% of the white population was of English ancestry. Of the rest of the white population, about 10% was Irish, 8% Scotch, and 9% German in ancestry. By 1920 over 90% of the population was white, but only 44% of the white population was of English ancestry, while Americans of Irish ancestry were about 11% of the population, and the proportion of German Americans had nearly doubled to about 16%. Also, by 1920 other ethnicities—Italian, Polish, Russian, and Spanish, for example—accounted for almost 30% of white Americans. By 1990 about 80% of the population was white, but only about 25% of the white population was of English ancestry; Irish Americans, however, now accounted for about 20% of the white population, and German Americans matched those of English ancestry at about 25%.

The great post-Civil War transformation was especially noticeable with respect to wealth. When Tocqueville published the second part of *Democracy in America* in 1840, there were not even twenty millionaires in the entire United States, and he was entirely correct when he wrote that "though there are rich men, the class of rich men does not exist; for these rich individuals have no feelings or purposes, no traditions or hopes, in common; there are individuals, therefore, but no definite class" (Tocqueville, 1945, p. 160). But the industrialization of America helped change this situation. In the thirty years between 1870 and 1900 the national wealth quadrupled, and the number of millionaires grew enormously. By 1893 it was estimated that there were over four thousand millionaires in the United States, and at least one hundred and twenty men who were worth over ten million dollars each. In fact, in 1892 the U.S. Census Bureau estimated that about 9% of American families accounted for over 70% of the nation's wealth. This trend towards accumulating wealth has continued, and in this regard, it is notable that according to the Spectrum group, there were 10.4 million households in the United States in 2016 worth over one million dollars. It is also worth noting that among America's 540 American billionaires listed in *Forbes* for 2015, there were a few WASPs such as Henry Lea Hillman, but many more self-made men. And while David Rockefeller, Laurance Spelman Rockefeller, and Paul Mellon represent a few old-money families, John Werner Kluge, Samuel and Donald Newhouse, Ronald Perelman, Ted Arison, Edgar Bronfman, Leslie H. Wexner, Jay and Robert Pritzker, Samuel LeFrak, Kirk Kerkorian, and Milton Petrie, among others, represent the enormous drive and achievement of talented individuals from religious and ethnic groups which have been excluded from the precincts of the Protestant Establishment, but have succeeded in leaving most old-stock families trailing in the dust.

Inclusion

While today great wealth is scattered among millions of families of all racial, ethnic, and religious backgrounds, during the period of the status revolution it was concentrated in the hands of relatively few. This newly created wealth formed the basis of a new class of rich men, a largely WASP business aristocracy of the sort that Tocqueville had said was absent from American society as late as the 1840s. Writing in 1955, sociologist Talcott Parsons described the process by which this business aristocracy had come into existence as follows:

> There is a continuing tendency for earlier economic developments to leave a 'precipitate' of upper groups, the positions of whose members are founded in the achievements of their ancestors, in this case relatively recent ones. By historical necessity these groups are strongest in the older parts of the country. Hence the cities of the Eastern seaboard have tended to develop groups that are the closest approach we have…to an aristocracy. They have generally originated in business interests…
> (Parsons, 1955b, p. 125)

Following Parsons, Baltzell (1957), showed how the newly rich industrialists and their families eventually formed a national upper class, which then drifted apart from local community roots.

This new national upper class was formed in American cities in the latter part of the nineteenth century when successful moneymakers—businessmen, merchants, and bankers—many of whom came from low social class backgrounds, founded families whose individual members through marriage, private education, and club membership associated themselves with old-money families. Through these associations, generation after generation, they came to constitute a business aristocracy in which upper-class values, wealth, and power were preserved. This business aristocracy, as Baltzell put it, "too often placed the desire for material comfort and security above the duties of political and intellectual leadership" (Baltzell, 1957, p. 5). Nevertheless, up to the Second World War, upper-class WASP families, living in fashionable neighborhoods and listed in the *Social Register*, helped to shape the business and cultural life of cities across the country. They educated their children at private prep schools, such as The Taft School, Groton, Hotchkiss, St. Mark's, St. Paul's, Foxcroft, and Choate, and colleges such as Princeton, Harvard, Yale, Vassar, and Smith among other elite colleges. They belonged to exclusive clubs—there are over two hundred and fifty listed in the *Social Register* today, from the Acorn in Philadelphia and the Algonquin in Boston to the Wilmington Country Club in Delaware and the Yale Club in New York—and helped shape the business and cultural life of cities across the country. At the beginning this WASP upper class was relatively open to new talent, and assimilated newly arrived individuals and their families into its ranks, but within a short time upper-class status appeared to be limited to old-stock Protestant families, which led Baltzell to ask, "what is the future function of a predominantly Anglo-Saxon and Protestant upper class in an ethnically and religiously heterogeneous democracy?" (Baltzell, 1957, p. 395).

Exclusion

This question invokes the image of declining class authority in America reminiscent of a similar situation described in Tocqueville's *Ancient Regime* (1955), which showed that when new men of talent, wealth, and power were refused membership in the French aristocracy by noblemen who drew a caste line making membership a matter of birth alone, class authority failed and set the stage for the French Revolution. A similar crisis of leadership in America had developed by the mid-twentieth century because the white, Anglo-Saxon, and Protestant national upper class had, by excluding talented individuals and their families from membership because they were from ethnic and racial minority groups, become a privileged caste rather than an authoritative establishment.

The old local upper classes had been, by and large, based on social considerations of family, rather than on business connections and wealth, and they had been open to newer ethnic groups as well as to old-stock Protestant Americans of Anglo-Saxon heritage. Thus, as late as the 1870s, Jews were assimilated into the local upper classes of American cities such as Boston, where Louis D. Brandeis, the future Justice of the U.S. Supreme Court, could join exclusive patrician clubs. The son of a wealthy Jewish merchant who had immigrated to Louisville, Kentucky from Prague in 1848, Brandeis entered Harvard Law School in 1875, and immediately rose to the top of his class. He soon became friends with many Boston brahmins, such as Dennis Warren, Jr, the son of a rich manufacturer, with whom he founded a law firm after graduation. Brandeis had no difficulty in joining the Union Club, or the Exchange, nor did anyone object to his joining and eventually becoming one of the directors of the Union Boat Club (Baltzell & Schneiderman, 1991). Brandeis's experience was hardly singular, for before the 1880s and the coming of a new national WASP upper class, wealthy Jews, especially German Jews, were able to assimilate into the local upper classes of most American cities. Thus, the Morgenthaus, Ochses, Sulzbergers, Strauses, Lehmans, and Guggenheims—families which are still well-known today—were an integral part of the nineteenth century New York establishment.

The new national upper class that formed in the 1880s was different than the old local upper classes. For one thing, it was clearly anti-Semitic. Historians and sociologists have suggested that WASP anti-Semitism was a reaction to the enormous number of immigrants from Eastern Europe, and some have tried to distinguish this upper-class bigotry from other types by calling it "genteel," or "social" anti-Semitism, although there is hardly a difference. In 1880 there were only about a quarter of a million Jews in America, but by 1920 there were over four million, and over 350,000 cramped into New York City's Lower East Side alone. About 80% of the four million American Jews in 1920 were of East

European, as opposed to German, extraction. These new immigrants brought with them very different values, languages, and cultures than did the German Jews who were already well established here by the 1880s. Whatever the reasons, the new national upper class now became exclusively white, Anglo-Saxon, and Protestant, and began excluding Jews from the institutions which were associated with it. As Baltzell has shown, "upper class anti-Semitism was perhaps more blatantly displayed in the five decades after 1880 than at any other time in our history" (Baltzell & Schneiderman, 1991, p. 48).

By the 1890s Jews were being excluded from membership in patrician clubs throughout the country. In 1893, New York's Union League blackballed the son of one of its Civil War-era founders, Jesse Seligman, because he was Jewish. And by 1913 President Woodrow Wilson decided against having Louis Brandeis in his cabinet, after opposition to his appointment was voiced by patrician New Englanders who had invited Brandeis into their social circle in the 1870s and 1880s. Bankers, lawyers, real estate magnates, railroad tycoons, stockbrokers, and others from families such as the Astors, Baldwins, Cuttings, Depews, Elliotts, Fishes, Griswolds, Hewitts, Iselins, Jaffrays, Kanes, Livingstons, Martins, Newbolds, Otises, Posts, Roosevelts, Schuylers, Twombleys, Vanderbilts, and Winthrops were part of the national metropolitan WASP upper class, as were the Harrimans, Rockefellers, Tafts, Cabots, and Lodges. There were no Jews or other ethnic minorities among them.

This national WASP upper class paid more attention to wealth than to family, and was more conscious of ethnicity than the earlier local upper classes throughout America. Excluding all but WASPs, this national upper class gained a profound self-consciousness through a network of exclusive clubs, boarding schools, resorts, and Ivy League colleges which promulgated a subculture of common values, and common norms of behavior, that is to say, common morals and manners. The need for commonality can be easily understood. The geographic distribution and larger numbers of the new national upper class required criteria beyond the geographical propinquity, face-to-face dealings, and local intermarriages that had prevailed in the pre-industrial local upper classes. In spite of its anti-Semitic and anti-ethnic bigotry, however, this new national upper class served an important purpose in America: it provided a pool of national leaders generally committed to liberal democracy. This was of no small value, for as political scientist, V. O. Key, the author of *Southern Politics in State and Nation*, wrote in 1949,

> ... the operation of democracy may depend on competition among conflicting sections of the 'better element' for the support of the masses of voters. Hence, the workings of democracy require a considerable degree of disagreement within the upper classes....In the absence of popular leadership from the 'better element,' the breach may be filled by persons and groups with few scruples and often little ability.
>
> (Key, 1949, p. 181)

Political Leadership

Nothing illustrates Key's point better than Theodore Roosevelt's succession to the presidency in 1901, which marked the beginning of a cycle of presidents of upper-class origins, a cycle that lasted forty-four years, ending with the death of Franklin Delano Roosevelt in 1945. This cycle, which began at the turn of the century, reflected a new national upper class's contribution to the political leadership of the nation. The patrician reformer Theodore Roosevelt, having inherited considerable wealth, had a certain loathing for the self-made millionaires of his day, whom he said "made the till their fatherland." He was followed in office by two other establishment presidents, Taft, a Republican as was Roosevelt, and Wilson, a Democrat (Schneiderman, 1989).

The election of 1912 shows the remarkable range of the new WASP upper class's interest in politics, and of its capacity to compete for the support of the masses as Key suggested it must. In this election, the three patricians who served, or would serve, as president from 1901 to 1921 were all candidates, and represented different political parties and different political platforms. Theodore Roosevelt running as a Progressive outpolled Taft, the incumbent Republican, but lost the election to the Democrat, Woodrow Wilson. Following Wilson's administration, the Twenties were presided over by presidents of upper middle-class backgrounds, Harding, Coolidge, and Hoover, thus interrupting, but not ending, the cycle. Franklin Delano Roosevelt and a host of fellow patricians of inherited wealth and privileged backgrounds came to Washington in the Thirties and Forties, thus keeping the cycle going until at least 1945. Although big government was here to stay by the beginning of the century, the entry of the patrician into national political life infused it with a new sense of noblesse oblige (Baltzell & Schneiderman, 1989). Establishment figures such as Theodore Roosevelt, Taft, Wilson, and FDR entered political life to see that the huge machinery of government was administered honestly and efficiently.

Not all members of the new upper class, however, contributed to the leadership of the nation. In fact, relatively few did. Many observers actually felt that there was a shameful lack of responsible leaders in this country at the turn of the century. For example, James Bryce, author of *The American Commonwealth*, concluded that the majority of citizens pay so little attention to public affairs that "they willingly leave all but the most important to be dealt with by the few" (Bryce, 1921, p. 557). Attributing this lack of interest to individualistic tendencies, Bryce suggested an individual's interests and priorities are ordered by, first occupation, second, family relatives and friends, third, by religion, fourth, by personal tastes, and fifth, by a sense of civic duty. Although Bryce was aware that the order of these interests varies from citizen to citizen, he was certain that civic duty would almost always rank last. As he said, "individualism, the love of enterprise, and the pride in personal freedom, have been deemed by Americans not only their choicest, but their peculiar and exclusive possessions" (Bryce, 1988, pp. 406–407). That these very American values born of democracy should be an obstacle to fulfilling the democratic spirit was an irony not lost on Bryce any more than it had been on Tocqueville before him.

In a famous lecture at Yale University in mid-October 1908—just before the election in which Taft was elected to the presidency, replacing Roosevelt, and preserving the WASP establishment's hold on the nation's top office—Bryce blamed the privileged classes for their inattention to civic duties. Such indolence, in his eyes, "made it a government of the many who don't care by the few who do." Noting the effect of selfishness in a business civilization such as our own, Bryce said that

> ... absorbed in business or pleasures, we think little of what our membership in a free nation means. The eloquent voice of a

patriotic reformer sometimes breaks our slumber, but the daily round of business or pleasure soon fills the mind and public duty again fades into the background of life.

(Bryce, 1993, pp. 92–93)

But Bryce's chief complaint was that among the educated classes, as he called the privileged upper-middle and upper classes, there was too much reluctance by "the fellows who are too good to run for minor offices," to take the lead in governing their local communities, states, and the nation. This was an old complaint against democracy, one which Tocqueville had thought was basic to the destruction of the Ancient Regime in France, and which Bryce had lodged against the "better classes" in America many times before. Basic to this complaint was an understanding that, as Bryce later said, "as a rule, that which the mass of any people desires is not to govern itself, but to be well governed" (Bryce, 1921, p. 501).

Also of concern to Bryce was that the higher status, better-educated classes from which public leaders were most likely to be drawn were most apt to be affected by the love of money. Bryce, who was the British Ambassador to America, and who was well acquainted with many members of the upper classes, observed that they had the duty to, and in practice did, set the moral standard for all the rest. Indeed, he called the leading political stratum drawn from the upper classes "the tone-setting class," because he believed that it is this class that "forms the standard not only for those who conduct public business but also to a great extent for the whole community." A tone-setting class, or what we would today call an establishment should, according to Bryce, set a high standard. If it sets a low standard, tolerates base motives and actions, "it depraves the morality of the community…and politics are defiled and debased, selfishness and trickery are taken to be natural, and public life becomes the favorite hunting ground of unscrupulous and reckless men" (Bryce, 1993, p. 119). Once the moral or civic standard is lowered, it is difficult to raise it again, and Bryce advocated legislation to prevent men from getting rich through public life.

Like his Establishment friends, such as Henry Adams and Theodore Roosevelt, Bryce was clearly an advocate of responsible leadership by the "better" classes, and to him this did not mean successful moneyed classes per se, but, rather, solidly educated achieving classes willing to take the lead in civic duty. His ideal in this was his good friend Roosevelt who, he told his audience at Yale, as a young man "more than twenty years ago did not consider himself above going to the lower house of the New York Legislature and who has now become an eminent statesman" (Bryce, 1993, p. 32).

But Roosevelt, who had served as the police commissioner of New York City from 1895 to 1897—just a few years before becoming President of the United States—was indeed the exception in terms of local politics. And while the WASP upper class contributed men such as Roosevelt to national business and politics, it effectively abandoned local politics to men of other ethnic backgrounds. As America grew, there was plenty of room for talented individuals from outside this class to exercise their talents, especially in the cities of America. While a few cities, such as Philadelphia, which did not elect an Irish Catholic mayor until 1964, maintained WASP leadership through most of this century, most, such as Milwaukee, which elected its first Irish Catholic mayor in 1863, or Boston, which followed suit in 1885, were dominated by ethnic elites since the latter part of the nineteenth century. Thus New York City elected its first Irish Catholic mayor, William Grace, in 1881, its second, Hugh Grant, in 1889, followed by Thomas Gilroy, in 1893. With the exception of two WASP mayors, Seth Low and George McClellan, who were in office from 1902 to 1909, New York had an unbroken string of seven Irish Catholic mayors from 1910, when William Gaynor was elected, through 1934 when an Episcopalian, Fiorello LaGuardia, son of a lapsed middle-class Italian Catholic father and an Austrian Jewish mother, was elected to the office. LaGuardia, who was mayor until 1945, was followed by another Irish Catholic mayor, William O'Dwyer, then by an Italian Catholic, Vincent Impellitteri, an upper-class German Catholic, Robert Wagner, and finally, after a half century of ethnic mayors, by a WASP, John Lindsay, in 1966. Following Lindsay's departure in 1973, New York elected its first Jewish mayor, Abraham Beame, in 1974, and its second Jewish mayor, Edward I. Koch, in 1978. Koch was followed by New York's first black mayor, David Dinkins.

If many of the great American cities were governed by ethnic minorities during the last hundred or so years, what effect did these new power holders have upon the authority of the Protestant Establishment? For one thing, the old-stock establishment based its authority on deference, in much the same way that Walter Bagehot said the English aristocracy had in the nineteenth century. Ironically, this process was at work in the Democratic Party, which has been in this century, by and large, the party of immigrants, ethnics, and minorities. In the words of Andrew Hacker, a political scientist,

> Ed Flynn might boss the Bronx, but he would defer to Franklin D. Roosevelt (of Harvard); Carmine De Sapio rides behind Averill Harriman (of Yale); and Jake Arvey cleared the way for Adlai Stevenson (of Princeton). The seeming inconsonance of the fact that the party of the immigrant accepted old-stock patricians as its leaders is good evidence of the deference that was paid to the *ancien regime*.
>
> (Hacker, 1957, p. 1015)

The Protestant Establishment might not have governed the cities of America, but for the first half of this century it set the tone and the atmosphere of culture and politics at the national level.

But if the WASP establishment set the tone and atmosphere for the exercise of national authority, how and why had it been able to do so? Asked another way, what is an establishment? Simply put, it is a group of leaders within an elite whose families are part of an upper class. Those few members of any upper class who form an establishment stand in contrast to the majority who are satisfied to have high status but little or no authority, in other words, with those who form a caste. The American Establishment has been made up of WASP families such as the Adamses, Bayards, Breckinridges, Frelinghuysens, Harrisons, Lees, Livingstons, Lodges, Roosevelts, Stevensons, Tafts, and Washburns, who have followed the aristocratic ethos that emphasizes the duty to lead, rather than the snobbish caste ethos which emphasizes only the right to privilege. Just four families, the Adams, Harrison, Roosevelt, and Taft families, for instance, have not only provided the nation with seven presidents among them (thus accounting for more than one-sixth of all our presidents), but have also contributed eleven governors, ten ambassadors, ten U.S. Senators, twenty-seven members of the U.S. House of Representatives, six cabinet officers, and two justices of the U.S. Supreme Court, not to mention five mayors of major cities, and over fifty state and local legislators and officials.

These four families are representative of the sort of leadership provided by the Protestant Establishment. In fact, the U.S. Presidency, the most visible position of leadership in the nation, has been dominated by establishment figures. Of our forty-one presidents, seventeen—Washington, both Adamses, Jefferson, Madison, Monroe, both Harrisons, Polk, Tyler, Taylor, both Roosevelts, Taft, Wilson, Kennedy, and Bush—have come from clearly upper-class backgrounds. And even though Kennedy is still our only Catholic president, he was clearly upper class and educated as a WASP. But aside from the presidency, establishment families have provided more than their share of governors, justices and chief-justices of the U.S. Supreme Court, diplomats, U.S. Senators and Congressmen, and cabinet officers.

Hegemony

A moral force within the putatively amoral world of politics and power elites, an establishment of leaders drawn from upper-class families can protect freedom in modern democratic societies. Such an establishment of political, business, cultural, religious, and educational leaders succeeds in its moral function when it sets, follows, and enforces rules of fair play in contests of power and opinion. This point was brought home by the German sociologist, Ralf Dahrendorf, in his brilliant analysis of the post–World War II political elite in Germany. "This elite is a mere sociological category without social reality," he wrote, and

> ...it is my thesis that the German political class has developed from unity without plurality, to plurality without unity, and that both these states are highly detrimental for the constitution of liberty... Liberal democracy demands an established political class... [and] a democratic elite has to be united in status, and divided in politics.
> (Dahrendorf, 1967, p. 277)

Similarly, in one of his most penetrating insights into the sociological functions of an establishment, Tocqueville wrote that "a powerful aristocracy does not merely shape the course of public affairs, it also guides opinion, sets the tone for writers, and lends authority to new ideas" (Tocqueville, 1955, p. 142). In other words, it has hegemony over society. Whereas Marxists see hegemony as a social evil, Tocqueville, like Dahrendorf, saw it as necessary to the well-being of society. Establishments give coherence to society. They do not eliminate conflict, but prevent it from ripping society apart.

One of the ironies of American history is that while power has been accessible to many, its sources remain hidden from the sight of most. This irony did not escape the eye of Reinhold Niebuhr, a leading theologian and social critic. "The knight of old knew about power. He sat on a horse, the symbol of military power," wrote Niebuhr,

> but the power of the modern commercial community is contained in the 'counters' of stocks and bonds which are stored in the vaults of the bank. Such a community creates a culture in which nothing is known about power, however desperate the power struggles within it.
> (Niebuhr, 1952, pp. 12–13)

Those who have and control power in America are, as Niebuhr well knew, often protected from sight just below the edge of public scrutiny by egalitarian mores and traditions which create ambiguous feelings about power and authority, and often deny that the powerful should exist.

Decline

It is this blind edge of the power structure of American society which marks the line between the upper-class authority of the establishment and the power elites. The genius of an establishment lies in its capacity to put moral brakes on power by applying an upper-class code of conduct and responsibility to it. This capacity was at work, for instance, when Joseph Welch, senior partner in the old-stock, patrician Boston law firm of Hale and Dorr, serving gratis as the U.S. Army's special counsel, stood up to Senator Joseph McCarthy and finally brought him down, ending the career of one of the most dangerous demagogues in American history. Nevertheless, McCarthyism marked the beginning of the end of establishment rule in American national politics. After all, it was the establishment itself which McCarthy attacked. Alger Hiss, a patrician from an old-stock Baltimore family, a graduate of Harvard Law School, was associated with other establishment figures, such as U.S. Supreme Court Justice Oliver Wendell Holmes, for whom he clerked, President Franklin Roosevelt, for whom he was a special advisor at Yalta, his friend former Secretary of State Dean Acheson, and the new Secretary of State, John Foster Dulles. In 1950 Hiss was convicted of perjury for denying the accusations that he was a Communist made by Whittaker Chambers. That same year Senator McCarthy began his four-year campaign to rid the government of Communist sympathizers, and his attack on the establishment, especially on patricians such as Dean Acheson whom McCarthy branded "a pompous diplomat in striped pants, with a phony British accent." It finally took the courageous establishment lawyer from Boston, Joseph Welch, who was unafraid to stand up to McCarthy, to help end one of the most disgraceful, and dangerous, episodes in our history. But the Protestant Establishment was beginning to lose its legitimacy, which it finally lost in the anarchic 1960s, when authority itself was broadly called into question in this country.

During the 1960s legitimacy and authority came into question and began to fail, fostering the growth of cynicism about many hierarchical elements of society, including the Establishment. This cynicism has carried through to the present. Thus, in *Cultural Literacy* E. D. Hirsch listed "the Establishment" as one of the ideas literate Americans should know. But for all the charges of elitism against him, Hirsch defined "the Establishment" in a cynical manner his critics would applaud. In the *Dictionary of Cultural Literacy* (1988), he described the Establishment as follows: "Individuals and institutions that exercise social, economic, and political authority over a society. The term has a pejorative connotation because it suggests that political and economic power is in the hands of the few." Perhaps all would agree with the first part of this description, but only a few would openly disagree with the pejorative connotation attached to the term.

A deceptive myth in liberal democracies like America is that civil liberties and freedom of expression are valued by most members of society, and most certainly by those at the bottom and middle of the social structure. But as Samuel Stouffer amply demonstrated in his classic study, *Communism, Conformity, and Civil Liberties* (1955), and as others have found since, this is not the case. Such freedoms are always most highly valued and protected by the elite few who are better educated, and who believe in the liberal democratic tradition, and the last bulwark of freedom may well be, as Baltzell has suggested,

> ... a unified Establishment from within which the leaders of at least two parties are chosen, who, in turn, compete for the people's votes of confidence, from differing points of view and differing standards of judgment, yet both assuming the absolute necessity of using fair means in accusing their legitimate opponents of fallibility rather than treason.
> (Baltzell, 1964, p. 293)

The sociological alternatives to rule by establishments have been, historically, rule by functionaries and bureaucrats or rule by demagogues, neither of which has proven satisfactory in protecting freedoms.

During this last century America has undergone a social revolution in leadership. Whereas the WASP upper class dominated America's political, economic, and intellectual elites up to the late 1940s, thus controlling the nation, today WASPs no longer have that control, nor perhaps does any other group. Thus, Peter Schrag ended his cogent book, *The Decline of the WASP*, by suggesting that

> America is not on the verge of becoming two separate societies, one rich and white, the other poor and black. It is becoming, in all its dreams and anxieties, a nation of outsiders for whom no single style or ethic remains possible.
> (Schrag, 1970, p. 255)

American leadership has for the last half century been increasingly dominated by atomized elites, like those in Germany described by Dahrendorf, rather than by an establishment. The difference is of some consequence, because an establishment is a real group, a *gemeinschaft*, or community, subject to all the forces of social control that at least potentially can instill and enforce moral standards in its members, if not society at large. An elite, however, is a *gesellschaft*, not a real group, but merely a convenient sociological category not subject to the forces of social control, and not a moral entity.

The caste-like exclusivity and bigotry of the Protestant Establishment served to destroy its class authority. Yet America's best democratic traditions might still be best served by having an establishment of some sort to provide moral authority and leadership to the nation. Of course, those traditions dictate that we should choose the most talented available men and women to represent us in positions of moral and political leadership, regardless of their class, religious, ethnic, or racial backgrounds. But we should not be surprised if these individuals try to pass on to their children all the advantages they can, nor if these individuals and their families intermarry with each other and constitute a new establishment—albeit one more open to talented newcomers, and less exclusive than its predecessor.

A New Establishment?

If the Protestant Establishment's values of achievement, conscience, industry, anti-sensuality, and civic-mindedness have become the backbone of American values, as Richard Brookhiser, in *The Way of the WASP* (1991), makes the case that they have, since the 1960s they have been challenged by a new emphasis on ascriptive values. No establishment can survive without deference, and there can be no deference without a commonly shared culture which maintains at least a modicum of consensus. Throughout this century successful individuals, and their families, of Irish, Jewish, Italian, and black backgrounds, were excluded from the WASP upper class; therefore, they established their own upper classes. And according to Nelson W. Aldrich, Jr in *Old Money: The Mythology of America's Upper Class,* they bought into WASP culture even as they founded their own

> schools, summer resorts, clubs—and bred their own patricians and aristocrats. They also established their own suburban enclaves and cultivated their own ethnic consciousnesses. Still, it seemed that these non-WASPs not only wanted to imitate WASP culture but yearned somehow to *be* WASP.
>
> (Aldrich, 1988, p. 280)

This may no longer be the case.

American society has become increasingly fragmented, and there is little or no consensus to be found regarding our political, business, and cultural life. Deference for the authority of the Protestant Establishment, or for any establishment for that matter, has been replaced in many quarters by an active, conscious hostility and opposition. Power will probably replace deference to authority if we adhere to no common set of social standards, obey no collective moral injunctions, and subscribe to no single culture. This situation was analyzed with great insight by Francis Fitzgerald in *America Revised*, in which she says that the message of most contemporary textbooks is that

> Americans have no common history, no common culture, and no common values, and that membership in a racial or cultural group constitutes the most fundamental experience of each individual. The message would be that the center cannot and should not hold.
>
> (Fitzgerald, 1980, p. 104)

Under these conditions it is difficult to imagine the resuscitation, or reconstitution of the establishment. Then again, there are still countless Irish, Italian, black, Jewish, Polish Indian, and other ethnic families who have adopted the WASP values of achievement and success, even while American society seems to be increasingly emphasizing blatantly ascriptive values in their place. As such, they may represent our brightest prospects for the future. As of now, it is too early to tell whether they will be successful in recreating an establishment, especially one open to all talented individuals and their families, no matter what their racial, ethnic, or religious backgrounds, or whether the fragmentation of our society now underway will preclude such a development.

13

STRESS, CRISIS, AND PSYCHOHISTORY

Over two decades since his death in 1994, Richard Nixon remains an enigmatic and fascinating figure in American political history. Bruce Mazlish's *In Search of Nixon* stands out as an early and innovative effort to use psychohistory to uncover the man and his motives.

Continuous interest in our thirty-seventh president makes it invaluable to understanding one of the strangest and most conflicted men ever to occupy the Oval Office.

One might well ask why this book is still worth reading so long after it was originally published, in 1972. Actually, Bruce Mazlish gave me a good answer to this question in an interchange of letters between us. *In Search of Nixon* is still relevant because, as Mazlish says, Nixon had a "convoluted personality" and a "complicated record." But while people sensed Nixon's personality traits in 1972, it was not until after his resignation in 1974 as a result of the Watergate scandal, and later, during his efforts at self-rehabilitation as a writer and an advisor to his successors about foreign policy, that Nixon was more fully revealed.

As for Nixon's record as president, most of it was still to come after the publication of *In Search of Nixon*, thus making this book something of a prequel, if not an anticipation of how Nixon's presidency might turn out. Mazlish had no crystal ball, but his analysis of Nixon's personality and behavior leads the reader to think that Nixon's success and failures in foreign and domestic policy, and his monumental meltdown in the disgraceful Watergate affair were, if not predictable, at least no surprise, because what Mazlish says about Nixon in 1972 could have helped predict Nixon's performance in office and beyond.

When *In Search of Nixon* was first published it received a number of unfavorable reviews from other historians. Looking backward over the more than four decades that have since passed, it is clear that Bruce Mazlish's "psychohistorical inquiry," as he called it, deserved a better reception than it first received. Indeed, Mazlish's "inquiry" into the character of America's thirty-seventh president helped lay the foundation for the now well-established psychohistorical approach to history. What makes *In Search of Nixon* doubly interesting today is not only that it is a pioneering work in psychohistory, but also that it was written in the midst of the Nixon presidency, before Richard Nixon became the only president who resigned from office. The insightfulness of *In Search of Nixon* may well be judged, at least in good measure, by its author's ability to help the reader to understand the self-destructive actions that led Nixon to resign in the face of the Watergate crisis.

Indeed, "crisis" is a term that Nixon himself used to define the most momentous events in his political life. A mere ten years before Mazlish's book was published, Nixon's first book, *Six Crises*, appeared in print. *Six Crises* is a highly selective autobiographical statement in which Nixon carefully discusses his place in six politically charged events that he says helped form his character leading up to his presidency. As Mazlish notes, however, what Nixon elects to leave out of these accounts is as revealing as what he includes. Given the manner in which Nixon embraces his part in these events, I am tempted to think of his book as being more aptly titled, *My Six Crises*. The irony here, of course, is that looking back, it was Nixon's unanticipated seventh crisis—Watergate—that made the largest impact on his life, and the life of the nation.

What were the six crises that Nixon described? First was the Alger Hiss case, during which, in 1948, Nixon served on the House of Representative's Un-American Activities Committee that was investigating communism in America. Second was what he labeled the Fund Crisis, in which Nixon was running for vice president on Dwight Eisenhower's ticket in 1952. He was accused of having an illicit campaign fund, and Eisenhower was considering dropping Nixon as his running mate. Nixon saved himself and became vice president by delivering the famous "Checkers speech" (referring to the dog named Checkers), in which Nixon averred his innocence, and said he would never give the dog back to its donor. The third crisis was precipitated by President Eisenhower's heart attack in 1955, when Vice President Nixon became, in his words, an "acting president" for a few weeks. Nixon's fourth crisis took place in 1958, when he and his wife were attacked in their limousine by a mob in Venezuela. The fifth crisis was Vice President Nixon's so-called "kitchen debate" with Nikita Khrushchev in Moscow in 1959. The final crisis described by Nixon was the 1960 presidential campaign, which ended with John F. Kennedy winning the presidency by a slim margin.

Mazlish discusses Nixon's six crises, and sees each of these as revealing something about his character. A superior theoretician, well-versed in psychoanalytic concepts, as well as in the literature of social science, Mazlish helps us to understand Nixon's personal psychology, as well as the temper of his time. In many if not most ways, Nixon was a typical American in his hopes and fears for America in the Cold War era. Beyond the standard-issue reactions to a new post-war world, however, Nixon projected his own characteristic self-image onto new waves of Communist enemies, and in Mazlish's words, "Nixon pictured himself as the warrior preserving the American way of life." This warrior self-image allowed Nixon to normalize what Mazlish calls "his paranoid fear of Communism with a heavy-handed ideological strategic stance to take on communism, and to defeat it." Pulling together one example after another from their random dispersal, Mazlish shows that Nixon's paranoia extended beyond Communists to his political opponents who were seen as "enemies," crooks, "bums," and other "cynical seekers of power." In this regard, Mazlish provides us with a powerful insight into Nixon's constant ambivalence about friends and enemies. That ambivalence is demonstrated in Nixon's proclamation that "I'm a pragmatist with some deep principles that never change," and in Mazlish's pointed remark that Nixon simply needed enemies onto whom he could "project aggressive feelings" (Mazlish, 2016, p. 85).

This canny observation about the duality of Nixon's sometimes ambivalent stances led Mazlish to speculate as to why and how Nixon could disentangle his unyielding and extreme feelings about Communists from his pragmatic stance towards them. The answer is that Nixon subordinated his dislike and fear of communism to what he saw as a larger national interest. When he wrote about this, Mazlish could not have anticipated one of the most interesting turnarounds in Nixon's career, namely his visit to China that eventually led to the normalization of relations between the United States and this Communist foe. Nixon's new accord with China in 1972 is a clear example of how psychohistory can sometimes explain forward behavior that could otherwise not be expected given the historical moment as a point in a given political trajectory. As Mazlish understands so well, Nixon's crises have little if anything to do with so-called "identity crises." Nixon has no need to deal with a crisis of identity. Rather than finding himself, according to Mazlish, Nixon needed to test himself, time and again. These tests are Nixon's self-proclaimed crises.

Indeed, there is a brilliant and still-growing social science literature on those who, like Nixon, thrive on stress and especially on overcoming it in one test of will after another. Georg Simmel's astonishing 1911 essay on adventurers, "Das Abenteuer," demonstrates that the adventurer synthesizes the "antagonisms and compromises between chance and necessity" (Simmel, 1971, p. 191). Without directing the reader to Simmel's text, Mazlish's description of Nixon's characteristic ambivalence suggests that he came most alive when finding himself on the edge of adventurous and stressful risk-taking. To Simmel we may add Max Weber's work on charismatic leaders. While one would be hard-pressed to see Nixon as a perfect example of a charismatic leader, he shared with such leaders the hunger for stressful crises, and often seemed to precipitate such crises, from the "Fund Crisis" in which he risked remaining Eisenhower's running mate in 1952, to the Watergate affair, which led to his resignation from the presidency in 1974.

Mazlish fearlessly dives right in to the deep well of Nixon's character as an impediment to good decision-making when he asks, "Why does Nixon seem to experience such difficulties in making decisions, and why, when he does make them, are they such unusually 'lonely' decisions?" Nixon, in Mazlish's view was "one of the most tightly self-controlled" presidents ever to hold the office. Not only was Nixon a so-called control freak, but he was also characterized by extraordinary ambivalence, worried, on the one hand, about being thought of as "strong and potent," and on the other hand, "compassionate and peace-loving" (Mazlish, 2016, p. 4). Indeed, Nixon's ambivalence was underscored, as I said above, by his reputation as an extraordinarily pragmatic politician, but also as an inveterate daydreamer. To discover the real Nixon, so to speak, is Mazlish's quest.

So, what does Bruce Mazlish's psychohistorical inquiry yield in terms of understanding the affinities between Nixon's background, character, and political behavior? In other words, can Nixon's stress-seeking ambivalence be explained through psychohistorical analysis? To answer this question, we may turn to Nixon's family and its roots. As Mazlish says, "Nixon seems the prototypic rootless, homeless American" (Mazlish, 2016, p. 43). The future president's father, Frank Nixon, worked a variety of blue-collar jobs in California, including working on an oil well and as a farmhand. He was thirty-five years old when Richard Nixon was born in 1913, and soon after he began to run a family-owned grocery store and gasoline station in Whittier, California. Frank Nixon was married to Hannah Milhaus, whom Richard Nixon tearfully called "a Quaker Saint" during his resignation speech in 1974. Neither of Nixon's parents was well educated, and the family lived a lower-middle class lifestyle.

If Nixon's mother was a saint—Mazlish says that she was a dedicated Quaker, and generally a pacifist—what was Nixon's father like? Frank Nixon seems to have been an opinionated, rough-and-ready father. There are intimations that he was mentally and perhaps physically abusive, beating his five sons—two of whom died young of tuberculosis. Mazlish notes that Richard Nixon wrote that if his father had not left school after merely six years because of illness in his family, and if he had had better opportunities to advance in life, he would probably have surpassed him in accomplishments. More to the point for a psychohistorian, according to Nixon, his father "loved the excitement and the battles of political life" (Mazlish, 2016, p. 29). Richard Nixon too, as emphasized above, loved the storm and stress of politics. In *Six Crises*, Nixon comes right down to it when he says that his father had a "fierce competitive drive and intense interest in political issues." Furthermore, Nixon said, guiltily, "I was determined not to let him down" (Mazlish, 2016, p. 97).

While Nixon seems to have thrived as a stress-seeker, we must ask if this is a trait peculiar to Nixon's character, or if it is, along with Nixon's extreme narcissism, a trait found in most politicians. In rereading *In Search *of Nixon*, it was difficult not to ask, time and again, if Nixon's narcissism, perhaps bordering on megalomania, as suggested by Mazlish, and his associated risk-taking and stress-seeking is not endemic to all those who test themselves on a public stage. When athletes, politicians, actors, intellectuals, and others who stride before public audiences lose their nerve, avoid risking failure, and shy away from competition, they are ruined. This obviously was not Nixon's problem. Watergate and its aftermath, including Nixon's resignation, were yet to come when Mazlish wrote *In Search of Nixon*, but what brought him down was his overconfidence, not his fear of failure. This makes *In Search of Nixon* such a provocative book, leading the reader to use Nixon as a springboard for thought about why Weberian charismatics or Simmelian adventurers often do themselves in by lack of caution, when caution is clearly called for at the edge of a cliff.

Psychohistory received its initial institutional thrust forward when William Langer made it the central concern of "The Next Assignment," his inaugural lecture as President of the American Historical Association, in 1957. During this post-WWII timeframe Freud's legitimacy within the social and historical sciences was paramount, and the final chapter of *In Search of Nixon*, "The Psychohistorical Approach," explores the relationship of psychoanalysis and history. This chapter was written at the dawn of psychohistory's appearance as a legitimate method and subcategory in the historical sciences. Since it was written, psychohistory has become a full-bodied incarnation of a way of doing history that supersedes either history as a chronologically oriented way of seeing the past, or psychoanalysis as a way of understanding the present by reconstructing the past. Both approaches necessarily rely on collecting the relevant facts of a person's life, because, after all, psychohistory is about real historical figures, the biographical details of whom are grist for the psychohistorical mill.

In the case of Nixon at the time that Mazlish wrote about him, most of the specific details of his early life were then unknown to us. The intense interest in Nixon during and since Watergate and its aftermath have caused biographers to dig more deeply. Thus, Mazlish is correct when he writes that Nixon's "relations with his mother, father, and siblings could not readily be analyzed in terms of classical psychoanalytical theory about the Oedipal complex." That would still be true today, when we know so much more about Nixon, because as Mazlish demonstrates, psychohistory's conclusions cannot, nor should they be presented in summary terms. This is Mazlish at his most careful best, acknowledging that psychohistory is limited by not itself being psychoanalysis. Both history and psychoanalysis aim to reconstruct the past. Together, as in the case of *In Search of Nixon*, they may succeed step-by-step to cobble together what Max Weber called an ideal type, an overarching précis of a person playing a role in life. Nixon, for all his faults and his virtues, was and remains an ideal typical politician: brash, overestimating his own powers, and coming alive under the stress of political battles.

14
HINDRANCES TO GOOD CITIZENSHIP

"What is Everybody's business," Lord Bryce wrote, "is Nobody's business" (Bryce, 1921, p. 547). *The Hindrances to Good Citizenship* is a brilliant analysis of the democratic dilemma: the more power becomes diffused throughout the citizenry, the less individuals are likely to take responsibility for the governance and well-being of the polity. In this book, first presented as a series of lectures at Yale in 1908, James Bryce addresses the special problems of civic duty in a democracy. Bryce lived one of those remarkably full and fruitful nineteenth-century public lives that remains a wonder today. Best known as the author of *The American Commonwealth*, he was also an important jurist, essayist, diplomat, and a member of Parliament. Engaged in public affairs as deeply as he was, it is not surprising that Bryce's model citizen was somewhat like himself, an energetic and self-sacrificing participant in the governance and well-being of the community.

Bryce never really bothered to define what he meant by "good citizenship" in these essays. He just seems to take for granted that anyone reading them will know what the term means. But in a much earlier essay, "The Teaching of Civic Duty," Bryce defined and commented upon the duties of citizenship (Bryce, 1893). Lamenting that there was no exact English equivalent for the French word *civisme*, Bryce suggested that the French term summed up all the qualities of civic duty: love, respect, attachment to country, liberty, right, justice, family, and community. He even coined a beautifully turned phrase to clarify the meaning of civic duty: "the home side of patriotism" (Bryce, 1893, p. 14). Bryce knew that love of one's country ran highest in the face of threats from external enemies, and that such threats brought out patriotic self-sacrifice as could no other. But love of one's country has a domestic side as well, according to Bryce, a side which is proud to be well governed, peaceful, just, and free. This home side of patriotism, the basis of all good citizenship, is essential for the well-being of democracies, but it is fragile, and, as he brings out in this book, liable to suffer from certain difficulties.

In Bryce's estimation, the fundamental causes of bad citizenship are indolence, selfish personal interest, and party spirit. Of these hindrances to good citizenship he deems indolence to be the most widespread, selfish personal interest to be the most pernicious, and party spirit to be the most excusable, but also the subtlest and most likely to affect those classes from which most leaders are drawn. Bryce discusses these obstacles to good citizenship, and finally offers his thoughts on what can be done to remove them. Although he was writing in the early twentieth, Bryce speaks to us as if a contemporary and has much to offer us today.

The Hindrances to Good Citizenship is a classic of late nineteenth-century liberal social analysis, undergoing eight printings from 1909 to 1931, a clear indication of its popularity and value beyond its author's own lifetime. It then went out of print for some sixty years. Nonetheless, I argue that Bryce's life and his place in the history remain significant to the social sciences.

Although the social sciences have followed separate courses of development throughout much of this century, they remain set firmly on the foundations laid by the founding generation in the late nineteenth and early twentieth centuries. While some of the founders like Weber and Durkheim are justly credited with the influence they have continued to exert over social science from the start, others, like Bryce, have become, perhaps less justly, mere footnotes in its history. But since such histories remain plastic in the hands of revisionist and elaborative scholars, there are always opportunities to rescue a reputation like Bryce's and restore such influence as he once had to a central place in social science discourse.

After Tocqueville's *Democracy in America*, the next-best book about American society is Bryce's *The American Commonwealth*. Given its continued importance, as well as many of Bryce's other accomplishments, it is strange that he has become one of the forgotten great men of the social sciences. While our fascination with Tocqueville goes beyond his ideas and includes the story of his life, comparatively little is known about Bryce, who is yet to be the subject of a modern biography. But he was famous during his life and remained so after his death for his accomplishments as a writer, scholar, jurist, and diplomat. How Bryce accomplished what he did as a man of affairs, and yet had the time to write as many important books and articles as he did is itself a mystery.

Bryce was born in Belfast, Northern Ireland, in 1838, to solidly middle-class parents of Scotch-Irish descent. When his father, a well-known mathematician and geologist, was appointed a master at Glasgow High School, Bryce and his family moved to Scotland. At age sixteen, young Bryce began his studies at Glasgow University, where his grandfather, father, and uncles had studied before him.

At Glasgow, Bryce studied Latin, Greek, mathematics, and logic. But as he said later, no history was taught, nor was English literature, nor any branch of the natural sciences. During summer vacations Bryce spent much time wandering in western Scotland and northern Ireland, and his lifelong passions for travel, mountain climbing, and botany were awakened. In fact, Bryce eventually managed to visit and write about all the inhabited continents. Elected to the Alpine Club in 1879, Bryce climbed mountains all over the world, and was quite famous for doing so; Mount Bryce in the Canadian Rockies was named after him in 1898. Rounding out his avocations, Bryce was an avid botanist who discovered a number of new species of plants.

After three years at Glasgow, Bryce was awarded a scholarship at Trinity College, Oxford, where he studied law, and made many friends who, like himself, would leave their marks upon the world. Among these future jurists, philosophers, art critics, poets, and educators were Albert Venn Dicey, T. H. Green, Walter Pater, Matthew Arnold, A. C. Swinburne, and Benjamin Jowett.

In 1862 Bryce entered Lincoln's Inn, and a year later continued his study of law at Heidelberg. During that same year he won the Arnold

Historical Essay Prize at Oxford for his essay on the Holy Roman Empire, which was published in 1864 in a much revised and expanded form. The publication of *The Holy Roman Empire* earned Bryce an international reputation as a scholar. He was called to the bar in 1867, and became a successful lawyer. Soon after, he began his long career in public service by serving on a royal commission studying education.

In 1870 Bryce was appointed Regius Professor of Law at Oxford, a post he held until 1893, and in which he did much to revive the study of Roman law. Many of his best essays were written during this period, and these were collected in his *Studies in History and Jurisprudence,* published in 1901. At any rate, 1870 was important to Bryce for another reason as well, for it was then that he took his first trip to America (which I shall discuss below), hence marking his first interest in this country, the study of which would make him famous beyond his time.

Elected to Parliament in 1880, Bryce gave up his law practice two years later, and then began working on the manuscript of *The American Commonwealth*. He had returned to America in 1881 and again in 1883, and these trips gave him yet more insight into his subject. But Bryce's time was being taken up with increasingly pressing public duties. All during this time he continued to serve in Parliament, and in 1886 he served as Under Secretary for Foreign Affairs in Gladstone's government. But finally, in 1888, he published *The American Commonwealth*, the book which made him famous in his own day and beyond.

Bryce again served in Gladstone's government in 1892, when he helped draft the Home Rule Bill for Ireland. In 1907, he was appointed as British Ambassador to the United States, and was very successful in this post, which he held until 1913, when he resigned at age 75. A year later he was raised to the Peerage as a viscount, and entered the House of Lords. But Bryce was not yet done with public service, and chaired an international committee to look into German war atrocities in Belgium. In 1915 and 1916 he was instrumental in fostering the idea for the League of Nations. In 1921 Bryce published his last book, *Modern Democracies*. He died a year later.

Like Tocqueville before him, Bryce first visited, and later wrote a famous book about, America. So similar yet different were the visits and consequent observations of these men that the two deserve comparison. Tocqueville came to America in 1831 to make a report on prisons for the French government. He was a well-educated, relatively young man of twenty-six years of age, accompanied by a friend, Gustave de Beaumont, also a young lawyer. In their ten-month journey Tocqueville and Beaumont traveled extensively, met and interviewed many Americans including President Andrew Jackson, former President John Quincy Adams, U.S. senators such as Daniel Webster, and writers such as William Ellery Channing and Jared Sparks. In 1835, three years after returning to France, Tocqueville published the first volume, which was followed by the second in 1840, of *Democracy in America*, still widely hailed as the best book ever written about that subject.

While Tocqueville made only one trip to America, Bryce made several. In 1870, almost four decades after Tocqueville's, Bryce made his first journey to America. At thirty-two he was only slightly older than Tocqueville had been. He too was very well educated and trained in the law, and had in fact just been appointed Regius Professor of Civil Law at Oxford.

Like Tocqueville, Bryce was accompanied by a soon to be famous friend, Albert Venn Dicey, who like Beaumont was also a lawyer. Dicey, as Beaumont before him, went on to become notable in his own right as an author, and published his great classic, *Lectures on the Relation between Law and Public Opinion in England during the Nineteenth Century*, in 1905. While Beaumont had a career in the French Parliament and as an author, Dicey became the first Vinerian Professor of English Law at Oxford, and wrote treatises on constitutional law that are considered classics.

This first trip whetted Bryce's interest, and he returned twice before beginning work on *The American Commonwealth* in 1883. Again, like Tocqueville, Bryce benefitted from conversations with many knowledgeable Americans, including a future President of the United States, Theodore Roosevelt, a future United States Supreme Court justice, Oliver Wendell Holmes Jr, and many journalists, jurists, politicians, and academics. Unlike Tocqueville, Bryce took a long time to write his book; with his election to Parliament, and his service in Gladstone's government, it was hard for him to find time to work on his massive manuscript. *The American Commonwealth* was finally published in 1888, and has often been hailed as the second-best book ever written about civic culture in America, after Tocqueville's *Democracy*.

From the time of its first publication in 1835 through the rest of the century, both popular and academic interest in Tocqueville's *Democracy in America* ran high. But as one of Tocqueville's best biographers, George Pierson, put it,

> ... as the nineteenth century passed away in America, and as the nationalized, industrialized era of the twentieth century came in, swiftly to sweep away the traces of the farmer democracy that Tocqueville had known, it seemed a little as if Tocqueville and his thoughts were at length outmoded. In the United States one no longer read his book in school. Apparently, even with scholars, *Democracy in America* was at last fading out of the content of political thought.
>
> (Pierson, 1938, p. 792)

Just as Tocqueville's *Democracy* was waning in importance, Bryce's *American Commonwealth* was taking center stage. *The American Commonwealth* was met with praise everywhere, as exemplified by the long and gracious reviews it received here and in England in 1889, specifically, from Woodrow Wilson in the *Political Science Quarterly*, and from Lord Acton in the *English Historical Review*.

Both Wilson and Acton compared Bryce's work to Tocqueville's, and while the former seemed to prefer Tocqueville's style and incomparable judgment, he nevertheless said that *The American Commonwealth* "is a great work, worthy of heartiest praise" (Wilson, 1889, p. 153). Like Wilson, Acton also realized that Tocqueville's and Bryce's books were to be judged on their own separate merits, and that if Bryce "has not the chill sententiousness of his great French predecessor, his portable wisdom and detached thoughts, he has made a far deeper study of real life…" (Acton, 1889, p. 388). But for all the praise Tocqueville got, Bryce carried the day. For the next fifty years Bryce's book was ubiquitous. It went through a number of revisions and was abridged for use in schools and colleges, and over 200,000 copies were sold. Bryce was quoted everywhere, and excerpts of his work were a solid part of many of the best social science textbooks, such as Park and Burgess's *Introduction to the Science of Sociology*.

Although he is often referred to as Lord Bryce, he was and remained a commoner throughout his life until 1914, after he retired as Ambassador to the United States, when he was elevated to viscount. Bryce was actually offered a peerage earlier, just before he was about to take on his duties as ambassador, but fearing that accepting a title would offend democratic sentiments of equality in America he declined the offer. Three years later, while he was ambassador, he was again offered a title, and again declined for the same reason. Both he and his wife had always felt reluctant to take a title, but upon returning to England and thinking that he could be useful in the House of Lords, he reconsidered and accepted when offered a peerage for the third time. But no matter what his social standing, Bryce was no mere gentleman scholar. While he is remembered as a man of practical affairs, a politician, a statesman, a world traveler and mountain climber, an orator, and especially as an author, he is hardly remembered at all for the important part he played in the institutional history of modern social science.

Remarkably there is no modern biography of Bryce, in fact there have only been two books ever written about him: H. A. L. Fisher's *James Bryce* written in 1927 is Bryce's only biography, and Edmund Ions' monograph, *James Bryce and American Democracy* written in 1968 gives some biographical details while concentrating on Bryce's relationship to America (Fisher, 1927). While Fisher does discuss Bryce's key role in founding the *English Historical Review* with his friend Lord Acton, neither he nor Ions even mentions that in 1904 Bryce helped found and was the inaugural president of England's first sociological association, the Sociological Society of London (Mitchell, 1968).

Neither do Fisher nor Ions mention that Bryce was an early member of L'Institut International de Sociologie founded in 1893 by the French sociologist Rene Worms. In fact, Bryce was elected and served a term as vice president of the institute, an honor shared over the early years by such famous social scientists as Gabriel Tarde, Ludwig Gumplowicz, Lujo Brentano, Alfred Marshall, Ferdinand Tönnies, Georg Simmel, Wilhelm Wundt, Albion Small, Thorstein Veblen, E. A. Ross, and Woodrow Wilson (Clark, 1973). Finally, while Bryce is cited, almost in passing, by Ions for his service in 1909 as the fourth president of the American Political Science Association, nothing much is made of it. But Bryce's contributions to social science deserve more attention than they have received.

Although today he is largely remembered only for *The American Commonwealth*, in his own day Bryce was a well-known scholar. It is noteworthy that beyond the professional honors accorded him, he was asked to lecture at colleges and universities throughout America including Harvard, Yale, Chicago, Columbia, Brown, Berkeley, Stanford, Haverford, Tuskegee, Amherst, Union, Rutgers, and many others.

Bryce's university lectures all show an active, scholarly, and practical mind at work. Bryce knew America as well as anybody, perhaps even better than anybody, and his lectures, insofar as they touched upon American subjects, are superb. In these Yale lectures on citizenship Bryce addresses the problems of civic duty in both general and specific terms. They remain valuable not merely for their historical interest as sketches of how the problems of citizenship were viewed at the beginning of this century, but more so for the insights they provide us for understanding the permanent problems of civic duty in modern democracies even as these have evolved in ways Bryce could not have anticipated. At this century's end Bryce's *Hindrances* should be at least as interesting as they were upon first publication in 1909.

A society's standard of civic duty, according to Bryce, is shaped and influenced by the relationship of two universally opposing principles: "the principle of Obedience and the principle of Independence, the submission of the individual will to other wills and the assertion of that will against other wills." Looking backward to centuries past, Bryce suggested that if taken to extremes, the principle of obedience leads to despotism, and the principle of independence leads to anarchy. Little did he know how apt this theory would be in the century which lay ahead. Nevertheless, Bryce saw that what he called "the reasonable mean" between these two principles was imperative for the creation and survival of modern democratic states (Bryce, 1888, pp. 406–407).

While the principle of obedience is indispensable for the survival of any form of government, democracies, like no other, depend on both the principle of obedience and the principle of independence. Bryce understood that, unlike any other form of government, democracy requires that members of the state "be capable of citizenship" (Bryce, 1888, pp. 406–407). The citizen of a democracy must be capable of the following: understanding the larger interests of the community as well as his own, judging when his own interests must be subordinated to those of the community, and having a sense of civic duty, by which Bryce meant serving the community by voting, working, or holding office.

But Bryce also knew that in the history of modern democracies, the principle of independence had become associated with the most powerful and alluring political prize, namely, "rights." As such, the principle of independence almost always exerts the strongest pull upon the individual. Or, as Bryce said, the struggle for political liberty was everywhere begun under the banner of rights, which were "something claimed by the citizen as due to him, to be held and exercised for his benefit and satisfaction" (Bryce, 1888, pp. 406–407).

Although citizens of democracies may prefer to exercise their rights rather than attend to their civic duties, the "civic relation," as Bryce called it, depends on the latter as much as the former. "Benefit and burden, power and responsibility, go together," he said, and even if citizens favor being reminded of their rights rather than their duties, "a democracy which the bulk of its members did not care to join in directing would not be a democracy at all, but a government of the many by the few" (Bryce, 1888, pp. 406–407).

Although often characterized as a more objective and less philosophical observer of American civil society than was Tocqueville, Bryce was no less a moralist than was his notable French predecessor. Both Tocqueville and Bryce agreed that individualism was distinctively part of the American character, and that it stood in the way of those civic virtues which support democracy, without which it would crumble. Recognizing individualism as a characteristic problem for democracies, both Tocqueville and Bryce angled their visions of America obliquely, to produce a parallax view of the relationship of the citizen to society.

Looked at from one angle, American individualism is independence writ large, appearing as something romantic, slightly anarchic, even revolutionary; it signifies personal freedom and autonomy, and the maintenance of a healthy distance between an individual and blind obedience and conformity to societal authority. Viewed from another angle, however, individualism assaults the very essence of democracy, and thus threatens those precious freedoms associated with it.

This second, or parallax view, shifts the interpretation of individualism from one of romantic description to one of moral concern. While individualism might be seen as a moral virtue to those, like Emerson, who saw in it the roots of that self-reliance so vital to the democratic spirit, to others, like Tocqueville and Bryce, it represented a moral canker which confronted the democratic ideal with apathy and personal self-interest.

The most famous definition of individualism is Tocqueville's in *Democracy in America*:

> Individualism is a mature and calm feeling, which disposes each member of the community to sever himself from the mass of his fellows and to draw apart with his family and his friends, so that after he has thus formed a little circle of his own, he willingly leaves society at large to itself.
> (Tocqueville, 1945, p. 98)

But Tocqueville did more than name individualism, he showed its connection to both anarchy and despotism which are caused by "that general apathy which is the consequence of individualism" (Tocqueville, 1945, p. 368).

If Tocqueville was the first to point out the dangers of individualism to the agrarian democracy of the early nineteenth century, Bryce followed suit a half century later by showing how individualism continued to degrade the democratic ideal in the industrial democracy of the late nineteenth and early twentieth centuries.

In "Oligarchies within Democracies," a brilliant chapter in his *Modern Democracies*, Bryce concludes that the majority of citizens pay so little attention to public affairs that "they willingly leave all but the most important to be dealt with by the few." Attributing this lack of interest to the same type of individualistic tendencies as did Tocqueville, Bryce suggests that an individual's interests and priorities follow the following order:

> ... first, the occupation by which he makes his living..., secondly, his domestic concerns, his family and relatives and friends,

thirdly,... his religious beliefs or observances, fourthly, his amusements or personal tastes, be they for sensual or for intellectual enjoyments, fifthly, his civic duty to the community.

(Bryce, 1921, p. 547)

Although Bryce was aware that the order of these interests varies from citizen to citizen, he was certain that civic duty would almost always rank last. As he said in *The American Commonwealth*, some fifty years after Tocqueville, "individualism, the love of enterprise, and the pride in personal freedom, have been deemed by Americans not only their choicest, but their peculiar and exclusive possessions" (Bryce, 1888, pp. 406–407). That these very American values born of democracy should be an obstacle to fulfilling the democratic spirit was an irony not lost on Bryce any more than it had been on Tocqueville. Both these foreign observers indicted American society for its individualism, but in these lectures on citizenship Bryce combines moral discourse and political analysis to help us understand what is at stake when indolence, self-interest, and party spirit stand in the way of the fulfillment of civic duty.

First presented at Yale University during a few days in mid-October 1908, Bryce's lectures on citizenship were considered important news, and were covered in *The New York Times* (1908). They were not as polished as they were when published a year later as *Hindrances to Good Citizenship*, but Bryce's more basic and streamlined original lectures offer us the seed from which the finished product grew.

In his first lecture, as reported in the *Times*, Bryce blamed the "educated classes of America" for their indolence in civic duties. Such indolence in his eyes "made it a government of the many who don't care by the few who do" (1908). Echoing one of Tocqueville's, as well as one of his own famous observations in *The American Commonwealth*, Bryce noted the effect of selfishness in a business civilization such as our own. "Absorbed in business or pleasures, we think little of what our membership in a free nation means. The eloquent voice of a patriotic reformer sometimes breaks our slumber, but the daily round of business or pleasure soon fills the mind and public duty again fades into the background of life" (Bryce, 1888, pp. 406–407). Tocqueville had observed this same individualistic spirit in America about seventy-five years earlier.

Bryce's chief complaint was that among the educated classes, as he called the middle and upper classes, there was too much reluctance by "the fellows who are too good to run for minor offices," to take the lead in governing their local communities, states, and the nation. This was an old complaint against democracy, one which Tocqueville had thought was basic to the destruction of the Old Regime in France, and which Bryce had lodged against the "better classes" in America many times. The *Times* reported that he indicated several reasons for the reduced interest of the citizen in his civic responsibilities. Among these was,

> the more indulgent temper of our times, which takes everything and everybody easily. Another arose from the vast growth of population which made each man's share in government seem so small. A third was that competition with public duty of new tastes, pursuits, and interests which the more changeful character of business, the increasing knowledge of science and liking for art, and above all, the passion for amusement and all that is called 'sport' had brought.
>
> (Bryce, 1993, p. 23)

Indolence, of course, transcends politics. The same indifference, or apathy, which hinders good citizenship causes many of the wasted opportunities of life which leave failure in place of success. Having led a tirelessly active life himself, Bryce reflects pitilessly upon those who allow "*fortune*" to have settled what "*will*," ought to have settled. But if in their private lives people are so sluggish as to let the happy moment slip, how, wonders Bryce, could it be otherwise in the discharge of civic duty?

Paradoxically then, apathy is both an enemy as well as a product of democracy. Reminding us that "the theory of democracy assumes a far higher level of good sense, judgment, honest purpose, devotion to the public welfare…than is needed in a [despotic oligarchy]," Bryce also argues that since shared civic duties, as such duties invariably are in a democracy, seem less personal, the sense of obligation is weak. Thus, since public affairs are of less personal importance for the average citizen than are private ones, indolence is the rule, and diligence the exception. Besides, "the average man," as Bryce was wont to say, "judges himself by the average standard, and does not see why he should take any more trouble than his neighbors." Only for "the best sort of citizen," in Bryce's words, does civic duty exceed personal duty. The basic fault of democracy was therefore summed up for Bryce in the dictum, cited above, "what is Everybody's business is Nobody's business" (Bryce, 1993, p. 73).

Whereas one might have supposed that under the increased influence of education and the press, civic apathy would have decreased, according to Bryce such indolence actually increased. Among the general causes of this increased apathy Bryce cited gentler manners and less anger. "A chief duty of the good citizen is to be angry when anger is called for," said Bryce, lamenting the decline of righteous indignation, a decline which signaled a deterioration in the standard of civic virtue. Yet today we may not only be experiencing this decline, but rather celebrating it as tolerance of "diversity"—a survival strategy in the cultural polyglot that is modern America (Bryce, 1993, p. 73).

Although Bryce was no Anglo-conformist like his friend Theodore Roosevelt, who once wrote that

> …we have no room for any people who do not act and vote simply as Americans and nothing else… where immigrants, or the sons of immigrants, do not heartily and in good faith throw in their lot with us, but cling to the speech, the customs, the ways of life, and the habits of thought of the Old World which they have left, they thereby do harm to both themselves and us,

he had a more unified moral vision of citizenship and nationality than our cultural pluralists have today (Baltzell & Schneiderman, 1991, p. 218). Bryce was in fact closer in outlook to Frederick Jackson Turner, his one-time assistant, who, in "The Significance of the Frontier in American History," wrote that "the frontier promoted the formation of a composite nationality for the American people" (Baltzell & Schneiderman, 1991, p. 220). It is interesting to note that in 1908, the same year that Bryce presented these lectures on citizenship at Yale, "The Melting Pot," a play by Israel Zangwell, opened in New York. In it the hero says, "America is God's crucible, the great Melting Pot where all races of Europe are melting and reforming," thus giving rise to one of the most powerful American self-images, one, in fact, shared by Bryce (Baltzell & Schneiderman, 1991, p. 219).

Anticipating what is now a common explanation of public apathy, Bryce also argued that the growth in size of modern democracies "made the share in government of the individual citizen seem infinitesimally small." This was a seminal insight by Bryce. Thus, echoing many of the findings of voting researchers, Robert Kuttner, writing in *The New Republic* in 1987, said "The decay of civic participation is a circular problem. People stop voting because they feel they can't make a difference, and then the entire political system seems somebody else's property" (Kuttner, 1987, p. 21).

Bryce also had another theory, now commonly held, that attributed civic indifference to the advent of various forms of mass entertainment which divert citizens from their more arduous civic duties. That Bryce wrote before the invention of radios, televisions, motion pictures, VCRs, and personal computers is significant. He saw a new and widespread interest in literature, art, and science as "reducing the interest in public affairs among the educated classes," and the burgeoning interest in organized athletics among all classes, but especially among the less educated, as serving the same diverting function (Bryce, 1909, p. 76). In this Bryce went beyond Tocqueville, who thought that Americans considered literature, theater, and poetry as "transient and necessary recreation amid the serious labors of life" (Tocqueville, 1945, p. 59). For Bryce, these had replaced for many Americans an interest in participating in the civic life.

Whatever its causes, however, indolence reduces the sense of public duty, and manifests itself as an increased unwillingness to participate in the common forms of civic life: voting, thinking, being well-informed, persuading, leading, and holding office.

After indolence, private self-interest stands as the next greatest impediment to good citizenship. Less widespread than apathy, selfish personal interest is more harmful to democracy.

The tendency to expand government action had begun during the mid- to late nineteenth century, but by 1908 Bryce recognized that many diverse groups were demanding even more government interference with enterprises which were normally left to the private domain. He had no personal quarrel with this tendency, but he believed it had a bearing upon good citizenship. As the role of government expands, Bryce said, and

> ... interferes with the conduct of private persons of any matter in which money can either be made or spent, the more grounds does it supply to private persons for trying to influence its action in the direction which will benefit such persons.

These people will, therefore, have private interests which differ from the larger public interests, and these private interests will tempt them to act "with a view, not to the common good, but to their own pockets" (Bryce, 1993, p. 97).

There are various forms in which private self-interest manifests itself, thus perverting civic duty. First among these is bribery, which corrupts not only the public official whose vote or influence has been bought, but also the briber who has subverted the common interest in favor of his own.

Second among the manifestations of self-interest is the tendency of whole classes of citizens to try to shift tax burdens from themselves and onto others. It is interesting that Bryce devoted as much space as he did to examining taxation as an arena for the perversion of civic duty. After all, he was writing before there was a federal income tax—the 16th Amendment to the Constitution, which authorized the Congress to levy a federal income tax, was not ratified until 1913—and also before many states levied income taxes. Nevertheless, Bryce, an astute observer of democracy in America, as well as in Great Britain and elsewhere, understood that all questions about taxation "are apt to present themselves to the individual citizen rather as affecting his own pocket than as matters of general policy" (Bryce, 1993, p. 29).

Other spheres in which private self-interest manifests itself to the detriment of civic duty are tariffs and tariff policies which give advantages to home producers by disadvantaging foreign competitors, appropriations of public money for local projects, government franchises for railroads, gas-works, water supplies, and other public utilities, government contracts for military supplies, government employment, and all sorts of legislation in which pecuniary and power interests are affected. In all of these spheres of government activity, according to Bryce, there is a temptation for individual citizens to "turn governmental action to private ends" (Bryce, 1993, p. 29). But while there may have been a time when this privatist ethos was consistent with democracy and citizenship, with the industrial transformation of America, those conditions had been emphatically altered.

Bryce was a well-respected commentator in America, and his thoughts about greed and corruption were newsworthy. Thus, under the headline "Bryce Sees Danger in Power of Money" *The New York Times* reported on his Yale lecture about self-interest. Expanding on this in *Hindrances*, Bryce understood that avarice, like indolence, goes well beyond politics, corrupting all parts of social life. But he saw avarice as especially detrimental to democratic societies. "The power of money is the root of all evil in government and is the real danger to democracy," Bryce told his listeners at Yale, and "the damage done by it is more than that done by apathy and indifference" (*The New York Times*, October 17, 1908, p. 9).

Bryce was also concerned that the higher-status, better educated classes from which public leaders were most likely to be drawn were most apt to be affected by the love of money. Like Tocqueville before him, Bryce observed that the upper classes set the moral standard for all the rest. Indeed, he called the leading political stratum drawn from the upper classes "the tone-setting class," because he believed that it is this class that "forms the standard not only for those who conduct public business but also to a great extent for the whole community" (Bryce, 1993, p. 118).

A tone-setting class, or what we might today call an establishment, should, according to Bryce, set a high standard. If it sets a low standard and tolerates base motives and actions, "it depraves the morality of the community…and politics are defiled and debased, selfishness and trickery are taken to be natural, and public life becomes the favorite hunting ground of unscrupulous and reckless men" (Bryce, 1993, p. 119). Once the moral or civic standard is lowered it is difficult to raise it again, and Bryce advocated legislation to prevent men from getting rich through public life.

Along these same lines, Bryce was an advocate of merely moderate fortunes—perhaps anticipating the bulging middle and upper-middle classes that grew in post-World War II America—which he thought would prevent class warfare between a small class of great wealth and an enormous class of the poor. He thought that the proliferation of moderate fortunes was an ideal buffer, because it would mean that the selfish interests of the rich and poor would not sway the very large classes of moderate fortune from the public interest.

Perhaps Bryce's advocacy of middle- and upper-middle-class democracy is not so hard to understand. He himself came from just such a solid middle- to upper-middle-class background. Although he was a fighting liberal in England, Bryce would have been considered a conservative, at least of the Mugwump sort, in America. Democracy, yes; populism, no. Bryce was clearly an advocate of responsible leadership by the "better" classes, and to him this didn't mean successful moneyed classes per se, but rather solidly educated achieving classes willing to take the lead in civic duty. His ideal in this was his good friend Theodore Roosevelt, who, he told his audience at Yale, as a young man "more than twenty years ago did not consider himself above going to the lower house of the New York Legislature and who has now become an eminent statesman."

Party spirit, or the spirit of faction, the third major hindrance to good citizenship, is also the most excusable. Bryce begins his discussion of factionalism most judiciously, reminding us that there has been little consensus among philosophers, historians, and politicians as to whether party spirit has been a help or a hindrance to maintaining a high standard of civic duty.

Recalling Thucydides' account of the massacres in Corcyra as an example of the excesses of factionalism, Bryce suggests that party spirit has been known to corrupt and do damage to public morals. Conspiracy, treason, and rebellion, as well as sedition, sectionalism, and mutual hatred have also been spawned by the spirit of faction.

Conversely, practical politicians and intellectuals who have themselves been deeply involved in politics—Bryce has Edmund Burke in mind—have been more likely to praise party spirit as essential for the maintenance of democracy. They argue, Bryce says, that party spirit brings out the electorate, brings people together to work for what they commonly believe in, and supports the power of free government. Some, like Burke, however, qualify their praise, and only see virtue in party spirit when it is associated with principles and policies "honestly advocated as being for the good of the community" (Bryce, 1993, 130). Party spirit is debased for such thinkers when it is associated with the blind following of leaders, and with efforts to secure either political power for its own sake, or the more tangible material spoils that come with it.

Parties, party spirit, and party formation, each of which he focuses on herein, are subjects which Bryce was pre-eminently qualified to discuss.

Writing before the publication of Robert Michels' *Political Parties*, and Moisie Ostrogorski's *Democracy and the Organization of Political Parties*, Bryce was the first social scientist to analyze political parties. In fact, both Michels and Ostrogorski, as well as Max Weber, were well acquainted with Bryce's chapters on parties in *The American Commonwealth*. As a practical politician and statesman, as well as a historian and political scientist, Bryce had spent much of his professional life observing political parties and party spirit at work. Thus, Bryce's own thoughts on these matters are of particular interest.

"Party Spirit" is Bryce's most personalized chapter in *Hindrances to Good Citizenship*; peppering it with personal anecdotes and reflections, Bryce pours himself into the subject with some passion. Like many other political thinkers before him, from Aristotle through Tocqueville, Bryce embraces moderation and abhors extremism. When taken to the extreme, party spirit is abusive and harmful to good citizenship, but when moderate party spirit animates a democracy, it promotes civic virtue.

After describing how parties are formed in a democracy, Bryce discusses their virtues, especially those which are indispensable in large-scale modern states where private self-interest and public apathy are likely to be present, and in which there is no obvious political ruling class from which potential leaders are automatically drawn, as in traditional and aristocratic societies. Among these indispensable functions are the ability to frame public issues and broadcast them to the community, to organize like-minded citizens to address issues of public concern, and to select and endorse leaders who are fit to hold office. Even while recognizing that these functions, especially the nominating function, extend the range and power of party actions, and in so doing open the possibility that eager, ambitious, and sometimes unscrupulous politicians will try to use the parties for their own devices, Bryce nevertheless understood that they tend to promote the public good.

When, however, parties are abused by self-interested politicians, or when party spirit is excessive and leads to blind faith in leaders, or hatred of the opposing party, the standards of good citizenship are hard to uphold. Citizens may find it impossible to make fair and unbiased judgments, loyalty to party may allow catchwords and cant phrases to replace critical reasoning as the basis for decision-making, and loyalty to the party may replace loyalty to the nation.

In the end, Bryce saw that in a democracy it is the average citizen, one who belongs to a party but is not an automaton of it who cuts short party excesses. Remarking that leadership is essential to a democracy, a theme he first brought up in *The American Commonwealth*, Bryce went on to say that "just as the multitude need leaders to inspire them and to think for them, so leaders need the great mass of sensible, well-intentioned followers to keep them in check" (Bryce, 1993, p. 155). How a democracy can ensure itself of having such a great mass of sensible and well-intentioned citizens, Bryce mused about in his concluding chapter, "How to Overcome the Obstacles to Good Citizenship."

Bryce offered two overarching approaches to overcome the obstacles to the fulfillment of civic duty: either improve the citizens, or improve the system of government. For the former, Bryce suggests "ethical remedies," for the latter, "mechanical remedies." Acquainted as he was with politics, Bryce was sure that the most concrete and enduring changes for the better in politics would require ethical remedies, meaning that the level of intelligence and virtue among the citizens would have to be raised. But he was equally certain that it would be a mistake to underestimate mechanical improvements to the structure of government. After all, said Bryce,

> to take away from bad men the means and opportunities by which they may do evil, to furnish good men with the means and opportunities which make it easier for them to prevent or overcome evil, is to render a great service.
> (Bryce, 1993, p. 159)

Before offering his own, Bryce comments upon two philosophical solutions to the problems of good citizenship popular at the time. First, while suggesting that they deserve consideration "because their doctrine represents a protest that needs to be made against the conception of an all-engulfing state in which individual initiative and self-guided development might be merged and lost," Bryce rejects the mechanical remedies of the philosophical anarchists (Bryce, 1993, p. 159). As he knew, they would cure the diseases of government by eliminating government itself. Clearly, Bryce thought that big government was itself somewhat of an obstacle to good citizenship, and maybe even a danger to democracy, but he had no faith in the goodness of human nature and brotherly love to allow individuals and families to live peacefully together without any government at all.

At the opposite end of the philosophical spectrum was the socialist solution, for which Bryce, who disliked big government, had little respect. The socialist answer to the problems of citizenship was to expand state power and authority until everyone relied on government officials for everything. Bryce conceded that under such a regime self-interest would be eliminated, but only because everyone's private business would vanish. But Bryce was no collectivist, and he feared that personal selfishness might actually become more dangerous if government had even more power than it then did. He also wondered if party spirit in a socialist state might not become yet stronger, and more pernicious than before. One can only imagine what Bryce might think about his own prescience had he lived through the twentieth century, with the coming of the welfare state in the West, and the rise of the enormous Communist one-party regimes of the Soviet bloc, and in China.

Moving on from this examination of philosophical designs for the wholesale reorganization of the modern state, Bryce turned his attention to more modest suggestions for reforming the structure of democratic governments to enhance active citizen participation and concern for the commonweal. Among these suggested reforms are a system of proportional representation, and direct popular voting in the form of the initiative (in which a certain proportion of the electorate may propose a law upon which the people vote), and the referendum (in which a law already passed by the legislature is brought before the electorate for final approval). Bryce mentioned that some countries have tried plans of obligatory voting to overcome the effects of citizen apathy, but quickly concluded that such schemes would violate the values and habits of political culture in places like America and England, and hence would have little popular support.

Like all else in *Hindrances*, the points Bryce made about voter participation are as relevant today as they were to his audience and readers at its beginning of the twentieth century. In November 1908, two weeks or so after Bryce presented these lectures at Yale, about two-thirds of the eligible voters in the United States voted in the national presidential election won by William Howard Taft. While the percentage of voters participating in that election was almost identical to the percentage of those who had voted in the previous election in 1904, which produced a victory for Theodore Roosevelt, it was considerably smaller than the percentage of eligible voters who turned out in each of the presidential elections since the Civil War, which averaged between 75% and 80%. With this in mind, we can see that Bryce's concern about citizen apathy was conditioned by the fact that since the Civil War, and actually well before, going back to the election of 1840, about three-quarters of the eligible electorate had come out to vote in U.S. presidential elections. Could Bryce have known or imagined that the percentage of eligible voters participating in presidential elections would never again even be as high as it was in 1908? With only about half the eligible electorate voting in the 1988 election, and not much higher a percentage having turned out in the four previous elections, voter apathy seems to have reached a level which would have shocked Bryce when he wrote *Hindrances to Good Citizenship*.

The picture of voter apathy is even gloomier if we look at off-year elections. In 1910, a year after Bryce published *Hindrances*, about 54% of the electorate voted, a percentage almost identical to that of the previous off-year election in 1906, and not much below the 57% who turned out in 1902. But from the time of the Civil War down to the election of 1898, not less than two-thirds of the eligible voters had voted in off-year elections. In contrast to the period up to the time that Bryce was writing this book, our contemporary electorate seems to be apathetic to the extreme. In 1986 only a little more than one-third of the electorate came out to vote, a not too much lower figure than that for the previous three off-year elections, in which the average turnout was just under 40% of the eligible voters.

Aside from the much greater voter apathy today, Bryce should also be interesting to us for his sound analysis of the problems confronting American democracy. For instance, although he understood that American political values would not support compulsory voting laws, Bryce was correct in assuming that such laws would serve to get the electorate involved in the democratic process. Thus, in Belgium and Luxembourg, where voting is compulsory, and in Italy, where, although voting is not compulsory, non-voting is recorded on citizens' official documents, the average rate of voter participation from the early 1970s through the mid-1980s was about 86% (Burnham, 1987).

Likewise, Bryce's advocacy of proportional representation is notable in terms of the relatively high voter turnout in countries that have such policies. In countries having proportional representation policies, such as Denmark, Finland, France, West Germany, Greece, Ireland, Israel, Norway, Spain, and Sweden, among others, the average rate of voter participation during the early 1970s through mid-1980s was about 82%. While this rate is below that of countries with compulsory voting policies, it is substantially higher than that of those countries that have district elections, where winners have a plurality on one ballot. These countries, like Canada, Japan, and the United Kingdom, had an average voter turnout rate of about 73% during the early 1970s through the mid-1980s. Then there is the United States, which during this same time period had a voter turnout rate of about 55% during presidential election years, and about 39% during off years (Burnham, 1987). Apparently there still are powerful hindrances to good citizenship at work in American political society.

As interesting and inviting as the mechanical remedies might be, Bryce was adamant that "the central problem of civic duty is the ethical problem." To alter the political system so as to invite greater participation in the democratic process was, of course, desirable, but it was what Bryce called "better conscience" which, he believed, would actually overcome the obstacles to good citizenship. "Indifference, selfish interests, the excesses of party spirit," Bryce wrote,

> will all begin to disappear as civic life is lifted on to a higher plane, and as the number of those who, standing on that higher plane, will apply a strict test to their own conduct and to that of their leaders, realizing and striving to discharge their responsibilities, goes on steadily increasing until they come to form the majority of the people.
>
> (Bryce, 1993, p. 173)

The most effective way to raise the level of the civic conscience, Bryce thought, was through education—moral education, that is. He believed that this was especially important because of the massive waves of immigrants coming to America at that time, "most of them ignorant of our language, still more of them ignorant, not only of your institutions, but of the general principles and habits of free government," Bryce lectured. But trends in the relationship between education and civic responsibility since Bryce's day show that perhaps he was too sanguine about the ability of education to raise the level of the better conscience among all citizens.

A survey of the political attitudes of American youngsters, conducted by People for the American Way in 1989, found that only about 7% of those surveyed believed that democracy was an important part of what made America a special place, that only about 12% believed that voting was a part of what made one a good citizen, and that less than one out of four believed that it was important to help improve the communities in which they live. The conclusion reached by the authors of this report, *Democracy's Next Generation*, is chilling, and reminds one of Bryce's warning that the defiant regard for rights over and against responsibilities was a constant danger to democracy:

> Consistent with the priority they place on personal happiness, young people reveal notions of America's unique character that emphasize freedom and license almost to the complete exclusion of service or participation. Although they clearly appreciate the democratic freedoms that, in their view make theirs the 'best country in the world to live in,' they fail to perceive a need to reciprocate by exercising the duties and responsibilities of good citizenship.
>
> (*Democracy's Next Generation*, 1989)

Obviously American political culture and its educational institutions—families, schools, churches, and media of communication—are failing to teach about civic duty, and to instill that home side of patriotism which Bryce thought necessary to the democratic enterprise. Indeed, this is consistent with what Robert Bellah and his associates called the "expressive" aspect of our individualist culture. "Its genius," they write in *Habits of the Heart*, "is that it enables the individual to think of commitments—from marriage and work to political and religious involvement—as enhancements for the sense of individual well-being rather than as moral imperatives" (Bellah, 1985, p. 47). One can only think that Bryce would have agreed with this assessment.

Not only do Americans seem to feel less responsibility to fulfill their civic duties, they also seem to know a lot less about how their government works, and who runs it for them. Recent surveys show that in spite of increasingly more and better education, the citizenry knows much less about politics than Bryce could have imagined. Only about two-thirds of those sampled in a 1989 survey knew which party controlled the U.S. House of Representatives, which was more than the 55% who knew which party had a majority in the U.S. Senate. This same survey showed that 71% of those sampled did not know who their U.S. congressman was, and that only 25% could name both U.S. senators from their state. Twenty-four percent did not know the name of their state's governor, and the same percentage did not know who the Vice President of the United States was. Questions about the Bill of Rights also yielded results that show a poor state of knowledge about the workings of the democratic process (Carpini & Keeter, 1991).

Individualism seems to have gotten even stronger than it was in Bryce's day. Bryce ends *Hindrances to Good Citizenship* on a hopeful note: "Here in America I am told that," he said, "the young men are more and more caring for and bestirring themselves to discharge their civic duties. That is the best news one can hear" (Bryce, 1993, p. 184). But the same obstacles to good citizenship that Bryce described in these lectures are still with us. If he was perhaps too optimistic about their eventual disappearance, he was right on the money about their effects. All the more reason to think anew about the problems of civic duty and popular government which Bryce struggled to understand.

This may not be easy, but it is essential. Churchill, it is said, called democracy the worst form of government, except for all the others. Bryce might well have appreciated such irony, because as a liberal he was forever hopeful about both democracy and human nature. But unlike Churchill, Bryce lived out the greater part of his creative life in a world quite different from our own. In 1908, when he presented his lectures on citizenship at Yale, there had been no Russian Revolution or Soviet Union; no Stalin or Hitler; no World War I or World War II; no Korean or Vietnam wars;

no Cold War or Atomic Age; no radio, or television, or talking movies, or VCRs; no Jazz Age or Prohibition; no Jet Age or jet setters; no Space Age or computers. In fact, his world was a small world: Commercial aviation was unknown, and there were not more than a handful of automobiles—and almost no paved roads on which to drive them—and more people lived in rural areas and small towns than anywhere else. In other words, Bryce's was still a small-town world capable of fulfilling the democratic dream of a citizen democracy.

In such a world, Bryce and fellow liberals still could hope that through education and self-sacrifice, citizens of democracies would yet master the prevailing individualism. Thus, Charles Horton Cooley, a brilliant American sociologist and virtual disciple of Bryce, could write, in the same year that *Hindrances* was published, that "a healthy democracy, is indeed a training in judgment and self-control as applied to political action" (Cooley, 1993, p. 152). But, judgment and self-control are the stuff of a particular type of deferential middle-class democracy, which may have predominated in Bryce's day, but does so less in our own age of seemingly endless bureaucratic government.

In Bryce's day, there was still a distinct line between state and society, that is to say, between government on the one hand, and other autonomous associations and social institutions on the other. The powers of the state had not yet reached into the orbits of morality, economics, and education, let alone into social institutions such as family, neighborhood, and occupational group. Citizens could respect the state because it was limited, and promoted freedom. From Tocqueville to Bryce and his friends Acton and Dicey, nineteenth-century liberal thinkers lauded a democracy set in the context of limited political power.

Today, of course, political power often seems limitless, and it has saturated American society from top to bottom. Under this changed condition, the hindrances to good citizenship are more varied, and perhaps more dangerous than in Bryce's time. For, as Tocqueville saw, perhaps better than anyone before or since, the relationship between political centralization, and the individualistic selfishness which Bryce saw as underlying the chief hindrances to good citizenship, could easily lead to despotism.

As secondary powers and associations such as family, social class, church, and neighborhood fade in importance, and as government increasingly stands in their place, "it every day renders the exercise of the free agency of man less useful and less frequent" (Tocqueville, 1945, p. 318). Under these conditions is it any wonder that individuals retreat from civic duty? As Tocqueville said, citizens of democracy

> ... can never, without an effort, tear themselves from their private affairs to engage in public business; their natural bias leads them to abandon the latter to the sole visible and permanent representative of the interests of the community; that is to say, to the state.
>
> (Cooley, 1993, p. 152)

While Bryce's America may no longer be our own, his critique of citizen apathy, personal self-interest, and partisanship is still applicable today. He raises the big issues, asks the right questions, and while, if his answers sound somewhat old-fashioned by our contemporary standards, nevertheless they may still provide a foundation for the continued examination of these problems. If anything, the increased power of government makes an examination of good citizenship more vital now than it was at the beginning of the century, for what may be at stake is freedom itself. As Bryce put it: "Political liberty is the participation of the citizen in the government of the community... It is an Active Right" (Bryce, 1921, pp. 54–55). An active right, indeed. Or as some contemporary wag might say: "use it, or lose it."

15

LEGISLATING SOCIAL AND POLITICAL MORES

William Graham Sumner is often credited as being the first sociologist in America, and as one of the most important of the early sociologists. I would argue that through *Folkways*, his most influential book, Sumner was actually a missing link between proto-sociology, and sociology per se. In "The Prospects of Sociological Theory," his 1949 American Sociological Society presidential address, Talcott Parsons labeled "all the theoretical endeavors before the generation of Durkheim and Max Weber as proto-sociology" (Parsons, 1950, pp. 3–16). To the sociological side of his generational list Parsons added Georg Simmel, and Americans such as Sumner, Robert Park, Charles Horton Cooley, W. I. Thomas, and George Herbert Mead. For Parsons, proto-sociology was marked by speculative systems, rather than by systems of theory. Later, Donald N. Levine used the idea of proto-sociology to good effect, and Philip Manning also revived the term as he used it as a base for another useful idea, namely, "proto-symbolic interaction" (Manning, 2005). In Chapter 7, I distinguish mostly descriptive proto-sociological ideas from analytical sociological ones. The latter are often built upon the foundational ideas of proto-sociology. I suggest that Sumner's *Folkways* is a missing link, so to speak, because although it is a compendious descriptive volume, it also introduces important, albeit pre-mature, concepts such as mores, folkways, ethos, ethnocentrism, and the like, making it just about a full-fledged sociological work.

In *Folkways,* Sumner either introduced or anticipated some of the big concepts that characterize modern sociology. Thus, he coined the term "folkways," and restyled the ancient Greek notion of mores into an almost scalpel-sharp concept. This in itself would have made his reputation, but Sumner went much further, giving us now indispensable concepts such as "ethos," "ethnography," "in-groups," "out-groups" and "we-groups," "ethnocentrism," "antagonistic cooperation," "strain of consistency," "conventionalism," "syncretism and diffusion," two types of institutions and of social change: "enacted" and "crescive," and most interestingly, because the term had never been properly attributed to him, "stereotype." Along with ethnocentrism, Sumner introduced the sociological term "stereotype" as we still use it today, meaning a widespread and simplified in-group idea about some out-group or other. As Sumner put it, stereotypes "seem to convey thought, especially ascertained truth, and they do it in a way to preclude verification. It is absolutely essential to correct thinking and successful discussion to reject stereotyped forms, and to insist on analysis and verification" (Sumner, 1906, p. 181). After *Folkways* was published, "stereotype" became part of the social science and philosophical literature, and was used prominently by sociologists, such as E. A. Ross, social psychologists and philosophers, such as George Herbert Mead, political scientists, such as A. Lawrence Lowell, and anthropologists, such as James George Frazer. Walter Lippmann, of course, popularized the term "stereotype" when he made it the central concept of his well-known and widely read 1922 book, *Public Opinion.* Soon the term "stereotype" was misattributed to Lippmann, who to this day is credited with coining it, by textbooks, Wikipedia, *The Oxford English Dictionary*, and the *International Encyclopedia of the Social Sciences*, among other sources.

However disparate these concepts may seem to be, they are all intimately linked by the fact that they constitute or are affected by "world views." Sumner emphasized the role of culture, values, and ideas in shaping our social behavior, rather than focusing more on the role of social structure. Robert Park and Ernest Burgess were among the first sociological theorists to note Sumner's influence on cultural sociology. Linking Sumner to Durkheim, and communication to social interaction, they say that

> ... as a part of the common life, there grows up a body of custom, convention, tradition, ceremonial, language, social ritual, and

public opinion, in short all that Sumner includes under the term 'mores' and all that ethnologists include under the term 'culture.'

Functionalism may have held sway in the 1950s and 1960s, but today American sociology relies at least as much on Sumner-generated or Sumner-inspired ideas about culture and values, as on functionalism's emphasis on structure and power. In this regard, it is significant that Byron Fox's coda to *The New Sociology* leaves us with the following:

> Sociology for the most part has not come to grips with the 'big-range' implications of political power. This failure is the result of historical developments, especially in the United States. It is interesting to ask, what would have been the course of American sociology had it taken its departure from the Marxian concept of power in political terms, rather than from Sumner in the form of folkways.
> (Fox, 1964, p. 480)

One of the most neglected aspects of Sumner's ideas about change is his concept of a "strain for consistency," which he began discussing in *Folkways*. Sumner's great contribution was to help shape our understanding of cultural and social change. Robert Cooley Angell noticed the usefulness of Sumner's observation that mores

> …tend to evolve in such a way that they remain adjusted to one another. Hence, if in a given society structural drift occurs in family relations, for instance, norms in the field of economic relations will tend to change slowly to fit.
> (Angell, 1958, p. 151)

Ironically, it is to this important contribution that Sumner owes a pivotal downturn of his reputation.

That Sumner's reputation as a *sociologist* has been tarnished, if not eclipsed, by none other than his own alter ego—as Sumner, a *polemicist*—is by now well-established. Mortimer Brewster Smith suggests that Sumner's reputational career

> … is a study in the irony of fame, a vivid example of how changing mores in thinking can dethrone the intellectual hero of

yesterday... he was a giant figure who cast a long shadow over the American political, economic, and social thinking of his time... [but] since his death in 1910 his influence has steadily diminished as his somewhat bleak and austere individualist philosophy has become intellectually unfashionable.
(Smith, 1950, pp. 357–365)

This turnabout has little if anything to do with Sumner's *sociological* writings, per se, but rather is due to his earlier polemical and often contentious writings on public issues and public policy in books such as *What Social Classes Owe Each Other*, and in essays such as "The Absurd Effort to Make the World Over." While these works established Sumner as one of the most prominent public intellectuals of his day, their conservative bent, as measured against progressive values in his own time, and radical-liberal ones today, has alienated him from more progressive-leaning sociologists and intellectuals.

Sumner has been branded a conservative so often that there is a certain taken-for-granted, if not reified, quality about seeing him in that light. Thus, while trying to pay Sumner a compliment, Philip Selznick says the following, which surely speaks for itself: "It was actually a conservative sociologist, William Graham Sumner, who introduced the idea of cultural relativity in America" (Selznick, 1992, p. 92). Certainly, not all sociologists think of Sumner as an archconservative. E. Digby Baltzell noted, "Sumner was an extremely independent individualist and by no means a consistent ideologist for the status quo or the values of the business establishment" (Baltzell, 1964, p. 103). Baltzell shows that Sumner often opposed parts of the business community, all forms of imperialism, restrictions on immigration, and racism. Therefore, any serious attempt to gauge his intellectual importance as a sociologist must also take into account his political and ideological influence.

Sumner's theory of the mores is much more refined and subtle than is usually understood. He even addresses the then current and useful distinction between the conscious and unconscious minds made popular by the German philosopher Eduard von Hartmann in his *Philosphie des Unbewussten* and introduced into the psychoanalytic framework by Sigmund Freud in *The Interpretation of Dreams*, in 1901. The unconscious character of the mores is actually one of their predominant qualities, according to Sumner, who said that it differentiated them from "products of intentional investigation or of rational and conscious reflection, projects formally adopted by voluntary associations, rational methods, consciously selected injunctions and prohibitions by authority, and all specific conventional arrangements." These he said "are not in the mores. They are differentiated by the rational and conscious element in them" (Sumner, 1906, p. 57).

Sumner's notion that the mores are unconscious restraints on behavior leads to obvious difficulties regarding volition. The unconscious element of mores is a quality shared with other forms of social control, as Sumner was wont to note. Indeed, early in this book, Sumner declared that all folkways are made unconsciously.

> The folkways, therefore, are not creations of human purpose and wit. They are like products of natural forces which men unconsciously set in operation, or they are like the instinctive ways of animals, which are developed out of experience, which reach a final form of maximum adaptation to an interest, which are handed down by tradition and admit of no exception or variation, yet change to meet new conditions, still within the same limited methods, and without rational reflection or purpose.
> (Sumner, 1906, p. 4)

This is a prime example of Sumner forming a bridge between protosociology and more fully articulated sociological analysis.

After Sumner, sociologists tried to analyze the qualities of the mores that he said compelled individuals to adhere to socially prescribed manners and morals. Thus, two generations after Sumner, Philip Rieff defined culture as "an institutionalized system of moral demands, elaborating the conduct of personal relations" (Rieff, 1966, p. 62). I note here in passing that Rieff's "moral career" as a sociologist is similar to Sumner's in that his brilliant and important ideas about the interdictory and remissive demands of culture have been obscured by his stigmatization as a conservative thinker by many sociologists and public intellectuals (Zondervan, 2005). Other well-known cases of conservative-branding include that of Irving Louis Horowitz, discussed in Chapter 7, and the radical attempts to brand sociologists Daniel Bell, Nathan Glazer, and Seymour Martin Lipset as neo-conservatives in the 1970s (Steinfels, 1979). Sumner, therefore, was one of the first of many important sociologists to have been the object of politicized witch hunts.

Sumner came close to articulating an analytic sociological theory of the laminating effect of combining cultural norms with individual conscience, but it was left to later generations of sociologists to actually generate effective theories of what George Herbert Mead, anticipating the work of Erving Goffman, Philip Rieff, and others, called "social control as operating in terms of self-criticism" (Mead, 1934, p. 255). While Mead does not appear to have cited Sumner's work in this regard, other University of Chicago-based Pragmatist sociologists, social psychologists, and philosophers openly quote from Sumner and demonstrate his influence on them (Dewey & Tufts, 1908).

If folkways generally, and mores in particular, have unconscious qualities, what distinguishes mores from the folkways of which they are a subgroup? The answer to this lies in how Sumner defines folkways as usages "which contain no principle of welfare, but serve convenience so long as all know what they are expected to do." Sumner cites the example of various Oriental cultures that show respect by covering the head, while uncovering the feet, while certain Western cultures do the opposite. He then says that,

> there is no inherent and necessary connection between respect and either usage, but it is an advantage that there should be a usage and that all should know and observe it. One way is as good as another, if it is understood and established.
> (Sumner, 1906, p. 57)

Folkways concerned with what Sumner calls public decency are mores, because, as he says, they "have real connection with welfare." With this understanding of mores Sumner hit upon a key element of many social norms which we might otherwise see as trivial.

> Fashions, fads, affectations, poses, ideals, manias, popular delusions, follies, and vices must be included in the mores. They have

characteral qualities and characteral effect. However frivolous or foolish they may appear to people of another age, they have the form of attempts to live well, to satisfy some interest, or to win some good.

(Sumner, 1906, p. 57)

The notion that mores associated with fashion and fads have in Sumner's words "characteral qualities" and "characteral effects" anticipates much of what we know about why people engage in what Thorstein Veblen, one of Sumner's former students, called conspicuous consumption, and why advertising is able to play upon our insecurities and desires to sell us things we otherwise would not need or desire. All these are, according to Sumner, "made with conscious ingenuity to exert suggestion on the minds of others" (Sumner, 1906, p. 57).

Thus, long before some of the major sociological studies of the twentieth century, from the Lynds' two works on *Middletown* to Paul Lazarsfeld's and Elihu Katz's *Personal Influence* to Robert Merton's *Mass Persuasion*, Sumner analyzed how mores could be manipulated to sell people one bill of goods or another. Sumner sounds as if he was talking about contemporary America when he says:

> The ways of advertisers, who exaggerate, use tricks to win attention, and appeal to popular weakness and folly; the ways of journalism; electioneering devices; oratorical and dithyrambic extravagances in politics; current methods of humbug and sensationalism—are not properly part of the mores but symptoms of them.
>
> (Sumner, 1906, p. 57)

Clearly Sumner's view of mores presents a view of morality as socially constructed, as we now say all too easily and in such a banal way. Sumner showed that mores differ from one society to another and from one time to another in the same society, making him one of the earliest theorists of the cultural relativism perspective. One of Sumner's major contributions to this perspective is his use of the ancient Greek term "ethos," which for him means "group character."

While some anthropologists have acknowledged Sumner's contribution in bringing "ethos" to the conceptual table, others have merely used the concept without citing Sumner at all. For example, Clyde Kluckhohn and E. Adamson Hoebel give credit to Sumner for his use of "ethos" (Kluckhohn & Hoebel, 1943). On the other hand, Clifford Geertz makes no mention of Sumner, as he famously uses the term ethos to stand for the moral and aesthetic aspects of a given culture, as opposed to a "world view," which stands for the cognitive and existential aspects of that culture (Geertz, 1973). Ethos, like many of Sumner's conceptual formulations in *Folkways,* has become so embedded in the discourse of sociology and anthropology so as to have gotten beyond the need for attribution. There are even sociology textbooks today that use and define "folkways" and "mores" with no mention of Sumner as their ultimate author. Sumner is given credit for coining the word "ethnocentrism," a bugbear of contemporary sociology, as well as in-groups and out-groups, also popular ideas for criticizing the exclusivity that American society often exhibits. Oddly, Sumner is not credited for his two most important terms, "folkways" and "mores," which are treated as artifacts of a "dominant ideology" maintaining "powerful social, economic and political interests" (Schaefer, 2010). Alas, poor Sumner.

Sumner was careful to distinguish ethos from ethnocentric notions of national character, and he understood that an ethos is "an overruling power for good or ill. Modern scholars have made the mistake of attributing to *race* much which belongs to the ethos with a resulting controversy as to the relative importance of nature and nurture" (Sumner, 1906, p. 74). At this point, Sumner underscores the sociological importance of his concepts: "The ethos," he says, "individualizes groups and keeps them apart. Its opposite is cosmopolitanism." With a purposeful nod toward Europe, Sumner further warns that the ethos of a society may degenerate into chauvinism and patriotic vanity, which he understood to be militant forms of ethnocentrism. Sumner died in 1910, before the outbreak of WWI, but his sections on ethos in *Folkways* seem to anticipate the aggressive ethnocentric chauvinism accompanying that war.

As I've said, Sumner is often regarded as a "conservative" sociologist, so it is ironic that he is barely noted for helping to establish a theoretical framework based on cultural relativism, one of the most liberal concepts in the discipline. An exception here is the noted anthropologist George Peter Murdock, who wrote that Sumner's "mores can make anything right still remains the most forceful and objective definition of cultural relativity" (Murdock, 1965, p. 145).

Of course, the idea that mores can make anything right has its obvious corollary, as pointed out by Ernest Burgess:

> William Graham Sumner has expressed this point of view in its most extreme form in his dictum, 'the mores can make anything right.' Conversely, they can make anything wrong. As an illustration of the validity of this principle, there seems to be no behavior that has been stigmatized as wrong in certain societies and subcultural groups that is not sanctioned as right in others. Examples are therefore legion. Among these are polygamy, polyandry, promiscuity, divorce, lying, stealing, infanticide, and murder.
>
> (Burgess, 1962, p. 389)

Probably the most quoted phrase in *Folkways* is that "the mores can make anything right" (Sumner, 1906, p. 521). Actually, the phrase is that "the mores can make anything right and prevent condemnation of anything." This is significant, since Sumner implies not merely that some behavior is allowed, but that criticism of that behavior is not allowed. The resonances here between the psychoanalytic understanding of the differences between shame and guilt should be obvious. The phrase has been quoted so many times that it has become a sociological cliché cited by some of Sumner's contemporaries as well as a host of sociologists one, two, or even three generations removed from Sumner, such as Robert Park, Ernest Burgess, Edward Shils, Talcott Parsons, Robert Merton, Robert Redfield, Arnold Rose, Philip Selznick, and Donald Levine among many others.

This phrase, and the set of ideas about social norms behind it, goes beyond theories of cultural relativity, and gets to the heart of how morals work. Even Norbert Elias, known for developing the concept of a "civilizing process," recognized Sumner's insight into the ethnographic discovery of what morality means (Elias, 1939). Interestingly, the year before Elias'

Civilizing Process was published in Germany, Bertram Doyle, a student of Robert E. Park, used Sumner's ideas to show that race-based patterns of etiquette not only persisted to keep blacks and whites apart, and to maintain white racial superiority and black inferiority, but mores-based etiquette also had the effect of minimizing friction and avoiding conflict between the races. Doyle's study seems to underscore Robert Park's quip, that "the mores have a harder time making some things right than others" (Doyle, 1937).

The chapter in *Folkways* titled "The Mores Can Make Anything Right," is brilliant in delaminating this concept, layer by layer. While mores set limits on behavior, these are "limits of toleration." As Sumner put it, "Literature, pictures, exhibitions, celebrations, and festivals are controlled by some undefined, and probably indefinable, standard of decency and propriety, which sets a limit of toleration on the appeals to fun, sensuality, and various prejudices" (Sumner, 1906, p. 521). One can easily argue that Sumner's very idea of folkways and mores makes the case against individualism, and in such a way as to take into account the ambivalence of social norms.

It is notable that Sumner wrote *Folkways* at a time when sociologists, anthropologists, and social psychologists were fascinated with questions about why and how collectivities influenced the ways that humans behaved. These were questions that Emile Durkheim, Marcel Mauss, Marcel Granet, and Gabrielle Tarde tried to answer throughout their careers in French sociology. The same can of course be said about Max and Alfred Weber, Georg Simmel, and Ferdinand Tönnies in Germany, and of Sumner, Charles H. Cooley, E. A. Ross, Robert E. Park, and others in American sociology. These sociologists were trying to solve the puzzle posed by the relationship of community and individuality. Sumner's *Folkways* is an important attempt to understand how individuality survives the onslaught of culture, mores, collective conscience, and what psychoanalysts call guilt. A very interesting acknowledgement of Sumner's role in this type of problem-solving can be found in Ruth Benedict:

> It is largely because of the traditional acceptance of a conflict between society and the individual, that emphasis upon cultural behavior is so often interpreted as a denial of the autonomy of

the individual. The reading of Sumner's *Folkways* usually rouses a protest at the limitations such an interpretation places upon the scope and initiative of the individual ... But no anthropologist with a background of experience of other cultures has ever believed that individuals were automatons ... no culture yet observed has been able to eradicate the differences in the temperaments of the persons who compose it.

(Benedict, 1934, p. 253)

While Sumner gives a host of examples of how a culture has made some behavior right whereas the same behavior would be forbidden in another culture, the value of his analysis can be seen perfectly in a classic example of anthropological ethnography, Bronislaw Malinowski's *Crime and Custom in Savage Society* (Malinowski, 2013). Indeed, Murdock ranks Malinowski on a par with Sumner, Marx, Freud, and Pavlov as one of the great innovators in the history of the behavioral sciences; furthermore, Malinowski knew and cited Sumner's *Folkways* (Murdock, 1943). More interesting yet is the early recognition of the affinity between Sumner and Malinowski. In the first edition of *Ethics*, Dewey and Tufts quoted copiously from Sumner's *Folkways*, which had been published only a year before. In the 1932 edition, they specifically cite Malinowski, and single out the example of Kima'i, a young Trobriander, committing suicide, which is clearly tied to Sumner's view of how mores function (Dewey & Tufts, 1932).

In 1914 with war breaking out in Europe, Malinowski began his anthropological fieldwork in the Trobriand Islands. Only a few months after arriving in the Trobriands, Malinowski met with his first case of death, mourning, and burial when he found that an acquaintance, Kima'i, a boy of sixteen years of age, had committed suicide. His first thought was to observe the rituals and ceremonies involved in what he called the mortuary proceedings, but his attention soon turned to the normative structure of Trobriand society that caused Kima'i to kill himself. Kima'i was committing incest with his maternal cousin, a practice that tribal mores made taboo. This in itself would not have been remarkable, but what Malinowski discovered was an ambivalence that marks mores everywhere, and that underscores Sumner's understanding that mores set limits on toleration. Of the incestuous affair, Malinowski remarks that "this had been known and generally disapproved of, but nothing was done until the girl's discarded lover, who had wanted to marry her and who felt personally injured, took the initiative." In other words, while disapproving of the incest, the community knew about and tolerated it. The limits to toleration were reached only when the jilted lover insulted Kima'i in public, and accused him of incest. The public accusation destroyed the community's tolerance, and left Kima'i with nowhere to turn. Toleration always implies some ambivalence between what is prohibited and what is actually done, and since mores set the limits on tolerance they control that remissive space that exists between complete prohibition and complete acceptance (Malinowski, 2013, pp. 97–99).

Before leaving Malinowski's account of Kima'i I would like to examine ritual, another aspect of the mores discussed by Sumner. According to Sumner,

> ... the mores are social ritual in which we all participate unconsciously. The current habits as to hours of labor, meal hours, family life, the social intercourse of the sexes, propriety, amusements, travel, holidays, education ... and innumerable other details of life fall under this ritual. Each does as everybody does.
> (Sumner, 1906, p. 62)

Malinowski observed that Kima'i had no choice but to follow custom and commit suicide in a highly-ritualized manner. The morning after having been publicly accused of incest, Kima'i "put on festive attire and ornamentation, climbed a coco-nut palm and addressed the community, speaking from among the palm leaves and bidding them farewell." He then "wailed aloud, as is the custom," and plunged some sixty feet to his death. The ritual of the mores was not over yet, however, since before leaping from the palm tree Kima'i appealed to the mores governing revenge, and told his clansmen that it was their duty to avenge his death, which they did by attacking the rival who had accused him of incest (Malinowski, 2013, p. 98).

As Malinowski's example of Kima'i suggests, sexual behavior and propriety are among the behaviors most likely to come under the realm of the mores, which means that they are among the most likely behaviors to generate edge-work between individual drives, desires, and proclivities, and socially insistent rules about what is and what isn't to be done. This is why sexuality and propriety generates so much ambiguity, ambivalence, and hypocrisy. Sumner realized this, and discussed "bundling" as his main example of how mores can make anything right, in that brief eponymous chapter. Bundling was a widespread centuries-old practice in parts of Europe, and eventually it became a custom in North America. Although Sumner briefly discusses various instances where strangers and extended families might sleep together for warmth, his discussion of bundling is really about a form of courtship in laboring and agricultural communities where there were few opportunities to meet and woo members of the opposite sex. Bundling meant sleeping together in the same bed. Sometimes a "bundling board," nothing more, really, than a glorified, thin, structural board, was place between a young man and woman by her parents, who according to custom would invite him to spend the night. Ostensibly this practice was to allow the young folks to get acquainted, with marriage hopefully in sight as a final result. Sumner introduces his discussion of this practice by calling it "one of the most extraordinary instances of what the mores can do to legitimize a custom which, when rationally judged, seems inconsistent with the most elementary requirements of the sex taboo" (Sumner, 1906, pp. 525–528). Sumner's discussion hints at deep ambivalence and disagreement about bundling among various institutional sectors of societies that either encouraged or tolerated it. But finally, Sumner gives the ultimate rationale for bundling when he quotes from a Royal Commission of the Marriage Laws held in Britain in 1868: "Their daughters must have husbands and there is no other way of courting" (Sumner, 1906, p. 529). Sumner clearly understood that mores are not monolithic and inflexible, but instead that they are plastic and often open to ambivalent reactions, as in the case of Kima'i above. The importance here of Kima'i and the incident of incest and suicide associated with him is that it demonstrates a key fact about mores of which Sumner himself was quite aware, namely their ambivalent qualities. As Malinowski discovered, everyone in the village knew about the incestuous affair, of which they disapproved. The widespread disapproval makes sense in Sumner's terms, but what about the fact that it was known? Sumner tells us that "a society is never conscious of its mores until it comes in contact with some other society which has different mores" (Sumner, 1906, p. 78). When this happens, a society becomes conscious of its social norms, and may begin to question them. Such questioning creates ambivalence, and more than ambivalence, it may create what Durkheim called "anomie," which often results when a culture begins to doubt its values. In the case of the Trobriands, we know that the Australian government sent magistrates to live near the villages, and English and Scottish missionaries also lived there. Kima'i and his cousin breached the mores governing sexual relationships because Trobrianders said one thing, but practiced another, as Sumner might well have anticipated.

Sumner's theory of mores, and Malinowski's observations about the ambivalent responses to breaches in mores are supplemented by the Freudian approach to ambiguities and ambivalence. "Hypocrisy is a precious thing in any culture… it may help build up those patterns of avoidance that swerve us from honest, but head-on collisions with one another" (Rieff, 1966, p. 57). Hypocrisy is clearly a defensive strategy for dealing with the ambivalence inherent in the mores. Wasn't Kitty Genovese as much the victim of her neighbors' hypocrisy and ambivalence as she was of their apathy or carelessness? This is another unambiguous indication of the multidimensional quality of the mores (Rosenthal, 1964, p. 49).

As I suggested above, one of the main thrusts of early sociology was discovery of the relationship of community values to individual behavior. Sumner chased after this Holy Grail, as did Durkheim and Malinowski, among many others. Durkheim's ideas about collective consciousness are remarkably close to Sumner's ideas about mores. They are both talking about shared communal values, and they both realize that these values ebb and flow, and more importantly, they change over time. It is notable, however, that Durkheim said many of the same things about social change as did Sumner, but he was never faulted for advocating against social and cultural change by theorizing about its difficulty. Some social scientists, such as Gunnar Myrdal, accused Sumner of archconservatism for observing that mores often got in the way of rapid social changes. Myrdal blatantly committed the fallacy of intentionality, claiming that Sumner intended to get in the way of change, when it is clear that Sumner did what sociology should do, namely discover and analyze change and resistance to it. Myrdal did not stop with this scurrilous critique of Sumner, but went on to tar and feather important sociologists such as Robert Park and William Ogburn. None of these sociologists showed personal bias in the way the Myrdal obviously did (Myrdal, 1944, pp. 1048–1049).

Rarely was Durkheim chastised for suggesting the same thing when he discussed the persistence of collective consciousness. Consider here one of Durkheim's most well-known pronouncements about this, in *The Rules of the Sociological Method*. After discussing the variability of law and morality from one society to the next, and within any given society, Durkheim says that these rules and norms can change within a given society so long as "the collective sentiments at the basis of morality must not be hostile to change, and consequently have but moderate energy." This observation led Durkheim to theorize that a culture in which morality, or what Sumner called mores, was so strong that it stifled all dissent, no originality or progress could make its mark (Durkheim, 1964, p. 71). Conversely, if values are so weak and ambivalent, anomie would prevail, and we would have what Philip Rieff would later call "an impossible culture," where everything would be true, and nothing prohibited (Rieff, 1970, p. 33).

The philosopher Dorothy Emmet adds a brilliant analysis to Sumner's theory of mores. She observes that mores as Sumner describes them are "capable of being internalized, i.e. a person may come to believe that he should observe them apart from external and overt pressures" (Emmet, 1966, p. 35). She later goes on to suggest that Paul Radin's classic work *Primitive Man as a Philosopher* "exploded the notion that no one in any primitive society asks questions about the mores." In fact, Radin was quite explicit here, and wrote that "early man instead of being enslaved to the group to the point of absorption in it was in fact highly individualistic" (Radin, 1927, p. xvi).

Because Sumner's sociology emerged as an accretion of proto-sociological descriptions, facts, and ideas we might ask how he came to write *Folkways*. In his preface, Sumner tells us that he began *Folkways* as part of a larger work in 1899. This larger project was to become a textbook of sociology composed of material he had collected and used in classes and lectures for at least a decade before he began writing. Given the importance of the mores as a concept, it is remarkable that Sumner had not published anything about them before he wrote *Folkways*. His self-stated intentions were therefore two-fold: to introduce, define, and illustrate the mores as a concept, and to publish his collected examples of the mores in a textbook. If he was successful, Sumner's first intention would advance our disciplinary understanding of social control, and his second one would provide a teaching tool for classes in sociology. There is no doubt that Sumner succeeded on both counts, but the value of his accomplishment goes far beyond intentionality.

The result of the publication of *Folkways* seems more interesting than his intentions in writing it, but here too we must beware of implied effects. In terms of Sumner's influence, first is, as I discussed above, the enormous impact of cultural relativism on the social sciences in general and sociology in particular. Along with the relativism of values is the changed meaning of morality that accompanies it. In Sumner's discussions "Morals is an impossible and unreal category. It has no existence, and can have none. The word 'moral' means what belongs or appertains to the mores" (Sumner, 1906, p. 37).

There are, however, two further conceptual goldmines that result from *Folkways*. The first of these derives from Sumner's discussions of in-groups, out-groups and "we" groups. These concepts add a structural component to Sumner's culturally-based sociology by situating mores and folkways in institutions and groups. Without moving too far afield, it is notable that Robert Merton gave credit to Sumner for both discussing the in-group and out-group dichotomy in and of itself, and for its influence on both reference group theory and the theory of relative deprivation (Merton, 1968, pp. 351–352). The lineage of these really important concepts, traced back to Sumner, gives *Folkways* a monumental place in the history of sociology.

Finally, I note Sumner's theory of social and cultural change, especially his dual concepts of crescive and enacted change, and their rootedness in the mores and folkways. Ultimately, it was Sumner's insistence that changes in the mores (crescive) must precede changes in legislated (enacted) law that led to his being branded as an archconservative, which blinded many sociologists to his important influences on the discipline, and threatened the formerly high and dry reputation Sumner enjoyed as one of the great founders of sociology.

Certainly, among modern sociology's focal points and its most controversial areas of interest is social and cultural change. It is in his discussions of change that Sumner proved himself to be one of the first sociologists to see that societies resist social and cultural changes, and he tried to create a descriptive taxonomy, and an analytic framework to understand it. By the time that Sumner began writing *Folkways* social change was becoming a topic of discussion among many sociologists, as evidenced by the work of Charles Horton Cooley, and E. A. Ross, among others. Sumner was hardly the first to recognize that changing social institutions was difficult because persistence and resistance to change were the norm, rather than exceptions to the norm, but his analysis is still solid today. Indeed, two works of lasting importance published soon after *Folkways*, William F. Ogburn's *Social Change*, and Frederick J. Teggart's *The Theory of History* cite Sumner, and make it clear that they see change as something difficult to achieve. Later, Robert Nisbet, Teggart's student, observed that "*Folkways* is another classic that might well be dusted off for use in courses in *social change* rather than for the familiar and tedious purpose of exemplifying 'obstacles to change'" (Nisbet, 2009, p. 326). All this points to Sumner as seeing that while social change meets resistance by persistent mores, overcoming those resistances is as normative as the resistances are themselves. Sumner's discussion of change begins in a subtle fashion with his discussion of "The Mores and Institutions," where he suggests that institutions and laws both emanate from the mores. Institutions, according to Sumner are either "crescive," or "enacted." Crescive institutions, and by implication crescive changes are shaped by the mores through long use in which they become "definite and specific." Sumner gives examples of crescive institutions, namely property, marriage, and religion, which began as folkways, developed into mores, and finally evolved into law (Sumner, 1906, pp. 45–56).

Enacted institutions, and changes in them, on the other hand, are "products of rational invention and intention." Later, in his well-known book *The End of Ideology*, Daniel Bell picked up on Sumner's dichotomy in order to analyze changes taking place in Soviet society and politics. Building on Sumner's theory of change, Bell showed that "crescive changes are those which surge, swell, go on willy-nilly, and develop with some measure of autonomy. They variously derive from organic growth of tradition, or from changes in values … or from technical imperatives." Bell furthermore analyzes enacted changes, which are "the conscious decisions or intents of legislators or rulers. Those who enact changes have to take into account the mores of the people and the resources at their disposal, but these serve only as limiting, not determining, factors" (Bell, 1962, pp. 346–347). Before Bell made use of Sumner's theory of change, Robert Redfield used the crescive and enacted dichotomy in his important article on folk society (Redfield, 1947, pp. 293–308). After this, many sociologists, such as Frank Knight, Jesse Bernard, Robert E. Park, Robert Cooley Angell, Peter Blau and Reinhard Bendix, made use of Sumner's dichotomy. John Hope Franklin, a historian who used the crescive and enacted change dichotomy, provides yet another example of liberal bias against Sumner: "The dictum of William Graham Sumner and his followers that 'stateways cannot change folkways,' convinced many Americans that legislating equality and creating one great society where race was irrelevant was out of the question." It is notable that Franklin never suggested who Sumner's supposed followers were, nor which or how many Americans believed this (Franklin, 1965, p. 56).

It is with his theory of change that Sumner eventually ran into the ideological wall of American sociology in the 1960s and beyond. To say, as he did, that mores have a persistent quality is one thing, but to say that "legislation cannot make mores," is another. In what turns out to be a quotation with pivotal implications for Sumner's reputation, he wrote that "legislation cannot make mores" (Sumner, 1906, p. 77). This quotation has been quoted time and time again by civil rights advocates and liberal sociologists as proof of Sumner's conservatism, and often of his mean-spirited recalcitrance to advocate change (Roche & Gordon, 1955). The most balanced and thoughtful analysis of Sumner's treatment at the hands of those who would use the law to create changes if the mores support these or not, can be found in "Law and Social Change: Sumner Reconsidered," an article published in the *American Journal of Sociology* in March 1962. The authors' conclusion was that "much of the criticism of William Graham Sumner's 'classic' formulation of the relationship between law and social change has been ill deserved" (Ball, 1962, p. 540).

Tiresome banalities about Sumner's "conservatism" have obscured just how important he was and remains for laying the cornerstone foundation upon which modern sociology is built, namely the ideas of ethnocentrism, and cultural relativism. The modern Western "ethos"—another of Sumner's important conceptual terms—is surely based on the relativity of values from one society to another that Sumner so brilliantly exposed in *Folkways*. When he coined the term "ethnocentrism," Sumner was hunting for a concept that would explain how it was that mores can make anything right. What he ended up doing was to help us see that cultural values are pertinent to a specific time and place, and that the morality which seems so universal and timeless in a given society is really one of many possible moralities that have arisen in some society or another. Culture not only explains why mores allow behavior in one society that would be prohibited in another, it helps to create the rational and intellectual basis for tolerance. After all, in a world in which people believe that theirs are the *only* proper ways of doing things, tolerance would be a remarkable feat. In a world in which we recognize that those who come from other cultures have different values than our own, we have the conditions for toleration. Of course, we also have the conditions to set in place a bunker mentality wherein a society feels that it is under attack by wrong-headed groups that do not share their values. Thus, while understanding that a multiplicity of moral values in the world is necessary for toleration, it is hardly sufficient to guarantee it. The case of a Denmark mother who left her baby in an unattended stroller outside a restaurant while visiting New York City in May 1997 is instructive. She was reported to police by patrons in the restaurant and then arrested on charges of child endangerment. The child was taken into custody by NYC Children's Services workers. This set up an international uproar, with Danes claiming that parents regularly leave their children unattended on the streets. A Children's Court judge finally agreed to tolerate the woman's behavior and return her child to her, proving that mores can sometimes trump the law (*New York Times*, 1997).

Over the last century sociology has provided us with an overarching framework upon which we could build our understanding of how society and social institutions give shape to life. Along the way sociologists have stood on the shoulders of previous generations, and they should once again read Sumner's *Folkways* to find out why he is worthy of respect for his insights into social control through mores and law, group identities, institutions, and change. In many ways Sumner has become the marginal man of sociological theory, criticized, on the one hand, by sociological liberals for his theory of social persistence and what they take to be his resistances to change through enacted legislation, and disparaged for his theories of ethnocentrism and ethical relativism by some sociological conservatives who see morals, customs, and traditions as so important as to deserve better treatment than they got from Sumner, whom they think relegated these to mere sociological inventions that societies use to remain functional. Of course, Sumner's importance to modern sociology lies beyond ideological stances and debates. In his preface to Mannheim's *Ideology and Utopia*, Louis Wirth applauded Sumner's achievement in advancing the cause of sociological objectivity.

> Outstanding in this respect is the work of William Graham Sumner, who, although he approached the problem somewhat obliquely through the analysis of the influence of the folkways and mores upon social norms rather than directly through epistemological criticism, by the vigorous way in which he directed attention to the distorting influence of ethnocentrism upon knowledge, placed the problem of objectivity into a distinctively concrete sociological setting.

If he had done nothing else, Sumner would still be important to us for this alone (Mannheim, 1936, p. xix).

Sumner's *Folkways* deserves a new look, from a new generation of social theorists, and I hope that this chapter will stimulate interest in this important transformational figure in the history of American sociology. As Lewis Coser said of Sumner, "the crisp and pithy prose... can still be read with considerable profit, especially by those who persist in believing that if there were only a law most human problems could be legislated out of existence" (Coser, 1978, p. 298).

16
PACIFISM AND UTOPIAN THOUGHT

Among the most important and representative sets of ideas about human relations developed by modern sociology are those concerning community bonds, and those concerning the results of moral and ethical motives and constraints on purposive action. These sets of concepts, exemplified in Emile Durkheim's study of suicide, were part and parcel of the ideas of the early generations of sociologists, and they are still important today (Durkheim, 1951). But a well-known and popular philosophical book, *Ends and Means,* by Aldous Huxley, runs so counter to sociological ideas developed in these two areas, that it deserves special attention, not merely because of its famous author, but even more for what he says about community, individualism, pacifism, and the relationship of ends and means in politics and war (Huxley, 2012).

It may fairly be said that one hallmark of an educated person from the beginning of the second half of the twentieth-century through today is having read Huxley's utopian novel, *Brave New World*, which, along with George Orwell's *1984* has been standard high school and college reading for decades. But Huxley's other less well-known works were once widely read and highly regarded: novels such as *Antic Hay*, *Point Counter Point*, *Eyeless in Gaza*, and *Island*. He also wrote over twenty collections of essays, such as *On the Margin, Vulgarity in Literature, Music at Night, Texts and Pretexts, The Olive Tree, The Art of Seeing, The Doors of Perception,* and *Brave New World Revisited*, all of which are still worth reading for their intelligence and literary form. Huxley wrote immensely readable and popular travel books too, and a parade of seemingly endless reviews and screenplays. In other words, Huxley was a professional writer whose breadth and depth was notable.

Among his now lesser remembered works, *Ends and Means* stands out for the issues it raises about the nature of politics and society in uncertain and violent times, when physical force is a standard means to achieve the ends of national safety, and even periods of peaceful accord in international politics. *Ends and Means* was first published in 1937, just around the time that sociologists such as Robert Merton, Talcott Parsons, Karl Mannheim, and Norbert Elias, were emphasizing the central role of community bonds, and of value-laden motives of political and social action on world events. Huxley's anti-sociological utopianism stands in marked contrast to these intellectual currents. As I will emphasize below, Huxley's work also stands in contrast to that of his contemporary, George Orwell, who was equally famous as a dystopian writer.

Born in 1894, Huxley was raised in one of those singular and rarified literary families that the English upper classes characteristically seem to breed. Among Huxley's numerous literary relatives was his mother's famed uncle, the poet and essayist Matthew Arnold, and Huxley's paternal grandfather, Thomas Henry Huxley, famous as the writer who coined the term "agnostic," and as a *force majeure*, in the struggle to get Darwin's theory of evolution accepted. As a young man, Aldous Huxley studied at Balliol College, Oxford, and for a short while after graduating, he took a job teaching French at Eton, and ironically had as one of his students George Orwell (then known by his given name, Eric Blair), whose *1984* is at least as famous as Huxley's *Brave New World*, the two forming bookends of dystopian literature in the last century. Huxley died of cancer of the esophagus in 1963.

A man of strong convictions and powerful ideas, Huxley was considered not merely an excellent writer and storyteller, but also a leader of opinion and a very important intellectual in his day. That *Ends and Means* challenges some major sociological ideas makes it an important statement in terms of social science, as well as an intriguing argument for pacifism in the face of Hitler's aggression in Europe.

Huxley's novel *Brave New World*, published in 1932, foreshadows one of his most sociologically controversial ideas, namely his praise for the so-called "non-attached man," given full treatment in *Ends and Means*. It is a long theoretical way from Albion Small's *General Sociology,* published in 1905, which states that "One man is no man" (Small, 1905, p. 561) to Huxley's *Ends and Means* which takes as its premise that "the ideal man is the non-attached man" (Huxley, 1950, p. 3).

From the sociological point of view, the very essence of society, any society, is to attach its members to it. Another vital function of civilization and culture is to provide meaning to social life and interaction that transcends individuals by providing forms and motives for living and dying well. The history of sociology as a discipline is intimately connected to discovering the forms that social groups take as they buffer the socially withering effects of individualism. Thus, among others, sociologists Ferdinand Tönnies, Georg Simmel, Max and Alfred Weber, in Germany, Emile Durkheim, Marcel Mauss, and Henri Hubert, in France, and Albion Small, William Graham Sumner, E. A. Ross, W. I. Thomas, Charles Horton Cooley, and Robert E. Park, in America, were immensely interested in the foundations of community.

As the founders of sociology knew, the unattached individual is something of a sociological anomaly. Durkheim went so far as to call a society of unattached individuals a "sociological monstrosity." Indeed, in his *Division of Labor in Society*, Durkheim wrote that,

> A society composed of an infinite number of unorganized individuals, that a hypertrophied state is forced to oppress and contain, constitutes a veritable sociological monstrosity… A nation can be maintained only if between the state and the individual, there is interlaced a whole series of secondary groups near enough to the individuals to attract them strongly in their sphere of action and drag them, in this way, into the general torrent of social life.
>
> (Durkheim, 1947, p. liv)

Following Simmel's famous essay on "the stranger" as a detached social type (Simmel, 1971, pp. 143–150), and Frederick Teggart's idea that social change occurs when individuals are "released" from the social bonds of their own societies, and then reintegrated into the mores and groups of another (Teggart, 1960), Robert Park saw that social detachment had an important function when it occurred periodically, and within the limits of release and reintegration. Detachment could punctuate the equilibrium of a society and create needed changes, as long as a new period of integration followed in a timely way (Park, 1928, pp. 881–893). Perhaps the strongest sociological statement about the unattached individual is again found in Albion Small's discussion of "the preposterous initial fact of the individual," which he says is "no longer a thinkable possibility" (Small, 1905, p. 443).

All of the sociological musings of the discipline's founders added up to the necessity of understanding individual attachment to the culture, mores, and intermediary groups in a society. After fifty years of the sociological tradition examining the importance of communal attachment, Huxley's *Brave New World* challenged the importance of community to social life. If ever there was a fictional account of what happens when a state takes over the intermediate social institutions of a society and destroys every spark of individuality, it is the sociological monstrosity Huxley called the "World State." One central character in Huxley's novel, John, also known as "the Savage," was born and raised outside the World State. For Huxley, the Savage is the ultimate detached individual because he has escaped the nighttime brainwashing of the World State, and thus has the ability to express unbridled emotions and think for himself. The Savage foreshadows Huxley's raising "non-attachment" to an exalted position in *Ends and Means*.

Ends and Means challenges sociology's architectonic ideas about the relationship of individual and community with the idea of the nonattached man. By the 1930s when *Ends and Means* was published, the increasingly specialized discipline of sociology was still eclectic and inclusive in its acceptance of works written by non-sociologists. Psychoanalysts, such as Karen Horney and Franz Alexander, literary critics, such as Kenneth Burke and Bernard DeVoto, philosophers, such as John Dewey and Richard McKeon, and historians, such as Louis Gottschalk and Crane Brinton, often wrote for and were reviewed in sociological periodicals. Deemed important enough for sociologists to know about, *Ends and*

Means was reviewed by Talcott Parsons in the March 1938 issue of the *American Journal of Sociology*. Parsons, whose *Structure of Social Action* made him one of America's leading sociologists of the time, obviously saw that Huxley's views on community and power could potentially undermine the sociological viewpoint, and argued against Huxley's anti-sociology in his review (Parsons, 1938).

Long before the publication of Huxley's book, justification of means by ends had been of interest to sociologists, and virtually all the notable founders of sociology made the relationship of ends to means an important part of their thinking. The ends and means schema appears in much of Durkheim's work, including *The Division of Labor in Society*, *Suicide* and *Professional Ethics and Civic Morals*. The same can be said of many of Durkheim's followers. Thus, Marcel Mauss employs this schema in *The Gift* and in *Sacrifice*, co-authored with Henri Hubert. In Germany, ends and means is a signature subject in Max Weber's work on both politics and the various forms of thought and social structure, such as *Economy and Society,* and in the essays on politics, such as "Politics as a Vocation." Ends and means also appear in much of Georg Simmel's work, including his magnum opus, *The Philosophy of Money*. In *Gemeinschaft and Gesellschaft*, Ferdinand Tönnies showed how meta-changes in social structure affected the way we used the ends-means schema. The list could go on and on, and could include the early American founders of sociology. Cooley, for instance, employed the ends-means schema in his work, as did William Graham Sumner, and Robert Park.

As the rise of Hitler and fascism in Europe in the 1930s made another world war increasingly probable, there was renewed and heightened interest among sociologists and others to the question of whether good ends could justify using violent means. Since Huxley's *Ends and Means* is ultimately a pacifist manifesto, it is not surprising that sociologists were interested in what he had to say. This is neither merely a tract for inspiring mass movements, nor a loose-jointed easy-to-read popular book. It is clearly a book meant to join the arguments for and against war and the use of violent means in a highly intellectual discourse.

Not one to be irresolute about what he is going to say, Huxley begins his book with a strong statement with which many might take exception, namely that there has been a general agreement for thirty centuries that "liberty, peace, justice and brotherly love" are the highest aims of civilization. The *terminus a quo* of this thinking, according to Huxley, are the biblical musings of the songs of Isaiah, and the *terminus ad quem*, the writings of Karl Marx. This is certainly a lively and controversial start. Having proclaimed that pacific ends are universally accepted, Huxley turns to means to achieve these and says flat out that it is here that "unanimity and certainty give place to utter confusion, [and] to the clash of contradictory opinions" (Parsons, 1938, p. 1).

It is at this juncture that Huxley introduces his invention of the "non-attached man." He cleverly posits two of the main ways of thinking about social change: change the machinery, or the structure of society, or change the hearts and minds of the individuals who compose it. He drops the former before the ink is dry, and chooses to only discuss changing the individuals who compose a society. For Huxley, Marx is out, and the songs of Isaiah are in. Thus, change for Huxley is a matter more amenable to psychoanalysis, education, and religion, than to structural reform or revolution. But the virtuoso attainments of self-insight, reason, and charisma are not for everyone. They are virtues of nonattachment, and, as Huxley says again and again, "the ideal man is the non-attached man." There is more than a hint of Eastern forms of mysticism, not to mention Rousseau-like idealism in Huxley's ideas about nonattachment. To make the world a better, freer place, we must disengage from society, attachment to which, after all, causes many of our woes. Huxley was a superior thinker and writer, but as for his own intellectual nonattachment, one could say that he is everywhere in chains to an antecedent line of philosophers who thought that they understood the world better than anyone else, and who criticized adherence to commonplace mores and philosophies with an almost astonishing self-certainty, if not downright snobbery.

Aside from being anti-sociological in terms of an individual's place in society, what exactly is nonattachment for Huxley? In the main it is disengagement with worldly values regarding wealth, education, inequality, politics, sexuality, and some forms of philosophy and religion.

> The Gospel of Jesus is essentially a gospel of non-attachment to 'the things of this world and of attachment to God. Whatever may have been the aberrations of organized Christianity and they range

from extravagant asceticism to the most brutally cynical forms of *realpolitik* there has been no lack of Christian philosophers to reaffirm the ideal of non-attachment.

(Parsons, 1938, p. 5)

To underscore his thinking here, Huxley lists Nietzsche, Marquis de Sade, Machiavelli, Hegel, and "contemporary philosophers of Fascism and dictatorial Communism" as eccentrics in political thinking who have denied the value of nonattachment. These thinkers and others that devalue non-attachment have little regard for charity towards mankind, or truth, for that matter. These thinkers, and their impact on Western thought, leave Huxley asking, "How can the average sensual man and the exceptional (and more dangerous) ambitious man be transformed into those non-attached beings, who alone can create a society significantly better than our own?" (Parsons, 1938, p. 8).

Unchained, as Huxley would have it, by new forms of education and religion, from attachments to worldly ends ranging from power to wealth to sexual desire, the nonattached are free to follow only good ends such as "liberty, peace, justice, and brotherly love." Good ends, and Huxley underscores this throughout the book, "can be achieved only by the employment of appropriate means. The end cannot justify the means, for the simple and obvious reason that the means employed determine the nature of the ends produced" (Parsons, 1938, p. 9). Huxley's idea here, that means drive the ends, raises an old issue regarding the relationship of the one to the other. Plato experimented with answering this question in the dialogue called "Thrasymachus," but reached no definitive conclusion.

Perhaps Huxley's contemporary, George Orwell, came closer when his main character in *1984*, Winston Smith, is being tortured and his tormentor says,

Power is not a means, it is an end. One does not establish a dictatorship in order to safeguard a revolution; one makes the revolution in order to establish the dictatorship. The object of persecution is persecution. The object of torture is torture. The object of power is power.

(Orwell, 1950, p. 263)

Although they might have agreed on this one point, we shall soon see that Orwell and Huxley were worlds apart on the question of pacifism, so central to *Ends and Means*.

Pacifism is a pivotal issue for Huxley in the late 1930s, no less than it was for Max Weber in the post-WWI period. While Huxley was famously in favor of pacifism, Weber was resolutely against it, and made pacifism a key to understanding why politics needed to follow an ethics of responsibility, sometimes employing violent means to achieve desirable ends. For Huxley, however, peace, along with liberty, justice, and brotherly love were umbrella values, and so far beyond debate that there was no point in his questioning them. These ends *could*, or, might we say, *should* never be supported by bad means, namely war, force, or violence. This meant that they could never be achieved politically, and that is at the heart of Huxley's anti-politics.

If the relationship of means and ends is at the core of moral philosophy and theology, it is just as or even more central to political philosophy and political sociology. Here lies the value of Huxley's book, for it exemplifies one of the major approaches to the means and ends schema in the sphere of politics, namely an adherence to what Max Weber called *Gesinnungsethik*, or an ethic of conviction, of which we shall discuss in more detail below (Weber, 1946). By the time Huxley published *Ends and Means* in 1937 he had already become an ardent pacifist, and, unyieldingly anti-political.

Ends and Means reveals Huxley's anti-politics even in the face of the obvious threat of armed aggression on Hitler's part. According to Huxley, war and violence were means that could never be justified by the ends they served, not even the end of peace itself. The 1930s, of course, were a time of challenges, transitions, and barbarities that sparked wildfires in the landscape of ideas. To hold tightly and uncompromisingly to a value, such as pacifism, was to ignore the larger political variations in ideas and ideologies. It was a time in which another now famous novelist, Robert Musil, could sensibly write in his partially complete novel, *The Man Without Qualities*, in 1932, that "One couldn't get along without ideas… but the right thing was a certain equilibrium between them, a balance of power, an armed peace in the realm of ideas, so that no side could set too much happening" (Musil, 1954, p. 71). There is a fascinating convergence between Musil's "armed peace in the realm of ideas," and Max Weber's question, "which of the warring gods should we serve?" (Weber, 1946, p. 153).

Huxley's writing on pacifism was not confined to *Ends and Means*. The year before, in 1936, Huxley had published a well-received novel, *Eyeless in Gaza*, and a widely-read pamphlet, *What Are You Going to Do About It? The Case for Constructive Peace*, both of which advocated his pacifist ideology. The next year, along with *Ends and Means*, Huxley published his *Encyclopedia of Pacifism*. It is interesting to note that Huxley's pacifist worldview seems to have arisen in response to violent world events, which seemed resolvable only by force being met with force. This raises a sociology of knowledge question of how and when utopian thinking awakens from dormancy. Here again we can learn much from Robert Musil, who in *The Man Without Qualities* asks us to consider why we "only attack history like an animal, when he is hurt, when things are on fire behind him? Why, in short, does he make history only in an emergency?" (Weber, 1946, p. 71). The storm clouds of war on the horizon of the 1930s seem to have brought out the pacifist in Huxley.

Indeed, Huxley's advocacy of pacifism shows the "utopian mentality" at work. The utopian mentality, of course, is one of the most important concepts in Karl Mannheim's classic study, *Ideology and Utopia*, published in English translation in 1936, through the cooperative efforts of Mannheim, Louis Wirth, and Edward Shils. That the *American Sociological Review* placed a review by Howard Becker of Mannheim's book right after a review of Huxley's *Ends and Means*, in its April 1938 issue, making them shelf-mates of a sort, only underscores the close intellectual bond between them. As Mannheim understood, "a state of mind is utopian when it is incongruous with the state of reality within which it occurs." Furthermore, utopian thought aims to "shatter, either partially or wholly, the order of things prevailing at the time." Similarly, Mannheim says that incongruous thoughts that aim to bolster the prevalent order of things, are also ideological (Mannheim, 1936, p. 173).

At this point we might well ask what Huxley's pacifism is all about. Throughout *Ends and Means*, as well as his other writings on this subject, Huxley seems to define pacifism either in terms of what it is not, or in terms of what it stands against. Thus, pacifism is not politics, indeed it is anti-politics; it is not nationalism; it is obviously not militarism; it is not imperialism; and it is not about competing for international prestige, wealth, and power. On the contrary, Huxley's pacifism is about brotherly love, reform, peace, cooperation, social justice, and more than less, it is about socialism and a leavening of wealth and power. In a word, it is anti-political. It is also, at least in large part, anti-sociological.

Huxley was aware of what sociology, or at least what some sociologists, had to say about these things that pacifism was or wasn't. Swept up by the seemingly unstoppable force of Vilfredo Pareto's sociological juggernaut in the 1930s, Huxley declared Pareto his mentor. What attracted Huxley to Pareto was his cynicism towards human stupidity, the cavalier attitudes societies adopt towards issues of power. It is this cynical attitude that helped Huxley to develop his pacifist values. Huxley was also acquainted with sociologists such as Emile Durkheim, Maurice Halbwachs, Thorstein Veblen, and Max Weber, all of whom he cites in *Ends and Means*. In the case of Weber, it is too bad that Huxley only mentions *The Protestant Ethic and the Spirit of Capitalism*, translated into English by Talcott Parsons, and published in 1930. It would have been interesting to see what Huxley might have made of Weber's essays on politics, which are so opposite his own thoughts on that subject.

Contrasting Weber and Huxley on pacifism and politics allows us to see Huxley from a different perspective than the one he wants to be seen from. Having no more use for democracies than fascist states, Huxley declares that "Twentieth-century political thinking is incredibly primitive" (Parsons, 1938, p. 40). We might well take this as the utopian atavism of an otherwise brilliant and progressive mind at work, but Weber was undoubtedly the more clear-minded and realistic thinker about politics.

Unlike Huxley, Weber was no utopian, but neither was he an ideologue. Sailing far from the relatively safe harbor of political philosophy, Weber navigated and charted the deeper waters of political sociology. He was far less interested in producing some political theory *de jure* than he was in analyzing the consequences of purposive political action.

For Weber, the relationship of ends to means was central to understanding politics. He realized that politics can be found in all manner of civil associations from unions to churches to families, but it is politics as found in the modern state that defines the usual boundaries of that term and what it represents. Since the state is the arena in which politics plays out, the nature of the state determines the nature of politics. For Weber, the state is never defined by its aims, which differ from state to state, but always by the means specific to it, namely physical force (Weber, 1946). From this Weber shows that since the state has the sole right to use physical force, which is the source of its power, politics "means striving to share power or striving to influence the distribution of power, either among states or among groups within a state" (Weber, 1946, p. 78).

This sociological view of the state, and of politics in and among states, gives us a stark contrast between Huxley's utopian mentality and Weber's realist sociology. Weber actually had much to say about the place of ethics in politics in general, and about pacifism and the ethic of the Sermon on the Mount in particular. But, to avoid veering too far afield by sharing with the reader more of what Weber says about ethics and politics than is relevant to Huxley, we should examine Weber's dichotomy pitting an "ethic of responsibility" against an "ethic of conviction." This will allow us to think about why Weber would probably call Huxley's otherwise brilliantly argued case for pacifism "an ethic of indignity."

The starting point, if not the *sine qua non*, for both Huxley's pacifism and Weber's ethic of conviction is the Sermon on the Mount, which Weber calls "an ethic of indignity" when applied to politics (Weber, 1946, p. 119). In an earlier book, *What Are You Going To Do About It?* Huxley's pacifism becomes manifest when he writes: "'The Church does not condemn war,' says an orthodox heckler. 'Why am I expected to be more pacifist than the bishops?' The Church does not condemn war; but Jesus did condemn it" (Huxley, 1936, p. 16). While Huxley seems to be unquestioning about Jesus' condemnation of violence and war, Weber invokes Dostoyevsky's "Grand Inquisitor," of whom he says,

> If one makes any concessions at all to the principle that the ends justify the means, it is not possible to bring an ethic of ultimate ends and an ethic of responsibility under one roof, or to decree ethically which end should justify which means.
>
> (Weber, 1946, p. 122)

The defining means for politics is violence. Weber's sociology of politics rests on this foundation. Much like Jacob Burckhardt, with whose work he had a well-known affinity, Weber had no problem agreeing with the Swiss historian that "the truth is… power is in itself evil" (Burckhardt, 1943, p. 115). Following from this point, Weber poignantly concluded that "he who seeks the salvation of the soul, of his own and others, should not seek it along the avenue of politics, for the quite different tasks of politics can only be solved by violence" (Weber, 1946, p. 126). In other words, an ethic of responsibility which causes a politician to take the consequences of acting or not acting seriously is the appropriate ethos for political action.

Huxley too sees power as an evil, but whereas Weber saw politics as a means to fight evil, perhaps by employing ethically dubious means, Huxley's view of politics was unconditional, namely, you should not fight evil with evil. He saw politics as a way of thinking in terms of "historicalness," or what we might call historical inevitability. Thus, for Huxley,

> this implicit identification of what ought to be with what is, effectively vitiates all thinking about morals, about politics, about progress, about social reform, even about art. In those who make the identification it induces a kind of busy, Panglossian fatalism.
> (Huxley, 2012, p. 68)

Because politics is intimately tied to "historicalness," Huxley believes that it allows, or even causes, evil. While Weber saw politics as a way of mediating the inevitable value conflicts over good and evil, Huxley saw politics, national and international alike, as an evil in itself. A contemporary man, says Huxley, is "ready, in a word, to tolerate or even actively engage in any wickedness or any imbecility, because he is convinced that there is some historical providence which will cause bad, inappropriate means to result in good ends" (Huxley, 2012, p. 69).

Whereas Huxley saw a polished foolishness in politics, Weber saw rough-cut wisdom. He distinguished between an ethic of responsibility, in which a politician must account for the probable and possible results of his actions, hence justifying the use of sometimes violent means to achieve presumably good ends, and an ethic of ultimate ends, or convictions, in which consequences are never taken into account. This distinction between the way ends and means are related has become a touchstone of modern political sociology, and is as important for the notion of ethical neutrality in sociological research, as it is for the study of politics. Huxley's forceful advocacy of pacifism in *Ends and Means* and other writings challenges the sociological understanding of politics and science as ways of turning ideas into motives for political action.

In the world of arts and letters, Huxley faced powerful, and seemingly an almost Weberian-type opposition to his pacifist values. The most fascinating opponent of Huxley's and others' pacifism was his fellow dystopian novelist, George Orwell. In his widely-read essay, "Pacifism and the War," published in a wartime 1942 issue of the *Partisan Review*, Orwell put it succinctly: "Pacifism is objectively pro-Fascist" (1942, p. 419). Unlike Huxley, Orwell had a more realistic, and, in Weber's sense, a more responsible understanding about the moral force of pacifism. Much like Weber, he understood that in international politics, power politics cannot be answered by moralizing, and an adherence to a pacifist ethos of conviction. Hence, he wrote "I am not interested in pacifism as a 'moral phenomenon'… Despotic governments can stand 'moral force' till the cows come home; what they fear is physical force" (1942, p. 420).

Even more telling was Orwell's direct question about pacifism and the Jews of Europe, in his devastating post-WWII essay, "Reflections on Gandhi" (1949, p. 85).

> In relation to the late war, one question that every pacifist had a clear obligation to answer was: 'What about the Jews? Are you prepared to see them exterminated? If not, how do you propose to save them without resorting to war?' I must say that I have never heard, from any Western pacifist, an honest answer to this question.
>
> (1949, p. 90)

No one interested in Weber's discussion of politics and ethics should ignore Orwell, who begins this essay in a way so close to Weber that one might almost mistake the one for the other.

> Saints should always be judged guilty until they are proved innocent… In Gandhi's case the questions one feels inclined to

ask are: to what extent was Gandhi moved by vanity… and to what extent did he compromise his own principles by entering politics, which of their nature are inseparable from coercion and fraud?

(1949, p. 86)

Ends and Means was published in 1937. Although Huxley had plenty of information about how Hitler was treating the Jews before the Holocaust began in deadly earnest, he only mentions the persecution of the Jews once, even though when Hitler was appointed Chancellor of Germany in 1933 it was well-known that he was putting anti-Semitic laws in place, and that anti-Semitic propaganda was destroying the place of Jews in German society. Hitler was very open about enacting anti-Jewish laws restricting their employment, citizen's rights, and even ability to marry outside their religion. Huxley mentions the persecution of the Jews in passing, as an example of the disastrous practical effects of wrong metaphysical beliefs:

> Hitlerian theology affirms that there is a Nordic race, inherently superior to all others. Hence it is right that Nordics should organize themselves for conquest and should do their best to exterminate people like the Jews, who are members of inferior races.

Unlike Orwell, Huxley shows not even the slightest hint of moral indignation, nor a hint of how pacifism should take the plight of the Jews into account (Huxley, 2012, p. 241). As author of *Ends and Means* Huxley was under no obligation to discuss the persecution of the Jews in Europe. But the fact that he extolled the virtues of pacifism, in spite of its consequences for the Jews, shows his utopian thinking as an ethic of conviction that is morally and politically distasteful, in a world in which the struggle between good and evil continues on a daily basis.

It is obvious that the issues raised by Huxley in the 1930s are still with us today. Contemporary intellectuals within the social sciences and sociology, as well as without, still struggle over the relationship of ends to means, especially as they appear in political discourse. Pacifism is still an important topic, as terrorism and dictatorial states abound. Many will find solace and justification of their points of view in Huxley's *Ends and Means*, others will find the book to be a case study in the sociological understanding of the relationship of ethics to politics. One way or the other, it is easy to agree with Talcott Parsons' assessment that *Ends and Means* "cannot fail to arouse the greatest interest" among social science intellectuals (Parsons, 1938, p. 833).

17

AUTHORITY VERSUS CONVICTION

In April 1910, Max and Marianne Weber moved into one of the biggest houses in Heidelberg, at Ziegelhäuser Landstraße 17. The riverfront house, right off the Neckar, had belonged to Weber's late grandfather, Georg Friedrich Fallenstein, and when the Webers moved in they rented the top floor to Max's friend and colleague, Ernst Troeltsch, and his wife Marta. This villa, now known as Das Max-Weber Haus, is an international student center at the University of Heidelberg. It might also be considered a landmark for the golden age of the sociology of religion. After all, Max Weber and Ernst Troeltsch were and remain two of the most important scholars in this discipline, and the fact that they lived in the same house at the height of their careers is nothing short of astonishing.

The friendship between Weber and Troeltsch predates their sharing the house at Ziegelhäuser Landstraße by almost a decade and a half. It includes, among other things, their shared trip to America in 1904 where both men addressed and participated in the Congress of Arts and Sciences in St. Louis, an international gathering of many of the most accomplished scholars of the day.

It was during this fertile intellectual period at the end of the nineteenth and the beginning of the twentieth centuries that Weber began writing the articles that would later be published in 1905 as *The Protestant Ethic and the Spirit of Capitalism*. The next year, in 1906, Troeltsch published

Protestantism and Progress. This time period was also notable for William James' *The Varieties of Religious Experience*, 1902, Georg Simmel's *Die Religion*, published in 1906 as part of Martin Buber's Die Gesellschaft series of sociological monographs, and Emile Durkheim's *Elementary Forms of the Religious Life*, published in 1912. In 1913 Freud published *Totem and Taboo: Resemblances Between the Mental Lives of Savages and Neurotics*. While one would not want to ignore or slight earlier works, such as Fustel de Coulanges' *The Ancient City*, published in 1864, or later works such as Freud's *The Future of an Illusion*, published in 1927, the nearly dozen or so years from 1902 to 1913 laid the foundation for the social study of religion as we know it today. This is underscored yet again by the reminder that Weber's essays in the sociology of religion, including "Economic Ethic of the World Religions," published in 1915, and "The Protestant Sects and the Spirit of Capitalism," published in 1906, among others, were written during this timeframe, as was Troeltsch's best-known work, *The Social Teachings of the Christian Churches*, which was published in 1912.

Of all the brilliant works on the sociology of religion published during this period, one stands out for having been neglected until recently, namely, *Protestantism and Progress*. This book was originally titled *Die Bedeutung des Protestantismus für die Entstehung der modernen Welt* ("The Significance of Protestantism for the Emergence of the Modern World"), which actually is a more accurate description of what this small volume attempts to explain (Troeltsch, 1906). Both Weber and Troeltsch were working out theories of social change involving the movement from a medieval world view and social structure—what Troeltsch calls "der kirchlichen Kultur," or "church civilization"—to a modern culture and society. In *The Protestant Ethic and the Spirit of Capitalism*, Weber showed the affinity of Calvinism to the rise of capitalism, and hence the modern economy. In *Protestantism and Progress*, Troeltsch shows the affinity between some branches of Protestantism and what he calls "*der modernen Welt.*" Thus, we must first ask what Troeltsch means by this phrase, "the Modern World" and then we must ask what he sees as the relationship of Protestantism and modernity.

First, Troeltsch makes it clear that his subject matter is not an overstretched idea, but a more limited conception of modern civilization as developed in Europe and America. Second, he states unequivocally that what he calls "modern" refers most importantly to a prevailing trend rather than a thing unto itself. This is because, as Troeltsch understands it, there has never been a clean break, or line of demarcation between the old church civilization and the new modern one that has seemingly overtaken it. This is a vital point for understanding Troeltsch's concept of change in *Protestantism and Progress*, because he sees evolutionary trends that suggest that the old civilization and the new one replacing it coexist. In this Troeltsch is very much a man of his time. He wrote about Darwin in his historical essays, and seems to agree with the well-known Darwinian principle *Natura non facit saltum*—"nature makes no leaps"—when he analyzes social change. If Darwin thought that evolutionary change involved very small changes taking place over long periods of time instead of the occurrence of large precipitous changes, Troeltsch seems to see social change in the same light.

For Troeltsch, therefore, modern civilization can only be defined in terms of that which preceded it, but did not necessarily replace it. Church civilization is based on the widespread cultural and institutional belief in an absolute divine revelation embodied in the Church—meaning, of course, the Catholic Church—as the fountainhead of redemption and morality. This shared belief was the basis for expanding Church authority over both supernatural, divine ends, and human, social ends. In other words, there was nothing that stood outside the purview and authority of the Church. This made church civilization "*eine Autoritätkultur*," or a "civilization of authority." The overarching authority of the Catholic Church over all walks of life led church civilization to develop an inherent asceticism that depreciated the everyday sensuous world. The picture that Troeltsch paints of the church civilization is that of a world marked by the authoritative, ascetic, world-condemning, religious influences of the Church.

Before moving forward to define modern civilization, however, Troeltsch warns the reader that these religious and church-directed factors are not the only determining factors of the Middle Ages. He describes a set of social and economic conditions that made church authority possible, thus avoiding the fallacy of the single cause. Among these factors were the guild system that restricted trade and industry in the early

Middle Ages, which helped contribute to a weak central authority in all spheres of life except those dominated by the church. Since many later interpretations of both Troeltsch's and Weber's work on Protestantism, capitalism, and modernity are characterized by one form of causal reductionism or another, it is notable that Troeltsch insists on seeing multiple causation at work here.

In contrast with its immediate predecessor, modern civilization is everywhere oppositional in nature. Modernity, in Troeltsch's sense, replaces a strong centralizing church authority with an "individualism of conviction," and under the sway of independent and rational convictions, divine infallibility and ecclesiastical intolerance necessarily give place to human relativity and toleration (Troeltsch, 2013, p. 91, p. 12).

Troeltsch enumerates the elements of modern civilization in terms of politics, economy, art, science, and finally, religion itself. Significantly, he clearly shows that Protestantism per se has almost no *direct* causal relationship to the making of modern civilization, but just as significantly Troeltsch shows that the indirect relationships are indispensable for its formation. Troeltsch's understanding of the complex intertwining of historical trends and events in affecting social and cultural change makes *Protestantism and Progress* a model for sociological analysis of change. In this Troeltsch shares the spotlight equally with his friend and colleague Max Weber. Alas, as time has passed, so has Troeltsch's reputation among sociologists, who generations ago found him to be among the pantheon of great thinkers, but now increasingly reduce him to mere footnotes about his famous Church-Sect-Mysticism typology. Troeltsch was famous in sociological circles during his lifetime, as evidenced by his prominence in the first congress of the German Sociological Society in 1910. Beyond this, he was touted as a key figure in sociology by Karl Mannheim and others of the second generation of German sociologists. In addition, Troeltsch was a prolific writer whose complete works were published right after his untimely death in 1923 at age fifty-eight. But while Max Weber became widely known in America when his works began being translated here before and after WWII, Troeltsch's more esoteric and learned books remained available only in German, as many of them still are today. This and the fact that he is still more widely known among theologians and philosophers has seemingly decreased his reputation as a sociologist in America today.

One of the most intricate relationships described in *Protestantism and Progress* is that between Protestantism and polity. After describing how Protestantism shattered the absolute autocracy of the Catholic Church in terms of its control over everything from sexual love to marriage and family relations, private morality, and civil law, Troeltsch gets down to the brass tacks of its relationship to the modern secularized state. Here, too, reiterating Troeltsch's refusal to engage in causal oversimplification is important. Thus, he says that for the development of the modern state we must guard against current exaggerations, because the secular state and the modern idea of the state are not creations of Protestantism. Furthermore, Troeltsch shows that while Protestantism freed the state from subordination to church authority, the state was still not nearly the independent secular institution we see it as today. The matter of state independence was still further complicated by the two main branches of the Protestant Reformation, with Lutheranism closer to church civilization's absolutism regarding the state, and Calvinism establishing independent theocracies based on covenantal agreements. Troeltsch argues, however, that Calvinism "successfully established the right of resistance, which must be exercised on behalf of the word of God in the face of ungodly authorities" (Troeltsch, 2013, p. 65). This right to resist state authority set in motion cultural tendencies that would later help ease the way for our modern conception of the secular state.

At this point in his analysis of the relationship of Protestantism and the modern state, Troeltsch brilliantly shows that the schisms among early New England Calvinists in America helped establish our modern ideas regarding toleration, liberty of conscience, and separation of church and state. Invoking the history of New England Calvinism, Troeltsch showed that "the parent of the 'rights of man' was not actual church Protestantism, but the sectarianism and spiritualism that it hated and drove forth into the New World" (Troeltsch, 2013, p. 69). This is one of the most interesting and ironic observations made in *Protestantism and Progress*, namely that while the original impetus of the Protestant Reformation was to break apart the authority of the Catholic Church, further developments within Continental Protestantism led to far more individualistic manifestations of spirituality. This in turn "brought about the end of the medieval idea of civilization, and coercive church-and-state civilization gave place to individual civilization free from church direction" (Troeltsch, 2013, p. 71). In other words, the religiously-based medieval church civilization was replaced by, or at least placed in competition with the proto-modern civilization fostered by early Protestantism, and then both of these found themselves faced with the development of a secularized, rational, skeptical, tolerant, utilitarian, and even more modern civilization that grew out of these earlier competing social and cultural forms.

In chapter after chapter Troeltsch demonstrates the indirect effect Protestantism had on the development of modern civilization. *Protestantism and Progress* clearly shows that Troeltsch stands as Max Weber's equal in his analysis of the relationship of Protestantism and the rise of modern institutional social forms. The two were friends and colleagues, and they obviously shared their work with each other and held each other's thoughts in the highest regard. Troeltsch's chapter on Protestantism and capitalism in this book certainly reflects Weber's influence upon him, as the latter's *Protestant Ethic and the Spirit of Capitalism* reflects Troelsch's influence upon it. Although Weber's book is more narrowly focused on the economy, and Troeltsch's *Protestantism and Progress* deals with a wider range of social and institutional developments, the two serve the same purpose, namely to analyze the cultural changes indirectly affected by Protestantism. For Troeltsch these include family, law, the state, economics, civil society, science, and art. It is notable that in *Science, Technology and Society in Seventeenth-Century England*, Robert Merton cited Troeltsch as many times as he did Weber as he analyzed the relationship of Protestantism to the development of science (Merton, 1970). Merton's reliance on Troeltsch is hardly surprising, since *Protestantism and Progress* shows that Protestant religious individualism became fused with scientific knowledge and freedom of thought. Here again we see the primacy of Troeltsch's work analyzing Protestantism's effect on modern civilization.

The one overriding value that emerges from the transition from what Troeltsch called "church civilization" to "modern civilization" is individualism. This was noticed, of course, in Weber's work, too, but it is analyzed precisely and deeply in *Protestantism and Progress*. Troeltsch was no stranger to the famous work of Alexis de Tocqueville, *Democracy in America*, and that of James Bryce, *The American Commonwealth*. Both of these books set forth a description and analysis of individualism that made it clear that America had become a society deeply imbued with the qualities of modern civilization. About the weakened bonds of community in modern societies Tocqueville wrote that,

> Men being no longer attached to one another by any tie of caste, of class, of corporation, of family, are only too much inclined to be preoccupied only with their private interests, ever too much drawn to think only of themselves and to retire into a narrow individualism, in which every public virtue is stifled.
> (Tocqueville, 1956, p. xv)

While Tocqueville and Bryce saw that the true genius of American politics has been to keep individualism balanced by a commitment to the larger community, Troeltsch's interest was only in tracing the roots of individualism back to Protestantism.

Nevertheless, one cannot imagine Troeltsch disagreeing with Tocqueville's description and definition of individualism as

> ... a mature and calm feeling, which disposes each member of the community to sever himself from the mass of his fellows and to draw apart with his family and friends, so that after he has thus formed a little circle of his own, he willingly leaves society at large to itself.
> (Tocqueville, 1945, p. 104)

Troeltsch not only uses the term "individualism" throughout *Protestantism and Progress*, he also sees that the principle of voluntary association fostered by Protestantism is the mechanism used by modern civilization to ward off the fragmentation of society caused by this alienating tendency.

The individualistic tendency of modern civilization manifests itself most dramatically in the last two areas discussed by Troeltsch—art and religion. In the section on art, Troeltsch works through the relationship of Catholicism, Protestantism, and the Renaissance before coming to the fascinating conclusion that, because of its ascetic tendencies, Protestantism "never elevated artistic feeling into the principle of a philosophy of life, metaphysics or ethics" (Troeltsch, 2013, p. 94). Asceticism is why Protestantism opposed the spirit of the Renaissance, and Troeltsch further reasons that "modern art everywhere proves the end of Protestant asceticism." It also proves the end of Protestant hegemony over the modern civilization that it helped to bring to life. The list of writers and artists—from Lessing to Byron and Shelly—who opposed institutional Protestantism is telling, as is Troeltsch's observation that Ruskin's "aestheticizing" of modern England signifies the end of Puritanism. Troeltsch was of course writing at a time when modern art was in the midst of replacing religion as the prevailing source of spiritual and philosophic truth for the educated classes of Europe.

From Art Deco, Bloomsbury, and Cubism to Dada, Expressionism, and Futurism, artists were seeing themselves and being seen as charismatic revolutionaries who would and more importantly should replace old moral elites as champions of something new—new personalities, new moralities, and new ways of living. Contrast the high art of church civilization to modern art as it existed in Troeltsch's day and you will see the war of values between one civilization and the other, just as Troeltsch did. That much contemporary art today makes the Expressionists of the early 1900s look tame demonstrates how close we may be coming to the end of what Troeltsch called modern civilization, and to the beginning of a postmodern one in which the idea of civilization itself comes under attack. Indeed, when we think of modernism and modern civilization today we are far more likely to think of art than religion, showing the prescience of Troeltsch's analysis.

But just as art became a battleground for the ascendency of modern civilization, religion itself occupies Troeltsch's final chapter in *Protestantism and Progress*. This final chapter on modern religious feeling not only meshes with similar analyses by Georg Simmel and Max Weber, but it also seemingly anticipates Philip Rieff's later idea of the triumph of the therapeutic:

> Christian culture survived because it superintended the organization of Western personality in ways that produced the necessary corporate identities, serving a larger communal purpose institutionalized in the churches themselves. Ernst Troeltsch was correct in his institutional title for the moral demand system

preceding the one now emerging out of its complete ruin: a 'church civilization' an 'authoritarian and coercive culture.' What binding address now describes our successor culture?

(Rieff, 1966, p. 19)

Troeltsch shows that having ripped institutional religion from its moorings, Protestantism in the early twentieth century had become the preeminent example of the religion of personal conviction and conscience, and as such it had adapted itself to a modern, individualistic civilization that had intensified the extension of individual freedom from all dogma, and the ascendency of personality over institutionally shaped character. Troeltsch's discussion of religion in modern civilization resonates with Weber's well-known discussions of the "Disenchantment of the World" (*Entzauberung der Welt*), wherein he sees the world becoming disenchanted, or Simmel's notion of "sterile excitation" (*sterile Aufgeregtheit*). Religious individualism had reached a stage in modernity that had in essence superseded the Protestantism that brought modern civilization into being.

I shall end here with an anecdote recorded in the proceedings (Verhandlungen) of the first conference of the German Sociological Society held in Frankfurt in 1910. The main speakers were Max Weber, Ferdinand Tönnies, Georg Simmel, Werner Sombart, and Ernst Troeltsch. After presenting his paper, "Stoic–Christian Natural Law and Modern Secular Natural Law," Troeltsch was asked by Simmel, who had introduced and moderated the session, whether he wanted to answer his critics, including Tönnies and Martin Buber. Troeltsch at first declined Simmel's invitation. However, encouraged by his friend Weber, he stated aloud that his colleague Weber said that "the Devil will have me if I don't speak" ("der Teufel sole mich holen, wenn ich nicht spreche"), so speak he did (*Verhandlungen*, 1911, p. 211). This exemplifies the physically, emotionally, and intellectually close relationship among these two German sociologists who presided over the institutional beginnings of modern sociology. That Weber and Troeltsch were so intellectually intimate was vital to the cross-fertilization of their ideas about the influence of Protestantism on the evolution of church civilization to modern civilization. In *Protestantism and Progress* Troeltsch traced that evolution and gave us a classic sociological monograph that is still well worth reading today.

References

Acton, L. (1889). "The American Commonwealth." *English Historical Review*, Vol. 4, p. 388.
Adams, H. (1931). *The Education of Henry Adams*. New York: The Modern Library.
Adams, J. T. (1921). *The Founding of New England*. Ithaca: Cornell University Library.
Adams, J. T. (1923). *Revolutionary New England*. Boston: The Atlantic Monthly Press.
Adams, J. T. (1926). *New England in the Republic*. Boston: Little, Brown.
Adams, J. T. (1927). *Provincial Society*. New York: Macmillan.
Adams, J. T. (1929). *Our Business Civilization*. New York: Boni Press.
Adams, J. T. (1930). *The Adams Family*. Boston: Little, Brown.
Adams, J. T. (1931a). *The Epic of America*. Boston: Little, Brown.
Adams, J. T. (1931b). *Tempo of Modern Life*. New York: Boni Press.
Adams, J. T. (1933). *The March of Democracy*. New York: Scribner's.
Adams, J. T. (1934). *America's Tragedy*. New York: Scribner's.
Adams, J. T. (1940). *Dictionary of American History*. New York: Scribner's.
Adams, J. T. (1969). *Album of American History*. New York: Scribner's.
Adams, J. T. (2012). *The Epic of America*. New Brunswick: Transaction Publishers.
Addams, J. (1902). *Democracy and Social Ethics*. New York: Macmillan.
Addams, J. (1909). *The Spirit of Youth and the City Streets*. New York: Macmillan.
Addams, J. (1910). *Twenty Years at Hull House*. New York: Macmillan.
Aldrich, N. W. Jr. (1988). *Old Money: The Mythology of America's Upper Class*. New York: Knopf.
Alsop, J. W. (1992). *I've Seen the Best of It: Memoirs*. New York: Norton.
Amory, C. (1947). *The Proper Bostonians*. New York: Dutton.
Amory, C. (1952). *The Last Resorts*. New York: Harper & Brothers.
Amory, C. (1960). *Who Killed Society?* New York: Harper & Brothers.
Anderson, P. (1968). "Components of the National Culture". *New Left Review*, No. 50, pp. 1–51.

Angell, R. C. (1958). *Free Society and Moral Crisis*. Ann Arbor: University of Michigan Press.
Arendt, H. (1968). *Between Past and Future*. New York: Viking.
Arendt, H. (1970). *On Violence*. New York: Harcourt.
Bagehot, W. (1867). *The English Constitution*. New York: Oxford University Press.
Bagehot, W. (1872). *Physics and Politics*. New York: D. Appleton and Company.
Ball, H. V. et al., (1962). "Law and Social Change: Sumner Reconsidered." *American Journal of Sociology*, Vol. 67, No. 5, p. 540.
Baltzell, E. D. (1958a). *An American Business Aristocracy*. London: Collier Books.
Baltzell, E. D. (1958b). *Philadelphia Gentlemen*. Glencoe: Free Press.
Baltzell, E. D. (1964). *The Protestant Establishment*. New York: Random House.
Baltzell, E. D. (1979). *Puritan Boston and Quaker Philadelphia*. New York: Free Press.
Baltzell, E. D. & Schneiderman, H. G. ed. (1991). *The Protestant Establishment Revisited*. New Brunswick: Transaction Publishers.
Baltzell, E. D. & Schneiderman, H. G. ed. (1994). *Judgment and Sensibility*. New Brunswick: Transaction Publishers.
Baltzell, E. D. (1995). *Sporting Gentlemen*. New York: Free Press.
Baltzell, E. D. (2013). *Sporting Gentlemen*. New Brunswick: Transaction Publishers.
Bauman, Z. (1989). *Modernity and the Holocaust*. Ithaca: Cornell University Press.
Beard, C. (1913). *An Economic Interpretation of the Constitution of the United States*. New York: Macmillan.
Beard, C. (1915). *An Economic Interpretation of Jeffersonian Democracy*. New York: Macmillan.
Bell, D. (1962). *The End of Ideology*. New York: Free Press.
Bellah, R. (1985). *Habits of the Heart*. Berkeley: University of California Press.
Bellman, L. (1975). "The Idea of Communication in the Work of Charles Horton Cooley." The Journal of Communication Inquiry, Vol. 1, No. 2, pp. 79–87.
Belloc, H. (1901). *Robespierre: A Study*. New York: Charles Scribner's Sons.
Benda, J. (1928). *The Treason of the Intellectuals*. New York: William Morrow.
Bendix, R. (1956). *Work and Authority in Industry*. New Brunswick: Transaction Publishers.
Bendix, R. (1960). *Max Weber: An Intellectual Portrait*. Berkeley: University of California Press.
Bendix, R. (1964). *Nation-Building & Citizenship: Studies of Our Changing Social Order*. New Brunswick: Transaction Publishers.
Benedict, R. (1934). *Patterns of Culture*. Boston: Houghton Mifflin.
Bentham, J. (1789). *Introduction to Principles of Morals and Legislation*. Oxford: Clarendon Press.
Bernard, L. L. (1934). *Fields and Methods of Sociology*. New York: Long and Smith.
Bershady, H. J. (2014). *When Marx Mattered: An Intellectual Odyssey*. New Brunswick: Transaction Publishers.
Bierstedt, R. (1974). *Power and Progress*. New York: McGraw Hill.
Birmingham, S. (1967). *Our Crowd: The Great Jewish Families of New York*. New York: Harper & Row.
Birmingham, S. (1968). *The Right People: The Social Establishment in America*. Boston: Little, Brown.
Birmingham, S. (1973). *Real Lace: America's Irish Rich*. New York: Harper and Row.
Birmingham, S. (1987). *America's Secret Aristocracy*. Boston: Little, Brown.
Blackstone, W. (1768). *Commentaries on the Laws of England, Vol. 2*. Oxford: The Clarendon Press.

Blau, P. (1955). *The Dynamics of Bureaucracy*. Chicago: University of Chicago Press.
Blau, P. (1986). *Exchange and Power in Social Life*. New Brunswick: Transaction Publishers.
Blaustein, A. P. & Mersky, R. (1970). *First One Hundred Justices*. New York: Oxford University Press.
Boorstin, D. (1953). *The Genius of American Politics*. Chicago: University of Chicago Press.
Boorstin, D. J. (1958). *The Americans: The Colonial Experience*. New York: Random House, Inc.
Bottomore, T. (1969). *Critics of Society: Radical Thought in North America*. New York: Vintage.
Bouglé, C. (1908). *Essais Sur le Régime des Castes*. Paris: Felix Alcan.
Boyd, J. (1950). *The Papers of Thomas Jefferson, Vol. 1*. Princeton: Princeton University Press.
Brinton, C. (1930a). "Clubs." *Encyclopedia of the Social Sciences*, Vol. 3. New York: Macmillan, 1930.
Brinton, C. (1930b). *The Jacobins: An Essay in the New History*. New York: Macmillan.
Brinton, C. (1934). *A Decade of Revolution*. New York: Harper & Brothers.
Brinton, C. (1938). *The Anatomy of Revolution*. New York: W. W. Norton & Company.
Brinton, C. (1941). *Nietzsche*. Cambridge: Harvard University Press.
Brinton, C. (1950). *Ideas and Men: The Story of Western Thought*. New York: Prentice Hall.
Brinton, C. (1954). "The Residue of Pareto." *Foreign Affairs*. Vol. 32, No. 4, pp. 640–650.
Brinton, C. (1959). *A History of Western Morals*. New York: Harcourt, Brace and Company.
Brinton, C. (1963). *The Shaping of the Modern Mind*. New York: New American Library.
Brinton, C. (1968). *The Americans and the French*. Cambridge: Harvard University Press.
Brinton, H. (1952). *Friends for Three Hundred Years*. New York: Harper & Brothers.
Brinton, C. (2011). *The Jacobins: An Essay in the New History*. New Brunswick: Transaction Publishers.
Brookhiser, R. (1991). *The Way of the WASP*. New York: Free Press.
Brooks, R. L. (1990). "What about Souter's Human Resume?" *The New York Times*, August 1990, p. 20.
Bryce, J. (1864). *The Holy Empire*. Oxford: T. & G. Shrimpton.
Bryce, J. (1888). *The American Commonwealth*. New York: Macmillan.
Bryce, J. (1893). "The Teaching of Civic Duty." *Contemporary Review*, Vol. 64, p. 14.
Bryce, J. (1901). *Studies in History and Jurisprudence*. New York: Oxford University Press.
Bryce, J. (1921). *Modern Democracies*. New York: Macmillan.
Bryce, J. (1993). *Hindrances to Good Citizenship*. New Brunswick: Transaction Publishers.
Burckhardt, J. (1943). *Force and Freedom*. New York: Beacon.
Burt, N. (1970). *First Families: The Making of an American Aristocracy*. Boston: Little, Brown.
Burgess, J. W. (1890). *Political Science and Comparative Constitutional Law*, Vol. II. New York: Baker and Taylor Company.
Burgess, E. (1962). "Social Problems and Social Processes." *Human Behavior and Social Processes*, ed. A. Rose. Boston: Haughton Mifflin.
Burnham, W. D. (1987). "The Turnout Problem." *Elections American Style*, ed. A. James Reichley. Washington: Brookings.
Burns, J. M. (1979). *Leadership*. New York: Harper Torchbooks.
Carpini, M. X. D. & Keeter, S. (1991). "Stability and Change in the U.S. Public's Knowledge of Politics". *Public Opinion Quarterly*, Vol. 55, No. 4, pp. 583–612.
Christopher, R. C. (1989). *Crashing the Gates: The De-Wasping of America's Power Elite*. New York: Simon and Schuster.

Cipriani, R. (2015). *Sociology of Religion*. New Brunswick: Transaction Publishers.
Clark, T. N. (1973). *Prophets and Patrons*. Cambridge: Harvard University Press.
Cohn, N. R. C. (1970). *The Pursuit of the Millennium*. New York: Oxford University Press.
Coleman, J. (1956). *Union Democracy*. California: Free Press.
Comte, A. (1851–1854). *System of Positive Polity*. Trans. Paris: L. Mathias, Carilian-Goeury, & Dalmont. London: Longmans, Green, and Co.
Cookson, P. W. Jr. & Persell, C. H. (1985). *Preparing for Power: America's Elite Boarding Schools*. New York: Basic.
Cooley, C. H. (1896). "Nature versus Nurture in the Making of Social Careers." *Proceedings of the 23rd Conference of Charities and Corrections*.
Cooley, C. H. (1902). *Human Nature and the Social Order*. New York: Charles Scribner's Sons.
Cooley, C. H. (1993). *Social Organization*. New Brunswick: Transaction Publishers.
Cooley, C. H. (1918). *Social Process*. New York: Charles Scribner's Sons.
Cooley, C. H. (1930). *Sociological Theory and Social Research*. New York: Holt.
Coser, L. (1978). "American Trends." *A History of Sociological Analysis*, eds. T. Bottomore & R. Nisbet. New York: Basic Books.
Coser, L. (1984). Review of C. Wright Mills: An American Utopian, by Irving Louis Horowitz. *The American Journal of Sociology*, Vol. 90, No. 3, pp. 657–658.
Coulanges, F. (1980). *The Ancient City*. Baltimore: Johns Hopkins.
Dahrendorf, R. (1967). *Society and Democracy in Germany*. Garden City: Doubleday.
Davis, K. & Moore, W. (1945). "Some Principles of Stratification." *American Sociological Review*, Vol. 10, No. 2, 1944 Annual Meeting Papers (April, 1945), pp. 242–249.
Degler, C. (1959). *Out of Our Past*. New York: Harpers.
Dewey, J. (1936). *School and Society*. Chicago: University of Chicago Press.
Dewey, J. (1947). *Problems of Men*. New York: Philosophical Library.
Dewey, J. & Tufts, J. (1908). *Ethics*. New York: Henry Holt.
Dewey, J. & Tufts, J. (1932). *Ethics*. Revised Edition. New York: Henry Holt.
Dicey, A. V. (1905). *Lectures on the Relation between Law and Public Opinion in England during the Nineteenth Century*. New York: Macmillan.
Domhoff, G. W. (1967). *Who Rules America?* New York: Prentice-Hall.
Domhoff, G. W. (1970). *The Higher Circles: The Governing Class in America*. New York: Random House.
Domhoff, G. W. & Zweigenhaft, R. (1982). *Jews in the Protestant Establishment*. New York: Praeger.
Doyle, B. (1937). *The Etiquette of Race Relations in the South: A Study of Social Control*. Chicago: University of Chicago Press.
Dumont, L. (1970). *Homo Hierarchicus: The Caste System*. Chicago: University of Chicago.
Dunne, G. T. (1977). *Hugo Black and the Judicial Revolution*. New York: Simon and Schuster, Ch. 17.
Durkheim, E. (1914). *Germany above All: German Mentality and War*. Paris: Librairie Armand Colin.
Durkheim, E. (1915). *Who Wanted War? The Origin of the War According to Diplomatic Documents*. Paris: Librairie Armand Colin.
Durkheim, E. (1922). *Professional Ethics and Civic Morals*. Illinois: Free Press.
Durkheim, E. (1947). *The Division of Labor in Society*. Illinois: Free Press.
Durkheim, E. (1951). *Suicide*. New York: Free Press.

Durkheim, E. (1964). *The Rules of the Sociological Method.* New York: Free Press.
Durkheim, E. (1965). *Elementary Forms of the Religious Life.* New York: Free Press.
Edwards, L. P. (1927). *The Natural History of Revolution.* Chicago: Chicago University Press.
Elias, N. (1939). *Über den prozess der zivilisation.* Basel: Haus zum Falken.
Elias, N. (1978). *The Civilizing Process.* New York: Urizen Books.
Emmet, D. (1966). *Rules, Roles and Relations.* Boston: Beacon.
Engels, F. (1894). *Anti-Dühring.* New York: International Publishers.
Ferrero, G. (1914). *Ancient Rome and Modern America.* New York: Putnam.
Ferrero, G. (1942). *The Principles of Power.* New York: Putnam.
Fisher, H. A. L. (1927). *James Bryce American Democracy.* New York: Macmillan.
Fitzgerald, F. (1980). *America Revised.* New York: Random House.
Fitzhugh, G. (1854). *Sociology for the South.* Richmond: A. Morris Publisher.
Fowler, D. (1989). *Democracy's Next Generation.* Washington, DC: People for the American Way.
Fox, B. (1964). "The Emerging International Sociology." *The New Sociology,* ed. I. L. Horowitz New York: Oxford University Press.
Franklin, J. H. (1965). "The Two Worlds of Race." *The Negro American,* eds. T. Parsons & K. B. Clark. Boston: Beacon.
Freud, S. (1930). *Civilization and Its Discontents.* Austria: Internationaler Psychoanalytischer Verlag Wien.
Freud, S. (1975). *Future of an Illusion.* New York: Norton.
Freud, S. (1950). *Totem and Taboo.* New York: Norton.
Friedrich, C. (1972). *Tradition and Authority.* New York: Oxford University Press.
Gardner, J. W. (1966). "The Anti-Leadership Vaccine." *Princeton Alumni Weekly,* Vol. LXVI, No. 29, p. 27.
Geertz, C. (1973). *The Interpretation of Cultures.* New York: Basic.
Gibbs, J. P. (1989). "Conceptualization of Terrorism." *American Sociological Review,* Vol. 54, pp. 329–340.
Giddings, F. (1900). *Democracy and Empire.* New York: Macmillan.
Giddings, F. (1918). *The Responsible State.* Boston: Houghton Mifflin.
Goffman, E. (1959). "The Moral Career and the Mental Patient." *Psychiatry,* Vol. 22, No. 2, pp. 123–142.
Gouldner, A. (1954). *Patterns of Industrial Bureaucracy.* Chicago: Free Press.
Gaustad, E. (1962). *Historical Atlas of Religion in America.* New York: Harper & Row.
Geertz, C. (1973). *The Interpretation of Cultures.* New York: Basic.
Hacker, A. (1957). "Liberal Democracy and Social Control." *American Political Science Review,* Vol. 51, No. 4, pp. 1009–1026.
Harrington, W. (1987). "Revenge of the Dupes." *Washington Post,* December 27, 1987.
Harrison, P. (1959). *Authority and Power in the Free Church Tradition.* Princeton: Princeton University Press.
Hartmann, E. (1869). *Philosphie des Unbewussten.* Berlin: Carl Duncker's Verlag.
Hartz, L. (1955). *The Liberal Tradition in America.* New York: Harcourt.
Hegel, G. W. F. (1821). *Elements of the Philosophy of Right.* Cambridge: Cambridge University Press.
Hegel, G. W. F. (1807). *Phenomenology of Mind.* Cambridge: Cambridge University Press.
Hennis, W. (1988). *Max Weber, Essays in Reconstruction.* London: Allen & Unwin.
Hess, S. (1966). *America's Political Dynasties.* Garden City: Doubleday.

Hirsch, E. D. Jr. (1987). *Cultural Literacy*. Boston: Houghton Mifflin.
Hirsch, E. D. Jr. (1988). *The Dictionary of Cultural Literacy*. Boston: Houghton Mifflin.
Hirschman, A. O. (2013). *The Passions and the Interests*. Princeton: Princeton University Press.
Hitchens, C. (1990). *Blood, Class, and Nostalgia: Anglo-American Ironies*. New York: Farrar, Straus and Giroux.
Hobhouse, L. T. (1911a). *Liberalism*. New York: Holt.
Hobhouse, L. T. (1911b). *Social Evolution and Political Theory*. New York: Columbia University Press.
Hobhouse, L. T. (1918). *The Metaphysical Theory of the State*. New York: Macmillan.
Hofstadter, R. (1955). *The Age of Reform*. New York: Vintage Books.
Hofstadter, R. (1973). *American Political Tradition and Those Who Made It*. New York: Knopf.
Holmes, O. W. (1989). *The Mind and Faith of Justice Holmes: His Speeches, Essays, Letters, and Judicial Opinions*. New Brunswick: Transaction Publishers.
Homans, G. C. (1941). "Anxiety and Ritual." *American Anthropologist*, Vol. 43, pp. 164–172.
Homans, G. C. (1967). *The Nature of Social Science*. New York: Harcourt, Brace & World.
Horowitz, I. L. (1961). *Radicalism and the Revolt against Reason*. London: Routledge.
Horowitz, I. L. (1964). *The New Sociology: Essays in Social Science and Social Theory in Honor of C. Wright Mills*. New York: Oxford University Press.
Horowitz, I. L, (1965). "The Stalinization of Fidel Castro." *New Politics*, Vol. 4, No. 4, pp. 61–69.
Horowitz, I. L. (1968). *Professing Sociology*. Chicago: Aldine.
Horowitz, I. L. (2014). *Professing Sociology*. New Brunswick: Transaction Publishers.
Horowitz, I. L. (1970). "Radicalism and Contemporary American Society." *Where It's At: Radical Perspectives in Sociology*, eds. S. Deutsch & J. Howard. New York: Harper & Row.
Horowitz, I. L. & Becker, H. (1972). "Radical Politics and Sociological Research." *American Journal of Sociology*, Vol. 78, No. 1, pp. 48–66.
Horowitz, I. L. (1977). *Ideology and Utopia in the United States: 1956–1976*. New York: Oxford University Press.
Horowitz, I. L. (1984). "Democratic Societies and Their Enemies, 1950–1984." *Bibliography of the Writings of Irving Louis Horowitz*. Privately printed.
Horowitz, I. L. (1992). "Morris Raphael Cohen and the End of the Classical Liberal Tradition." *The Faith of a Liberal*, ed. M. R. Cohen. New Brunswick: Transaction Publishers.
Horowitz, I. L. (1997). *Taking Lives: Genocide and State Power*. New Brunswick: Transaction Publishers.
Horowitz, I. L. (1999). *Behemoth*. New Brunswick: Transaction Publishers.
Horowitz, I. L. (2006). *The Idea of War and Peace*. New Brunswick: Transaction Publishers.
Horowitz, I. L. (2013). *War Game*. New Brunswick: Transaction Publishers.
Howard, J. W. Jr. (1968). *Mr. Justice Murphy*. Princeton: Princeton University Press.
Hughes, H. (1854). *Treatise on Sociology*. Philadelphia: Lippincott, Grambo & Co.
Huxley, A. (1936). *What Are You Going to Do about It?* London: Chatto and Windus.
Huxley, A. (1950). *Brave New World*. New York: Harper & Row.
Huxley, A. (2012). *Ends and Means*. New Brunswick: Transaction Publishers.
Ions, E. (1968). *James Bryce and American Democracy*. London: Macmillan.
James, W. (1880). "Great Men, Great Thoughts, and the Environment." *Atlantic Monthly*, Vol. 46, pp. 441–459.
James, W. (1902). *The Varieties of the Religious Experience*. New York: Longmans.
James, W. (1911). *Memories and Studies*. New York: Longmans.

Janowitz, M. (1960). *The Professional Soldier: A Social and Political Portrait*. London: The Free Press of Glencoe Collier-Macmillan.
Jones, R. (1966). *The Quakers in the American Colonies*. New York: Norton.
Kant, I. (1889). *Critical Philosophy*. New York: Macmillan.
Kant, I. (1949). *Immanuel Kant's Moral and Political Writings*, ed. Karl Friedrich. New York: Random House.
Key, V. O. (1949). *Southern Politics in State and Nation*. New York: Knopf.
Kluckhohn, C. & Hoebel, E. A. (1943). "Covert Culture and Administrative Problems." *American Anthropologist*, Vol. 45, No 2, pp. 213–229.
Knox, R. A. (1950). *Enthusiasm*. New York: Oxford University Press.
Kohn, N. (1970). *The Pursuit of the Millennium*. New York: Oxford University Press.
Konolige, K. & Konolige, F. (1978). *The Power and Their Glory: America's Ruling Class— The Episcopalians*. New York: Wyden.
Kuttner, R. (1987). "Why Americans Don't Vote." *New Republic*, September 7, 1987, p. 21.
Langer, S. (1942). *Philosophy in a New Key*. Cambridge: Harvard University Press.
Laski, H. J. (1919). *Authority in the Modern State*. New Haven: Yale University Press.
Laski, H. J. (1949). "American Presidency." *Parliamentary Affairs*, Vol. 3, No.1, pp. 7–19.
Lasswell, H. (1930). Psychopathology and Politics. Chicago: University of Chicago Press.
Lasswell, H. (1935a). *Politics: Who Gets What, When, How*. New York: McGraw Hill.
Lasswell, H. (1935b). *World Politics and Personal Insecurity*. New York: McGraw Hill.
Lasswell, H. (1936). *Politics: Who Gets What, When, and How?* New York: McGraw Hill.
Leahy, J. E. (1996). *Freedom Fighters of the United States Supreme Court*. Jefferson, NC: McFarland & Company.
LeBon, G. (1913). *The Psychology of Revolution*. New York: Putnam.
LeBon, G. (1921). *The World in Revolt*. New York: Macmillan.
Levine, D. N. (1995). *Visions of the Sociological Tradition*. Chicago: University of Chicago Press.
Levine, D. N. (1999). *Greater Ethiopia: The Evolution of a Multiethnic Society*. Chicago: University of Chicago Press.
Levine, D. N. (2017). Schneiderman, H. G. ed. (1994). *Dialogical Social Theory*. New Brunswick: Transaction Publishers.
Lewy, G. (1974). *Religion and Revolution*. New York: Oxford University Press.
Lincoln, A. (1864). Speech to the One Hundred Sixty-Fourth Ohio Regiment. *Abraham Lincoln Speeches and Writings 1859-1865*. New York: Penguin Random House, 2014.
Linton, R. (1936). *The Study of Man*. New York: Appleton.
Lippmann, W. (1929). *A Preface to Morals*. New York: Macmillan.
Lippmann, W. (1970). *Men of Destiny*. Seattle: University of Washington Press.
Lippmann, W. (1922). *Public Opinion*. New York: Macmillan.
Lipset, S. M. (1950). *Agrarian Socialism*. Berkeley: University of California Press.
Lipset, S. M., Trow, M. & Coleman, J. (1956). *Union Democracy*. California: Free Press.
Lipset, S. M. & Bendix, R. (1959). *Social Mobility in Industrial Society*. Berkeley: University of California Press.
Lipset, S. M. (1960). *Political Man: The Social Bases of Politics*. New York: Doubleday & Company.
Lipset, S. M. (1971). *Rebellion in the University*. Boston: Little, Brown.
Löwenthal, L. (1949). *Prophets of Deceit*. New York: Harper & Bros.
Lukes, S. (1978). "Power and Authority." *A History of Sociological Analysis*, eds. T. Bottomore and R. Nisbet. New York: Basic.

Lynd, R. S. & Lynd. H. M. (1929). *Middletown*. New York: Harcourt, Brace.
Lynd, R. S. & Lynd, H. M. (1937). *Middletown in Transition*. New York: Harcourt, Brace.
MacIver, R. M. (1917). *Community: A Sociological Study*. New York: Macmillan.
MacIver, R. M. (1926). *The Modern State*. Oxford: The Clarendon Press.
MacIver, R. M. (1931). *Society: Its Structure and Changes*. New York: Farrar and Rinehart.
MacIver, R. (1947). *The Web of Government*. New York: Macmillan.
Malinowski, B. (2013). *Crime and Custom in Savage Society*. New Brunswick: Transaction Publishers.
Mannheim, K. (1936). *Ideology and Utopia*. London: Routledge.
Manning, P. (2005). *Freud and American Sociology*. Cambridge: Polity Press.
Marlin, C. L. (1963). *The Preaching of Jemima Wilkinson*. Indiana University: Unpublished.
Marx, K. (1844). *Philosophical and Economic Manuscripts*. Moscow: Progress Publishers.
Marx, K. (1875). *Critique of the Gotha Program*. Moscow: Progress Publishers.
Marx, K. (1909). *Capital*, Vol. III. Chicago: Charles H. Kerr.
Marx, K. & Engels, F., ed. Feuer, L. (1959). *Basic Writings*. New York: Anchor.
Marx, K. (1992). *Early Writings*. New York: McGraw Hill.
Marx, K. (1994). *Selected Writings*. Indianapolis: Hackett.
Marx, K. (2012). "*On the Jewish Question.*" *Early Writings*. New York: McGraw Hill.
Mayo, E. (1933). *The Human Problems of an Industrial Civilization*. New York: Macmillan.
Mazlish, B. (2016). *In Search of Nixon*. New Brunswick: Transaction Publishers.
McCraw, T. (2007). *Prophet of Innovation: Joseph Schumpeter and Creative Destruction*. Cambridge: Harvard University Press.
McLachlan, J. (1970). *American Boarding Schools*. New York: Scribner's.
McLoughlin, W. (1971). *New England Dissent*. Cambridge: Harvard University Press.
Mead, G. H. (1934). *Mind, Self, and Society*. Chicago: University of Chicago Press.
Merton, R. K. (1938). "Social Structure and Anomie." *American Sociological Review*, Vol. 3, No. 5, pp. 672–682.
Merton, R. K. (1968). *Social Theory and Social Structure*. New York: Free Press.
Merton, R. K. (1970). *Science, Technology and Society in Seventeenth-Century England*. New York: Harper & Row.
Michelet, J. (1899). *Robespierre*. Paris: Calmann, Lévy.
Michels, R. (1915). *Political Parties*. New York: Free Press.
Milgram, S. (1974). *Obedience to Authority*. New York: Harper.
Miller, W. (1962). "American Historians and the Business Elite." *Men in Business*. New York: Harper & Row.
Mill, J. S. (1843). *A System of Logic*. Toronto: University of Toronto Press.
Mill, J. S. (1848). *The Principles of Political Economy*. London: Longmans, Green and Co.
Mill, J. S. (1859). *On Liberty*. London: Longman, Roberts & Green.
Mills, C. W. (1951). *White Collar*. New York: Oxford University Press.
Mills, C. W. (1956). *The Power Elite*. New York: Oxford University Press.
Mills, C. W. & Horowitz, I. L. ed. (1963). *Power, Politics and People*. New York: Oxford University Press.
Minogue, K. (1963). *The Liberal Mind*. London: Methuen.
Mitchell, G. D. (1968). *A Hundred Years of Sociology*. Chicago: Aldine.
Mommsen, W. (1989). *The Political and Social Theory of Max Weber*. Chicago: University of Chicago.
Morley, J. (1886). *Robespierre*. London: Macmillan.

Mosca, G. (1939). *The Ruling Class*. New York: McGraw Hill.
Murdock, G. P. (1943). "Bronislaw Malinowski." *American Anthropologist*, Vol. 45, pp. 441–451.
Murdock, G. P. (1965). *Culture and Society*. Pittsburgh: University of Pittsburgh Press.
Murray, R. K. & Blessing, T. H. (1983). "The Presidential Performance Study: A Progress Report". *The Journal of American History*, Vol. 70, No. 3, pp. 535–555.
Musil, R. (1954). *The Man without Qualities*, Vol. 2. London: Secker and Warburg.
Myrdal, G. (1944). *An American Dilemma: The Negro Problem and American Democracy*. New York: Harper and Row.
Naison, M. (1984). "Populism, Pragmatism, and Activism." *Commonweal*, April 20, 1984.
Nevins, A. (1968). *James Truslow Adams: Historian of the American Dream*. Urbana: University of Illinois Press.
New York Herald Tribune Book Review. (1935). June 9, pp. 1–8.
The New York Times. (October 16, 1908). "Bryce Sees Danger in Power of Money." p. 9.
The New York Times. (October 17, 1908). "Bryce on Civic Indolence." p. 12.
The New York Times. (October 24, 1908). "Bryce for Jail Sentences." p. 8.
The New York Times. (May 18, 1997). "They're Not in Denmark Anymore." P. E-2.
Niebuhr, R. H. (1929). *The Social Sources of Denominationalism*. New York: Henry Holt.
Niebuhr, R. (1943). *The Nature and Destiny of Man*, Vol. 2. New York: Scribner's.
Niebuhr, R. (1952). *The Irony of American History*. New York: Scribner's.
Nisbet, R. (1993). *The Sociological Tradition*. New Brunswick: Transaction Publishers.
Nisbet, R. (1999). *Tradition and Revolt*. New Brunswick: Transaction Publishers.
Nisbet, R. (2009). *Metaphor and History*. New Brunswick: Transaction Publishers.
Nixon, R. M. (1962). *Six Crises*. New York: Doubleday.
Novicov, Y. A. (1917). *The Mechanism and Limits of Human Association*. New York: American Sociological Society.
Obama, B. (2006). *The Audacity of Hope: Reclaiming the American Dream*. New York: Crown.
Ogburn, W. F. (1922). *Social Change*. New York: Viking.
Oppenheimer, F. (1914). *The State*. Quebec: Black Rose Books.
Ortega y Gasset, J. (1932). *Revolt of the Masses*. New York: W. W. Norton & Company.
Orwell, G. (1942). "Pacifism and the War." *Partisan Review*, August–September 1942.
Orwell, G. (1949). "Reflections on Gandhi." *Partisan Review*, January 1949.
Orwell, G. (1950). *1984*. New York: Penguin Books.
Ostrogorski, M. (1902). *Democracy and the Organization of Political Parties*. New York: Macmillan.
Pareto, V. (1935). *Mind and Society*. New York: Harcourt.
Park, R. & Burgess, W. (1921). *Introduction to the Science of Sociology*. Chicago: University of Chicago Press.
Park, R. E. (1928). "Human Migration and the Marginal Man." *American Journal of Sociology*, Vol. 33, No. 6, pp. 881–893.
Park, R. (1975). *The Crowd and the Public*. Chicago: University of Chicago Press.
Parsons, T. (1930). *Protestant Ethic and the Spirit of Capitalism*. Boston: Unwin Hyman.
Parsons, T. (1937). *The Structure of Social Action*. New York: McGraw Hill.
Parsons, T. (1938). "Review of *Ends and Means*." *American Journal of Sociology*, Vol. 3, No. 5, pp. 832–833.

Parsons, T. (1950). "The Prospects of Sociological Theory." *American Sociological Review*, Vol 15, No. 1, pp. 3–16.
Parsons, T. (1955a). *Family, Socialization and Interaction Process*. Glencoe: Free Press.
Parsons, T. (1955b). "Social Strains in America." *The New American Right*, ed. D. Bell. New York: Criterion.
Pessen, E. (1984). *The Log Cabin Myth: The Social Backgrounds of the Presidents*. New Haven: Yale University Press.
Pierson, G. (1969). *The Education of American Leaders*. New York: Praeger.
Pierson, G. (1938). *Tocqueville and Beaumont in America*. New York: Oxford University Press.
Polanyi, M. (1958). *Personal Knowledge*. London: Routledge.
Radin, P. (1927). *Primitive Man as a Philosopher*. New York: Appleton.
Redfield, R. (1947). "The Folk Society." *American Journal of Sociology*, Vol. 52, No. 4, pp. 293–308.
Rieff, P. (1959). *Freud: The Mind of the Moralist*. New York: Viking.
Rieff, P. (1966). *The Triumph of the Therapeutic*. New York: Harper.
Rieff, P. (1970). "The Impossible Culture." *Encounter*, Vol. 35, No. 3, p. 42.
Riesman, D. (1950). *The Lonely Crowd*. New Haven: Yale University Press.
Robinson, J. H. (1906). "Recent Tendencies in the Study of the French Revolution." *The American Historical Review*, Vol. 11, No. 3, pp. 529–547.
Robinson, J. H. (1912). *The New History*. New York: Macmillan.
Roche, J. P. & Gordon, M. M. (1955). "Can Morality by Legislated?" *New York Times Magazine*, May 22.
Rodell, F. (1955). *Nine Men: A Political History of the Supreme Court from 1790 to 1955*. New York: Random House.
Rosenthal, A. M. (1964). *Thirty-Eight Witnesses: The Kitty Genovese Case*. Berkeley: University of California Press.
Ross, E. (1907). *Sin and Society*. New York: Houghton Mifflin.
Ross, E. (1916). *Social Control*. New York: Macmillan.
Rossiter, C. (1956). *The American Presidency*. New York: Harcourt, Brace.
Russell, B. (1936). *Freedom and Organization, 1814–1914*. London: George Allen & Unwin.
Russell, B. (1938). *Power: A New Social Analysis*. London: George Allen & Unwin Ltd.
Russell, B. (1949). *Authority and the Individual*. Abingdon: Routledge.
Russell, B. (1950). *Unpopular Essays*. New York: Simon and Schuster.
Saint-Simon, H. (1825). *New Christianity*. Paris: Bossange.
Schaefer, R. T. (2010). *Sociology* (12th ed.). New York: McGraw Hill.
Schlesinger, A. M. (1948). "Historians Rate U.S. Presidents." *Life*, pp. 65–66, 68, 73–74.
Schlesinger, A. M. (1960). *The Politics of Upheaval*. Boston: Houghton Mifflin.
Schlesinger, A. M. (1962). "Our Presidents: A Rating by 75 Historians." *New York Times Magazine*, pp. 12–13, 40–41, 43.
Schlesinger, A. M. Jr. (1986). *The Cycles of American History*. Boston: Houghton Mifflin.
Schmalenbach, H. (1977). *On Society and Experience*. Chicago: University of Chicago.
Schmidhauser, (1979). *Judges and Justices: The Federal Appellate Judiciary*. Boston: Little, Brown.
Schneiderman, H. G. (1982). "Review of Wolfgang Schlucter, the Rise of Western Rationalism." *Sociology*, Vol. 9, No. 4., p 17–21.

Schneiderman, H. G. (1989). "Presidents, Privilege, and Performance." *Society*, Vol. 26, No. 3. pp. 12–15.
Schneiderman, H. (2009). "The Strange Career of Political Sociology in America." *Culture and Civilization*. Vol. 1, No. 1, pp. 96–123.
Schneiderman, H. & Troeltsch, E. (2013). *Protestantism and Progress Redux*. New Brunswick: Transaction Publishers.
Schrag, P. (1970). *The Decline of the WASP*. New York: Simon and Schuster.
Schumpeter, J. (1989). *Essays: On Entrepreneurs, and Innovations*. New Brunswick: Transaction Publishers.
Selznick, P. (1953). *TVA and the Grass Roots*. Berkeley: University of California Press.
Selznick, P. (1992). *The Moral Commonwealth: Social Theory and the Promise of Community*. Berkeley: University of California Press.
Shaw, G.B. (1961). *The Millionairess*. New York: Penguin Books.
Shils, E. & Young, M. (1952). *The Meaning of the Coronation*. Indianapolis: Bobbs Merrill.
Shils, E. (1956). *Torment of Secrecy*. Chicago: Free Press.
Shils, E. (1980). *The Calling of Sociology*. Chicago: University of Chicago.
Shils, E. (1981). *Tradition*. Chicago: University of Chicago.
Simmel, G. (1906). *Die Religion*. Frankfurth: Rutten & Loeing.
Simmel, G. (1908). *Soziologie*. Germany: Leipzig, Duncker & Humblot.
Simmel, G. (1950). *The Sociology of Georg Simmel*. New York: Free Press.
Simmel, G. (1971). *On Individuality and Social Forms*. Chicago: University of Chicago Press.
Simonton, D. K. (1987). *Why Presidents Succeed: A Political Psychology of Leadership*. New Haven: Yale University Press.
Small, A. W. (1905). *General Sociology*. Chicago: University of Chicago Press.
Small, A. W. (1924). *Origins of Sociology*. London: Russell & Russell.
Smith, T. V. (1934). *Beyond Conscience*. New York: McGraw Hill.
Smith, M. B. (1950). "W. G. Sumner: The Forgotten Man." *American Mercury*, September 1950, pp. 357–365.
Sohm, R. (1892). *Kirchenrecht*. Leipzig: Duncker & Humblot.
Sohm, R. (1895). *Outlines of Church History*. London: Macmillan.
Sombart, W. (1896). *Socialism and the Social Movement*. New York: E. P. Dutton & Co.
Sombart, W. (1976). *Why is There No Socialism in the United States?* White Plains: M. E. Sharpe.
Sorokin, P. (1925). *The Sociology of Revolution*. Philadelphia: Lippencott.
Stampp, K. (1969). *Reconstruction*. Baton Rough: Louisiana State University Press.
Stark, W. (1967). *The Sociology of Religion Part II*. London: Routledge.
Steinfels, P. (1979). *The Neoconservatives*. New York: Simon & Schuster.
Stone, L. (1971). "Prosopography." *Daedalus*, Vol. 100, No. 1, pp. 46–79.
Stouffer, S. A. (1949). *The American Soldier*. Princeton: Princeton University Press.
Stouffer, S. (1955). *Communism, Conformity, and Civil Liberties*. New York: Doubleday.
Sumner, W. G. (1883a). "The Absurd Effort to Make the World Over." *Forum*, Vol. 17 (March 1894), pp. 92–102.
Sumner, W. (1883b). *What Social Classes Owe Each Other*. New York: Harper.
Sumner, W. G. (1906). *Folkways*. New York: Ginn and Company.
Sumner, W. G. (2014). *On Folkways and Mores*. New Brunswick: Transaction Publishers.
Sydnor, C. (1952). *American Revolutionaries in the Making*. Chicago: Free Press.

Tarde, G. (1899). *Les Transformations du Pouvoir*. Paris: Felix Alcan.
Tarde, G. (1903). *Laws of Imitation*. New York: Henry Holt.
Tawney, R. H. (1921). *Acquisitive Society*. New York: Harcourt, Brace.
Teggart, F. J. (1925). *The Theory of History*. New Haven: Yale University Press.
Teggart, F. J. (1960). *The Theory and Processes of History*. Berkeley: University of California Press.
Thomas, W. I. (1921). *Old World Traits Transplanted*. New Jersey: Patterson Smith.
Thomas, W. I. (1927). *The Polish Peasant in Europe and America*. New York: Knopf.
Tocqueville, A. (1856). *The Ancient Regime and the French Revolution*. New York: Harper & Brothers.
Tocqueville, A. (1945). *Democracy in America*, Vol. 2. New York: Knopf.
Tocqueville, A. (1956). *The Ancient Regime and the French Revolution*. Oxford: Blackwell.
Tocqueville, A. (1998). *The Old Regime and the Revolution*. Chicago: University of Chicago.
Tönnies, F. (1963). *Community and Society*. New York: Harper.
Troeltsch, E. (1906). *Die Biedeutung des Protestantismus fur die Entstehung der modernen Welt*. Muchen: R. Oldenbourg.
Troeltsch, E. (1931). *Social Teachings of the Christian Churches*. London: Allen & Unwin.
Troeltsch, E. (2013). *Protestantism and Progress*. New Brunswick: Transaction Publishers.
Turner, V. (1974). *Drama, Fields, and Metaphors*. Chicago: Adline.
Veblen, T. (1899). *The Theory of the Leisure Class*. New York: Macmillan.
Verhandlungen des Ersten Deutschen Soziologentages. (1911). *Verhandlungen des Ersten Deutschen Soziologentages*. Tubingen: J.B.C. Mohr.
Wakefield, D. (1984). "Before His Time." *The Nation*, pp. 212–213.
Walker, L. R. (1997). "John Dewey at Michigan." *Michigan Today*, Vol. 29, pp. 2–19.
Ward, L. (1906). *Psychic Factors of Civilization*. Boston: Ginn and Company.
Warner, W. L. & Lunt, P. S. (1941). *The Social Life of a Modern Community*. New Haven: Yale University Press.
Warner, W. L. (1953). *American Life*. Chicago: University of Chicago Press.
Warner, W. L. (1959). *The Living and the Dead*. New Haven: Yale University Press.
Warner, W. L. (1963). *Yankee City*. New Haven: Yale University Press.
Warren, C. (1923). *The Supreme Court in United States History*, Vol. 2. Boston: Little, Brown.
Weaver, J. D. (1967). *Warren: The Man, the Court, and the Era*. Boston: Little, Brown.
Weber, M. (1922). *Wirtschaft und Gesellschaft*. Tubingen: C. B. Mohr.
Weber, M. (1946). *From Max Weber: Essays in Sociology*. New York: Oxford University Press.
Weber, M. (1958). *The Protestant Ethic and the Spirit of Capitalism*. New York: Scribner's.
Weber, M. (1968). *Economy and Society*. Berkeley: University of California.
Wecter, D. (1937). *The Saga of American Society*. New York: Scribner's.
Wesolowski, W. (1967). "Some Notes on the Functional Theory of Stratification." *Class, Status, and Power*, eds. R. Bendix & S. M. Lipset. New York: Routledge & Kegan Paul.
Westley, F. C. (1973). "Unfit to Rule." *London Spectator*, Vol. 230, p. 7.
Wilson, W. (1889). "Bryce's American Commonwealth: A Review." *Political Science Quarterly*, Vol. 4, No. 1, pp. 153–169.
Wisbey, H. A. (1964). *Pioneer Prophetess*. Ithaca: Cornell University Press.
Zangwell, I. (1908). *The Melting Pot*. New York: Macmillan.
Zondervan, A. A. W. (2005). *Sociology and the Sacred: An Introduction to Philip Rieff's Theory of Culture*. Toronto: University of Toronto Press.

INDEX

Adams, James Truslow 4, 14, 15, 66–68
Adventurers 216, 218
Alienation 86, 88 104, 116, 147
Ambivalence 215–217, 255–259
Anomie 4, 61, 259, 260
Antinomian 12, 42, 43, 52, 53, 57, 58, 115, 119
Anti-Semitism 200, 201
Arendt, Hannah 27, 102, 103, 118
Authoritarian 2, 3, 7, 116, 137, 289
Authority: Authority, bureaucratic 8, 10, 11, 19, 25, 135, 136, 144; Authority, charismatic 8, 10, 15, 18, 23–27; Authority, class 3, 8, 10–12, 126, 134, 135, 147, 151, 188, 208, 211

Bagehot, Walter 21, 98, 206
Bakunin, Mikhail 4, 5
Baltzell, E. Digby 126–139 and *sic passim*
Bell, Daniel 43, 96, 147, 251, 262, 263
Bendix, Reinhard 96, 102, 108, 263
Benedict, Ruth 130, 255, 256
Bershady, Harold 130
Bierstedt, Robert 25, 26

Blessing, Tim H. 158–161, 166–171, 176, 179, 182
Boorstin, Daniel 87, 101, 174
Bougle, Celestin 19
Brinton, Crane 45, 69–83, 169
Bryce, James 220–245 and *sic passim*
Buber, Martin 282, 289
Bund 24, 26, 32
Bundling 258
Burgess, Ernest 226, 247, 254
Burke, Kenneth 269

Caste 11, 19, 102, 126, 134, 136, 138, 141–143, 146–147, 151–153, 195, 199, 200, 206, 211, 287
Change, crescive 247, 261, 262, 263
Charisma *sic passim*
Citizenship 23, 47, 98, 220–245
Class: Class origins 155, 161, 163, 165, 166, 169, 175–189, 202; Class system 64, 194; Class, upper, American 47, 62, 126–139, 149, 151, 152, 155, 161, 164–170, 178, 181, 195, 198, 199, 200, 201–210

303

Cohn, Norman 40
Communism 84, 97, 116, 123, 209, 214–216, 272
Conflict 90, 99, 111, 112, 116, 120, 125, 208, 255, 277
Connecticut 45–59
Consensus 13, 57, 90, 112, 116, 117, 211, 212, 236
Conservatism 107–113, 115, 123–125, 263
Cooley, Charles Horton 15, 76, 87–95, 103, 110, 142–145, 244–246, 255, 262, 268, 270
Coser, Lewis 121, 122, 265

Davis, Kingsley 5
Deference 11, 12, 14, 15, 21, 28, 194, 196, 206, 211, 212
Degler, Carl 63
Democracy, defiant 12–15, 21, 135, 142
Dewey, John 90, 95, 106, 251, 256, 269
Dicey, Albert Venn 222, 224, 244
Domination 5, 8, 12, 17, 23–27, 106, 134
Dumont, Louis 19
Durkheim, Emile 4, 19, 16, 82, 87–89, 94–97, 103, 105, 106, 221, 246, 247, 255, 259, 260, 266, 268, 270, 282

Egalitarianism 2, 4, 104, 194
Eisenstadt, S.N. 43
Elias, Norbert 254–267
Elite 9, 10, 18, 20, 46–54, 62, 71, 78, 80, 83, 90, 98, 130–136, 151–153, 159, 187, 192, 195, 205–210, 219, 288
Emmet, Dorothy 260
Enthusiasm 33, 37, 39, 42, 44
Enthusiasts 33, 37
Establishment 8, 126, 129, 133–139, 147, 151–155, 167, 193–212, 235, 249
Ethnocentrism 246, 247, 253, 263–265
Ethos 3, 4, 47, 48, 54, 113, 117, 136, 151, 194, 206, 234, 246, 247, 252, 253, 263, 277, 278
Extremists 31, 74, 117, 118, 237

Ferrero, Guglielmo 12, 13, 20, 21
Freud, Sigmund 28, 69, 218, 249, 256, 259, 282
Friedrich, Carl 22
Functionalism 115, 248

Geertz, Clifford 28, 29, 34, 253
Gemeinschaft 24, 25, 210, 270
Gerth, Hans 96, 132
Gesellschaft 24–26, 210, 270, 282
Goffman, Erving 82, 107, 110, 111, 251
Gorton, Samuel 58

Harnack, Adolph 18
Hartz, Louis 114
Hegemony 11, 168, 170, 182–187, 194, 207, 208, 288
Hirschman, Albert O. 141
Hofstadter, Richard 162, 196
Homans, George 75, 76, 82
Horatio Alger myth 173–192
Horowitz, Irving Louis 107–125, 250
Hutchinson, Anne 42, 58
Huxley, Aldous 266–280

Ideal types 8, 48, 81, 219
Individualism 2–4, 13, 14, 48, 53, 59, 99–104, 136, 203, 228–230, 243, 255, 266–268, 284, 286, 287, 289
Inequality 5, 103, 104, 106, 194, 271
Interests 2, 26, 52, 55–59, 91, 92, 99, 102, 104, 131, 140, 141, 168, 170, 193, 198, 203, 228–231, 234, 235, 245, 253, 287

Jacobins 69–83

Kant, Immanuel 29, 34, 35, 88, 95, 104, 118
Kluckhohn, Clyde 253

Langer, Susanne 28, 29
Laski, Harold 21, 22, 157
Lasswell, Harold 22, 61, 69, 94, 95
Lazarsfeld, Paul 129, 252

Leveling 48, 64, 136, 174, 183, 191
Levine, Donald N. 246, 254
Lewy, Guenter 40
Liberalism 107–125
Liminal 43–83
Linton, Ralph 11, 142, 152
Lippmann, Walter 14, 101, 103, 145, 148, 149, 247
Lipset, Seymour Martin 96, 97, 102, 117, 147, 251
Log-cabin myth 155, 161–164, 176
Lukes, Steven 27
Lynd, Helen 61, 62, 69, 130, 131, 252
Lynd, Robert 61, 62, 69, 129, 130, 131, 252

MacIver, Robert M. 22, 95, 129
Malinowski, Bronislaw 256–259
Mannheim, Karl 9, 40, 69, 265, 267, 274, 284
Manning, Philip 246
Marx, Karl 4, 46, 79, 86–88, 94, 129, 136, 152, 256, 271
Mayo, Elton 82, 145
Mazlish, Bruce 213–219
McKeon, Richard 269
Mead, George Herbert 28, 246, 247, 251
Merton, Robert 34, 61, 63, 124, 125, 129–133, 146, 148, 149, 252, 254, 261, 267, 286
Michels, Robert 9, 10, 18, 74, 80, 89, 90, 94, 96, 98, 106, 237
Milgram, Stanley 29
Mills, C. Wright 49, 96, 112, 113, 121, 122, 124, 125, 129–131, 147, 148
Mommsen, Wolfgang 27
Moore, Wilbert 5–7
Moral career 39, 107, 110, 11, 116, 125, 250
Mosca, Gaetano 20, 89, 94, 98
Murdock, George Peter 254, 256
Murray, Robert K. 152–161, 166–171, 176, 179, 182
Musil, Robert 273, 274

Nationalism 22, 84, 85, 89, 275
Neoconservatism 115, 122, 124
Niebuhr, H. Richard 40
Niebuhr, Reinhold 62, 208
Nietzsche, Friedreich 29, 83, 88, 271
Nisbet, Robert 19, 23, 262

Obedience 4, 19–29, 34, 227, 228
Ogburn, William F. 260, 262
Orwell, George 266, 267, 272, 273, 278, 279
Ostrogorsky, Moisy 70–74, 80, 94, 96, 98, 237

Pacifism 266–280
Pareto, Vilfredo 20, 70, 71, 75–80, 82, 89, 94, 98, 275
Park, Robert 89, 93, 95, 226, 246, 247, 254, 255, 260, 263, 268–270
Parsons, Talcott 21, 22, 46, 69, 82, 95, 124, 125, 198, 254–267, 270–275, 280
Patriotism 221, 242
Pessen, Edward 161–170, 176, 177
Plutocracy 14, 147
Populism 116, 236
Propaganda 74, 76, 79, 279
Prophets 25, 31, 37, 43
Proto-sociological 86–92, 98, 100, 103, 104, 246, 260
Psychohistory 213–219
Puritans 47, 48, 58, 81

Quakers 39, 45, 47, 48, 51, 53, 56

Radicalism 8, 69, 80, 107, 108, 112, 115–119, 123, 125
Rhode Island 45–59
Rieff, Philip 28, 29, 34, 107, 250, 251, 259, 260, 288, 289
Riesman, David 97, 146, 148, 149
Ritual 43, 77, 82, 83, 110, 247, 256, 257
Robespierre, Maxillian 74, 75
Robinson, James Harvey 71–73

Ross, Edward A. 22, 90, 94, 143, 144, 226, 247, 255, 262, 268
Roth, Guenter 27
Russell, Bertrand 17, 106

Schlesinger, Arthur M. Jr 123, 156, 170
Schlesinger, Arthur M. Sr 156–160, 166, 168, 176, 179
Schmalenbach, Herman 24, 25
Schmidhauser, John A. 175, 176
Schumpeter, Joseph 25, 94
Shaw, George Bernard 11
Shils, Edward 12, 23, 25, 43, 96, 102, 254, 274
Simmel, Georg 18, 66, 76, 77, 88, 89, 94–96, 116, 146, 216, 218, 226, 246, 255, 268, 270, 282, 288, 289
Simonton, Dean Keith 160
Small, Albion 88, 100, 226, 268, 269
Social change 69, 72, 78, 106, 247, 248, 259, 262, 263, 271, 282, 283
Social detachment 269
Social mobility 62, 65, 96, 99, 104, 136, 187, 194
Socialism 63, 97, 136, 275
Sohm, Rudoph 18
Sombart, Werner 88–92, 95, 98, 289
Sorel, Georges 117, 119–121
Sorokin, Pitirim 22, 69, 135
Spencer, Herbert 74, 86, 87
Stark, Werner 40
Status, achieved 24, 25, 33, 40, 142, 143, 152, 170
Status, ascribed 23–25, 33, 40, 142, 143, 161
Stereotype 163, 247
Stouffer, Samuel 97, 209
Stratification 2, 5, 6, 12, 62, 86, 103, 104, 132, 133, 143, 144, 161, 195

Success 2–4, 14, 47, 61–67, 133, 135, 138, 140–154
Sumner, William Graham 9, 88, 94, 246–265, 268, 270

Tarde, Gabriel 19, 226, 255
Terrorism 9, 81, 84, 85, 116, 280
Tocqueville, Alexis de *sic passim*
Tönnies, Friedrich 24, 25, 88, 89, 95, 106, 255, 268, 270, 289
Transducers, social 27
Troeltsch, Ernst 2, 46, 281–290
Turner, Victor 43, 83

Unintended consequences 46, 59
Utopianism 116, 267

Veblen Thorstein 144, 226, 252, 275
Violence 74, 80, 116, 119, 120, 273, 276, 277
Voluntary associations 76, 77, 93, 100, 102, 104, 154, 250, 287

Warner, W. Lloyd 61, 62, 82, 130, 131
WASP (White Anglo-Saxon Protestant) 126, 134, 136, 168, 170, 182, 183, 185, 187, 193–212
Watergate 156, 157, 167, 213, 214, 216, 218
Weber, Max *sic passim*
Wesolowski, Wlodzimieirz 5–7
Wilkinson, Jemima 33–42
Williams, Roger 58
Wirth, Louis 61, 265, 274

Young, Michael 23

Zealots 25, 31